love

Finla xx

Breaking the Silence

Breaking the Silence

Martin Ridge
with Gerard Cunningham

Gill & Macmillan

Gill & Macmillan Ltd
Hume Avenue, Park West, Dublin12
with associated companies throughout the world
www.gillmacmillan.ie

© Martin Ridge 2008
978 07171 4397 9

Type design: Make Communication
Print origination by Carole Lynch
Printed and bound by ScandBook AB, Sweden

This book is typeset in Linotype Minion and Neue Helvetica.

The paper used in this book comes from the wood pulp of
managed forests. For every tree felled, at least one tree is
planted, thereby renewing natural resources.

A CIP catalogue record for this book is available
from the British Library.

5 4 3 2

Contents

Preface

This is a story of extraordinary betrayal and extraordinary survival which emerged when three separate child abuse cases surfaced almost simultaneously in a tiny corner of north-west Ireland. The cases involved fifty children and went back four decades. One of the abusers would prove to be Ireland's most prolific rapist. The Gardaí launched what would be described as successful investigations, and prosecutions followed, but this was no ordinary criminal activity. Like an iceberg, just a fraction of the reality was ever on view.

I stepped into the investigation by accident. I was asked to assist detectives from another district because their investigation involved more than one district. I became involved in two further investigations when survivors of sexual abuse approached me with their stories.

Sexual abuse had already been in the headlines in Ireland. The aftermath of the Fr Brendan Smith case had taken down the government of Albert Reynolds. But this was my first encounter with it, despite a thirty year career in An Garda Síochána. I had seen the consequences of terrorism during those years, but nothing I had seen prepared me for the fall-out from sexual abuse. There was no training for this, no guidelines from HQ.

The story began at Christmas 1997 when a west Donegal priest, Fr Eugene Greene, reported to the Gardaí that a local man had tried to blackmail him. Instead, Greene himself ended in the dock. His hubris set in motion a train of events that led to two successful prosecutions. The lead detective in the first case also brought a third case to a successful end. I was assigned to the case because that detective, John Dooley, had worked with me before.

Among the survivors of sexual abuse, word got out of what was happening. Victims came knocking on my door — none would come to the Garda station — and my house became the unofficial nerve centre of the investigation. Those who came to me were grown men, most in their mid-thirties and most flooded with shame and guilt. Over the next two years I became accustomed to meetings in car parks, along lonely country roads, harbour piers — never in the

Garda station. They didn't want to be seen, and so we met in quiet deserted places, ironically often in the same lonely spots where many of them had been secretly abused years earlier. The shame stalked them as they told me the dark secret, almost as if in confession.

Listening to their stories, I was held in shocked silence. Of the twenty-six men who came forward about Fr Eugene Greene, I dealt with sixteen, all from the tiny Gaeltacht parish of Gort an Choirce. I knew them, their wives and their parents. It was a curiously intimate investigation.

Not long into the Greene investigation, another young man knocked at my door and stood there half huddled in the shadows when I answered. 'I was also abused,' he said. His abuser was Denis McGinley, a local schoolteacher. McGinley had abused children systematically in his classroom over many years.

There were now three investigations running simultaneously. The third, in which I was also involved as victims approached me, was focused in Dooley's district. The Greene and McGinley cases both involved the Catholic Church, since McGinley was a teacher in a Catholic school answerable to religious managers.

As we probed, we learned that the Church had been told about the abuse in both cases decades before. One family had made a report as far back as 1976. Nothing was done. As a devout Catholic myself with close relatives in the Church, this causes me difficulty to this day. One night, early on, when I still had difficulty accepting what I was learning, I found myself standing in front of a mirror in my home shouting at myself, reminding myself of my duty to believe these men and not to be diverted by any other loyalty. I remain shocked and distressed at the role of the Church.

The force offered no support to the handful of officers involved in these cases. In contrast to police forces in the UK including the PSNI in Northern Ireland, there was virtually no logistical support. In the end I bought my own computer and taught myself how to use it, attending evening classes in a local hall in order to prepare an investigation file for the Director of Public Prosecutions (DPP). Neither was there any kind of professional support. At the end of the investigation when I asked for counselling, I was told I didn't need it. Such support is routine in the UK. It was symptomatic of the Irish force's attitude at the time. Maybe things have changed.

Of necessity the accounts in this book do not go into the full details of the horrors those young men endured while they were still children, but it is necessary to recount some of their experiences here in greater detail in order to show what lies behind by now familiar words like 'sexually abused', 'molested' or 'interfered with'. Young boys mostly aged between 8 and 12 were repeatedly raped by their abusers. In some cases the abuse lasted for years. Victims described how they were forced to masturbate their rapists or endure the indignity of being masturbated by them; boys were forcibly stripped, held down and repeatedly anally raped so violently that they bled for days afterwards; or forced to accept or perform oral sex, in one case so violently that the victim almost lost consciousness. Boys had to suffer their abusers' hands reaching inside their pants, touching their testicles and penis or anus and endure unwelcome hugs and kisses, often accompanied by the stench of stale alcohol. One young boy was effectively imprisoned for three days by his abuser.

More than anything else, this is a book about the victims, those who survived sexual abuse at the hands of Greene, McGinley and others, and their courage in coming forward and telling their stories. Without their courage, justice would never have been done. The same goes for their friends, families and spouses who stood by them and established support groups. To protect the identities of those victims, their families and their friends, aliases have been used throughout the book. Certain biographical and other details that might lead to their identification have also been altered. The names of other people in the book such as my fellow Garda officers, health board officials, priests and teachers are unchanged. The one exception is *John Reilly*, who was convicted in 1999 and who cannot be identified as his name was never made public in order to protect his victims.

There are many others whose advice and assistance were priceless in writing this book, not all of whom I can name here.

Thanks first of all to Fergal Tobin, Publishing Director, and all those at Gill & Macmillan for their encouragement and support in this project and for invaluable advice at crucial stages.

Darragh MacIntyre, a reporter with BBC *Spotlight*, lived for several years in Gort an Choirce and got to know as well as I did many of those who were sexually abused as children. His own investigations for *Spotlight* uncovered new information that highlighted the extent of the scandal within the Church. It was he who introduced me to Fergal Tobin.

John Dooley, who worked closely with me on these cases, was an inspiration with his professionalism and attention to detail. To him and to the other Gardaí who worked on these and other cases, my thanks and appreciation, along with their counterparts in the health services.

Gerard Cunningham provided insights into the workings of the Morris Tribunal, in which forum John Dooley came forward, as well as advice on how to structure this book.

I would also like to thank the many priests who provided valuable background and insight and who sometimes were just willing to listen.

This book, and the investigations it recounts, would never have been possible without the strength and courage of the survivors of sexual abuse who came forward and told their stories, and their families. I cannot name them here, but to each of them, my eternal gratitude. I would also like to thank Colm O'Gorman, the director of One in Four, whom I had the privilege to meet several times.

Finally this book would not have been possible without the patience and understanding of my wife Brid and my daughters Aoife and Cliodhna. And I would like to thank my granddaughters Ailbhe and Síofra for their bright smiling faces.

To all of you, for your patience and dedication as I talked to you through a torrent of anger and horror, my thanks.

Martin Ridge
February 2008

Glossary of placenames

Anagaire	Annagry
An Craoslach	Creeslough
An Fál Carrach	Falcarragh
Caiseal na gCorr	Cashelnagore
Cill Mhic Réanáin	Kilmacrennan
Cloich Cheann Fhaóla	Cloughaneely
Cnoc Fola	Bloody Foreland
Gort an Choirce	Gortahork
Gaoth Dobhair	Gweedore
Inis Bó Finne	Inishbofin
Leitir Mhic an Bhaird	Lettermacaward
Loch an Iúir	Loughanure
Machaire Uí Robhartaigh	Magheroarty
Toraigh	Tory

Chapter 1
Blackmail

Father Eugene Greene rang John Dooley's home first, but the Glenties-based detective garda was at work. He left a number and a message, and Dooley's wife phoned the Garda station to pass on the message.

It was just before 10 p.m. on the last Saturday before Christmas, 20 December 1997, when Dooley phoned back. Greene was a priest living in semi-retirement in the nearby town of Anagaire (Annagry). The priest told Dooley he had been the victim of a blackmail attempt. Dooley arranged to meet him the following afternoon and take a statement.

At 3 p.m. on Sunday, 21 December, Greene called to Glenties Garda Station and asked to see Dooley. Greene told him that the previous spring, on 15 April, he was in his home when the doorbell rang at around 6 p.m. He answered the door and found a young man standing there.

'Do you recognise me?' the young man asked.

'No,' Greene answered.

'I'm *David Brennan* from Leitir,' the man told him. 'You did something to me. I'll be back next Monday and you better have the money. Otherwise I'm going to the Guards. You have the money next Monday or else,' *Brennan* said, and left.

Brennan mentioned no amount, just 'the money', and he never said what it was the priest was supposed to have done, Greene told Dooley, adding, 'I did nothing wrong.' *Brennan* didn't show up the following Monday as promised, and Greene heard nothing more from him for several months. Then, on 16 December, *Brennan* called to his home again.

'Do you recognise me?' he asked.

'No,' Greene replied again.

Brennan reminded the priest that he had called before in mid-April. 'I'll be back on Monday, and you better have five grand,'

Brennan told the cleric, 'otherwise I am going to the Guards, then all Loch an Iúir (Loughanure) will know.'

Greene reported this confrontation to Dooley, but said he still didn't know what it was everyone would know. He decided to call *Brennan*'s bluff and told him to go to the Guards. He said that *Brennan* never mentioned during either visit what it was he was supposed to have done.

'I took *David Brennan*'s visit on 16 December 1997 very seriously when he demanded £5,000 from me,' Greene told Dooley. 'I considered how to deal with it for a few days. I came to the decision that I had no option but to report the matter to the local detective as I see this as blackmail.'

The following morning Dooley arranged to meet Greene in the car park of a local shopping centre. He handed the priest a small dictaphone and microphone to tape *David Brennan* if he showed up again. The detective also gave the priest his mobile phone number in case he needed to get in touch. That evening between 7 and 10 p.m. Dooley sat in his unlit car watching Greene's home in case *Brennan* should show up. It was an uneventful evening. *Brennan* never appeared.

At 9 a.m. the following morning Dooley briefed Superintendent Jim Gallagher on the events since the first phone call from Greene. That afternoon, along with Detective Garda David Moore, he arrested *David Brennan*. Dooley gave *Brennan* the standard police caution as he arrested him, warning him that he was not obliged to say anything, but that anything he did say would be written down and could be used in evidence.

'That bastard, Greene, sexually molested me,' *Brennan* blurted out.

The detectives took *Brennan* to Glenties Garda Station for questioning. Once there, he freely admitted that he had visited the priest twice and demanded £5,000 because he was sexually abused by the priest when he was an altar boy in west Donegal in the 1970s. The detectives asked him if anyone could back up his allegation. The only people he had ever told were his wife *Carol* and his best friend, *Alan Walsh*, he informed them.

Dooley knew *Alan Walsh*, who as it happened worked near by. While *Brennan* was still in custody, Dooley left the station to speak to *Walsh*, who confirmed that *Brennan* had told him he had been sexually abused by Greene when he was a child. *Walsh* was willing to make a statement to that effect.

Two hours into his arrest, *Brennan* made a full statement after being cautioned, admitting his blackmail attempt and outlining the abuse he had suffered as an altar boy. As he made the statement he became emotional and upset several times as he relived the pain of his abuse.

Greene often asked *David* to come up to the parochial house after weekday morning Mass and make him a cup of tea. At first *David* only had to make tea and he enjoyed the job because it meant he got to skip some early morning classes in school. Then, a few mornings in a row, Greene brushed against *David* while he made the tea, his hand grazing against the boy's penis. Finally one morning he took *David* to his bedroom and undressed him. *David* didn't understand what was happening. The priest warned him before he left the parochial house not to tell anyone. 'It's our secret,' he told the boy. 'Only God will know.'

'I was afraid to tell anybody about this,' *David* told the detectives. The abuse continued for several weeks until he could take no more. He told his parents he was getting too old to be an altar boy. 'I dreaded this sexual abuse but I was afraid to tell anyone about it because he had told me it was his and my secret and that God knows,' he said. 'The other reason I was afraid to tell it was because he was a priest. I always felt dirty and I still feel very ashamed about the abuse. This is the first time I ever told the full story. I never forgot the torture he put me through.'

In his Garda statement *Brennan* also named other altar boys who had served around that time. He told the detectives that the priest often sent him down to local pubs to buy bottles of whiskey. He said he hadn't seen Greene after the priest left Leitir Mhic an Bhaird (Lettermacaward) until one day in 1997 when he attended a funeral. At that time he was building a home for his family and money was tight. 'I felt that this bastard should pay in some way for all the abuse on me,' he explained. That was when he decided to call on Greene and demand money.

Greene had told the detectives he had no idea why a stranger at the door was demanding money. *David* gave a fuller account. When the priest opened the door, he invited *David* into a small study.

'Do you remember what you did to me as an altar boy in Leitir Mhic an Bhaird?' he asked.

'No, what did I do?' Greene replied.

'You fucking bastard, you sexually abused me when I was an altar boy in Leitir Mhic an Bhaird,' he told the priest.

'Ah no, I never did that,' Greene answered.

'You lying bastard, you know rightly that you did it,' *David* shouted, rising out of the chair in anger. He told the priest he was stuck for money and he would be back in a few days. He didn't follow up on it though until shortly before Christmas when he called again to the priest's home. Finances were stretched to breaking point finishing his new home, and his wife had spoken about cashing in her life insurance policy to pay the deficit. *David* didn't want her to lose the investment.

·   The priest again denied he had abused *David* and pleaded poverty, but *David* was having none of it. He told the priest he could get the money off the bishop, or he would make sure everyone in the county knew what had happened. It was an empty threat. *David* had already thought about going to a solicitor about the abuse he had suffered, but couldn't face the thought of having to tell someone else what had happened. As it transpired, his wife cashed in her insurance policy, solving the money crisis, so he didn't bother going back to the priest for the money.

'I would like to see this matter fully investigated and see that Fr Greene is brought to justice,' *David* told the detectives. 'I am willing to assist the Gardaí in any further enquiries in relation to my abuse. I can only say I regret demanding money from Fr Greene and I give an undertaking that I will not call to his house or approach him at any time again.'

'He had great difficulty in telling the details of the many incidents of sexual abuse inflicted upon him by Fr Greene in the parochial house', Dooley wrote later.

Brennan was released from Garda custody that evening while Dooley considered what to do next. A simple blackmail case had turned into something much bigger.

Chapter 2
A Trusting Time

I joined the Guards on 29 December 1966. I was 19 years old. I'm from Connemara, one of what was a typically large family at the time. I was wedged in, number seven of a family of ten. My mother had a total of fourteen children, but two were stillborn and two more died in infancy.

We lived beside Costelloe Lodge where the gentry came fishing. Bruce Ismay of *Titanic* fame built the lodge in the early 1920s. Just as an iceberg had taken so many of the *Titanic*'s passengers' lives, sometimes I think that what I later discovered in Donegal was like an iceberg: it destroyed so many lives and yet we only came across the tip of it, the one-tenth above the surface.

We were the fifth generation to live in the house. My father had a drink problem and we were evicted from that house when I was 7 years of age. I remember coming home from school one evening to see Joe Mór's big lorry pulled up at our house. We were being evicted by the owners of Costelloe Lodge.

Joe Mór's red lorry was packed with furniture and other belongings. We were moving to our new unfinished house beside the pier at Derrynea. I don't remember my father being there; I think he was working in England at the time. My mother was at home with us, a tower of strength to all ten of us. At the time, for someone in a small rural community like that, there was intense shame in being evicted. The cultural memory of the Great Famine and the shame of pauperism were still very real. The insecurity of that moment when we lost our home stayed with me for many years. We found somewhere else to live though our new house wasn't completely plastered on the inside when we moved in. But what I had to deal with in Donegal was far worse. The victims I met there lost their innocence.

Emigration was rife when I was growing up. All of my father's five brothers and two sisters emigrated to America bar one — Uncle

Paddy joined the British Army and was attached to the Irish Guards. He was killed in North Africa in April 1943 at the age of 28. The number on his tombstone reads: 2718348 Guardsman. My brother Tomás visited his grave and brought me back a picture of this tombstone. I never saw or met my other uncles, with the exception of my uncle Val who joined the Chicago Police Department and came home a number of times. He was a romantic figure to me when I was growing up, a living connection with the world of gangsters in comic books and films, and I think the stories he told us on his holidays were part of the reason I decided to join the Guards.

When I joined the Gardaí in December 1966, there were two December classes; about 300 of us entered the Garda College in Templemore that month. Training lasted six months: ninety lectures to study and three exams. Having been brought up a native Irish speaker, it was the first time in my life that I had to speak English full time. I was very conscious of that. If I made a mistake in Irish hardly anyone would notice or mind, but if I made a mistake in English everyone noticed. My English was quite good, although I found I was thinking in Irish and translating it into English before I spoke. But I got used to it after a while. There was a lot crammed into those six months: marching on the square, physical training in the gym and swimming, learning police duties. Wake-up call was at seven every morning. Breakfast at eight consisted of porridge or cereal and hard-boiled eggs. The dormitory floor had to be polished every morning, bedclothes folded neatly before we assembled on the square at 9 a.m. with shoes sparkling, uniforms neatly brushed and a very tight haircut. We had to get a haircut at least twice a week.

After Garda training in Templemore, my first station was in Milford, Co. Donegal. I was there from 1967 to 1973. I was only a few weeks in my first posting when I met my future wife. One of the Guards in Milford was doing a line with a girl from An Fál Carrach (Falcarragh), and he asked me to come along with him to a dance in the town. I can't remember who was playing that night, but it was the first time I met Brid.

Brid was studying to be a teacher in England. We got to spend time together during the summers and at holiday times and kept in touch by writing to each other during term. Nowadays it would be all e-mail and texts, of course. I remember one night I drove her home from a dance, and on the way back my car broke down. I saw a light in the distance and went up to the house and knocked at the door. When the owner opened the door I told him my tale of woe. I was a Guard; my car had broken down; could I make a phone call. I wasn't in uniform obviously and I didn't have any Garda ID, but he gave me the keys of his brand new Ford Cortina and told me to bring it back later. It was a different world, a trusting time.

I hated drink because I saw what it did to my own family. I swore I would never drink, but there was a football tournament in Conway and the cup came around afterwards. 'Go on, young Ridge, have a slug of it,' someone said. Within eighteen months I was hooked. I don't know if it was the stress of the job or something I inherited, but dealing with drink has always been a problem for me, sometimes more than at other times. There were a lot of things I didn't like about myself back then. Eventually I was lucky enough to find Alcoholics Anonymous. I have fallen off the wagon a few times but I'm sober now, thank goodness.

In 1973 I was transferred from Donegal to the Midlands. Brid joined me a year later and we got married. While we lived in the Midlands she taught in the Christian Brothers School in Portarlington. She is teaching at Caiseal na gCorr (Cashelnagore) now. She didn't pass the music exam in Ireland when she went for teacher training here, but she trained in England. It was one of those quirks I could never make sense of. She couldn't get into training here because she couldn't meet the Irish standards; yet once she got her degree in England she could apply to teach here. She had to do the Irish language test of course, but she is a native Irish speaker, just as I am and our children; it's something we were proud to pass on to them.

I was stationed in Portarlington from 1973 until 1980, working regular uniform duties. Portarlington Garda Station is close to Portlaoise, the biggest prison in the Midlands, perhaps the biggest in Europe. It held the top subversives in Ireland at the time. The IRA was a constant menace during my time there. One of my colleagues, Garda Michael Clerkin, was blown up in an explosion in October 1976. I think that was the worst day of my career. I remember picking up bits of his flesh at the scene afterwards. The biggest part left of him was his ankle. He was identified by the initials 'MC' on his signet ring.

We were dealing with terrorism. The so-called 'war' was on in full force. People forget now how bad it was, with ceasefires taken for granted and endless talks of choreography and agreements. I remember when Shergar was taken, and the decoys and phone calls from the North. I remember the Herrema siege, the endless days of waiting and the relief when everything was resolved peacefully.

In 1980 there was a reorganisation within the force. The powers that be decided to set up a new detective unit, a divisional task force, as part of the Special Task Force. I was reluctant to apply as I was still battling the bottle. It looks simple to leave a drink down, but it's not that easy. It gets a grip on you, consumes you. But when I wasn't drinking I would do the work of two or three people to make up for lost time. My work rate must have impressed somebody because I was told to apply for the task force. I spent fourteen years with the detective unit in the Midlands.

In the early 1990s I transferred back to Donegal, to the station in the border town of Castlefin. Most of my time there was spent on checkpoints and border patrols, routine police work for the area, with the occasional day spent as station orderly. In March 1994 I was transferred to An Fál Carrach.

I enjoyed coming back to where I started, though it had happened more by accident than design. Brid had wanted to move back to Donegal with the girls for some time, and when an uncle left her a plot of land where we could build a home, it was a perfect opportunity. I was glad to be back. I grew up near the coast, and it was good to be living close to the sea again after years spent in the Midlands. I had a certain love for the area, the place where I started my career and where I got to know the people, where I had played football and won a county junior medal. There were memories I wasn't so fond of too. It was the area that almost devastated my life as drink began to get a hold of me. It is hard to admit it, but I had a self-destruct mechanism inside and my mind was too hazy to see what I was doing to myself at the time. It was a trap, one I built myself, and hard to snap out of. Denial is a powerful force.

Around the time I came to An Fál Carrach, the BSE outbreak in England led to checkpoints for a different reason. The mad cow disease health scares meant we had to send out patrols to monitor cattle movements along the border and keep the country disease free after the government set up a ban on cattle imports. I was back in uniform again, back in Donegal where my career began, and only three years short of thirty in the force and approaching my 50th birthday. After my years in the detective unit I thought Donegal would be a winding down. I had done my share of hard policing, I had three years to go to my pension, and my girls were growing up. There was a small station party in An Fál Carrach — four guards and a sergeant. Steady as she goes to retirement, I thought. Donegal is beautiful, and An Fál Carrach is a particularly scenic spot, a small country station in the Gaeltacht. I couldn't think of a more secure and safe place to bring up my two children.

There were routine traffic checkpoints to run, inspections of local pubs at night at closing time, and dole forms, passports and other forms to fill out occasionally for people who called to the station. Dole day was always a source of amusement and amazement to me. Each week I would find some of the forms lying on the hallway floor for me to sign when I arrived at work in the morning, pushed hurriedly through the station letterbox because the claimant was in a hurry to get to work too! It was a quiet duty for the most part. I had to deal with traffic accidents, a sight all too common on our roads, and there were about five sudden deaths in the area. Several prominent members of Sinn Féin own holiday homes in the area, including the Party president Gerry Adams, and part of my duties included keeping an eye on their homes when they were here, just to see if there were any interesting visitors. The peace process was well under way. The IRA declared a ceasefire at the end of August 1994, so as you can imagine there were a lot of comings and goings. There was a marked change in the atmosphere since my detective days in the Midlands. Instead of watching the 'military men' and trying to figure out what they were up to, now I was keeping an eye on the peace process and more likely to notice a politician in the area, from local town and county councillors to TDS. By 1997 I had reached thirty years of service. I could retire if I wanted to. But as our family prepared for Christmas 1997, something happened a few miles away that would change my life.

On Saturday, 20 December, at around 10 p.m. Glenties-based Detective Garda John Dooley got a message to make a phone call to a priest living in semi-retirement in Anagaire. The priest told Dooley he had been the victim of a blackmail attempt. John arranged to meet the priest the following afternoon and take a statement. The arrest a few days later of the alleged blackmailer, *David Brennan*, led to one of the most successful paedophile investigations ever undertaken by An Garda Síochána. Ironically we learned later that Fr Eugene Greene first contacted Dooley after speaking to a solicitor who advised him to report the extortion attempt to the police. Somehow I doubt that Greene told the solicitor the full story when he asked him for advice on what to do, but either way his decision to report the incident illustrated his sense of absolute untouchability. Perhaps that sense of being above the law led him to feel that because of his clerical status the Gardaí would never investigate him. Whatever his reasoning, it is a perfect example of what the ancient Greeks called hubris, that particular mix of pride and arrogance that always comes before a fall, blinding him so that he could not see ahead to what would inevitably follow once Dooley began his investigation.

I was assigned to the case in January 1998. We got Greene's cv from the bishop, a history of his career. Greene had worked in Gort an Choirce (Gortahork) parish for several years, and my job was to find out if there were any victims on my patch. How do I start this assignment, I wondered.

Chapter 3
Where to Begin

Where do you start? You start with a casual conversation. My time back in uniform in Donegal paid off in a way I could never have foreseen when I transferred out of the Midlands detective unit a few years earlier. To the people who knew me in Donegal, I wasn't some remote detective from a district or divisional office sent in to investigate a case. I was Garda Martin Ridge. I had lived and worked here long enough to become a familiar face, signed passport applications and dole forms, handled the occasional traffic checkpoint and closing time in pubs. I was married to a local woman, my daughters went to school locally, I knew a lot of the people and they knew me. I wasn't a stranger; I was someone who could strike up a casual conversation.

I had worked with Detective Garda John Dooley on other operations over the years and I had a sense of what he was like. He had a reputation within the force for being a hard and diligent worker. I felt I could rely on him and I wasn't let down. His dedication to the work in hand was second to none. We both had detective branch experience and he still worked there. We gelled together well.

An Garda Síochána is a national police force with the country divided into six regions, each headed by an assistant commissioner. The northern region, like all the others, was divided into several divisions, including the Donegal division. The chief superintendent in charge of the Donegal division had his headquarters in Letterkenny. He oversaw several districts, each headed by a superintendent.

My area in Donegal was the Milford subdistrict of An Fál Carrach, the Gaeltacht area to the north-east of Errigal Mountain known as Cloich Cheann Fhaola (Cloughaneely), which included the rural parishes of An Fál Carrach and Gort an Choirce. The two towns are barely two miles apart, but their hinterlands cover a wide rural area. My Garda station in An Fál Carrach covered both parishes, both the towns and the outlying countryside. Cloich Cheann Fhaola is sparsely populated, but in area is the second largest Garda subdistrict in the country. Toraigh (Tory) and Inis Bó Finne (Inishbofin), two islands a few miles off the Donegal coast, were also part of the parish of Gort an Choirce. Toraigh was still inhabited all year round, but Inis Bó Finne was empty most of the year, although some of the islanders still went out there for their summer holidays.

Dooley brought me in on the Eugene Greene case when he found out that Greene had worked as a curate in Gort an Choirce for five years between 1976 and 1981. Although I was in the uniformed branch of the force, I had worked with him on a few cases since I got back to Donegal because of my detective branch experience. John knew I had been based in An Fál Carrach for a few years and had a fair grasp of the area. I knew a lot of young men of the right age to have been altar boys at that time. Most of them would have been in their early twenties by then. A conversation between Dooley and his superintendent, and a phone call to me from my superintendent, ending with the brief instruction to 'give John a hand on this', meant I was assigned to one of the most complicated and harrowing investigations of my career.

I put myself more or less on standby. At first I saw my task as no more than having a cursory look around the parish. We had Greene's cv from the bishop and I knew the time frame I had to deal with. I already knew Greene. I knew he was fond of a drink, but I was no stranger to that myself. I had often spoken to the man. He baptised one of our children in the mid-1970s. He was as drunk as a lord that day. Overall he seemed well liked. If anything, people felt sorry for him because of his drink problem.

I thought my task was to clear his name as far as the parish of Gort an Choirce was concerned. I couldn't imagine anything untoward happening to children in this area. I had read about clerical sexual abuse scandals in other parts of the country and abroad; it had brought the government of Albert Reynolds down in 1994; I was aware of abuse in the Midlands; but surely it could not happen in this lovely place.

To begin, I did what Guards do: I talked to people — nothing fancy, just a chat whenever I met anyone. I would maybe talk about what the priest said at Mass the previous Sunday or about schooldays in Gort an Choirce, an easy enough subject to bring a conversation around to since my wife Bríd worked as a teacher. Eventually you get to where you want to be in a casual chat. Do you remember Fr Greene? You'd have been an altar boy at the time, or maybe in a choir or youth club he supervised. What was he like? The response amazed me. 'He abused me.'

It was like igniting a flame. Little did I know that the flame would turn into a furnace. I felt as if I was hit in a raw nerve. It was happening here too, I thought, but at the same time part of my mind still protested: it couldn't be. I didn't want to believe it. I wanted to ask him, are you sure? I felt like a footballer playing for two opposing teams at the same time. My loyalty to the Church dragged me to one side, yet here was a victim giving me gruesome details of child sexual abuse.

What do I say? What do I do? I listened. I knew he wasn't lying, but I was ill prepared for his story. I could sense his shame and guilt as he blurted out his story as if it happened yesterday, every detail still fresh in his mind. The astonishing details were new to me, but not to him. I arranged to meet him later in a car park where he felt safe and could talk without worrying about being seen. He sat in my car, ducking whenever another car passed. The story gushed out with sadness and with some relief. It was agonising listening to him. This was his childhood, years of it, robbed and laid bare before us. He was ashamed of it. He was stagnating in hurt. I was shell-shocked at how fresh the details of the abuse were for him. He seemed to be reliving it as he spoke. Here was another tragic story kept buried for years due to fear, shame and guilt. All I could do was listen.

Dooley's enquiries had led him to several more victims in other parishes. I sat in while he took their statements. Watching John, I learned from him and applied the same approach in my own area. This was a sensitive investigation, given the subject matter. So if you go to see someone, don't go in uniform; go in plain clothes. Don't use a Garda car, not even an unmarked one; use your own car. Go slowly; be patient. If people want to talk to you, they will, and if they don't, don't press them. Given what they went through, people are going to be reluctant enough to talk anyway. The last thing they need is a Guard throwing his weight around. So you talk and, more importantly, you listen and you wait. If people want to talk, they will come to you.

Somehow, despite the secrecy of the investigation and the sensitivity of the allegations, word had got out. Another young fellow approached me and told me he was abused. One case led to another. Each one I spoke to knew someone else I could talk to. Not everyone wanted to talk to me and there were false leads, but slowly we were able to build a case file. One young man, *Edward Brown*, flew over from England to speak to me. He later told his story in a television documentary. A friend of *Edward* was also abused by Greene, and after they spoke on the phone about the investigation, *Edward* decided to come home and speak to me too. Most of the victims had been altar boys. For many of them, being sexually abused was the norm, something they had had to accept as a part of growing up. The way the horrors they described were accepted almost as part of the culture of childhood shocked me.

But at least now they were talking about it. They seemed relieved to finally let the cork out of the bottle, although none of them ever came to the Garda station to talk. Instead, we met in hotel rooms or at my home or in a deserted car park. I think they forgot I was a Guard. I didn't see myself as a policeman when I listened to them. Before this investigation started, they already knew me. I might have sworn a summons for them or taken care of a passport application or car tax. I dealt with them every day. They knew I would go down to the station for a form even if I wasn't on duty if they were in a hurry. That's the only explanation I can think of. I didn't have any particular expertise in this kind of investigation. My experience in the Midlands, and in Donegal before and after the Midlands, had never prepared me for this.

When I was stationed in the Midlands I had encountered child sexual abuse only once, and then only indirectly. It was a Saturday afternoon shortly after I was appointed to the detective branch, and I found myself alone in the offices with nothing much to do. I noticed a key on the wall, and out of curiosity more than anything else I took it down and tried it on some presses. They opened. To pass the time I took out some of the folders in the press, a few old brown files wound up with twine and covered in dust.

I opened up one or two of the files. They were past cases. There was one dealing with a murder in the area, several major crime cases and a few reports on 'subversive activity'. Then I came across one dealing with child sexual abuse in a local college. I was so shocked I almost dropped the file. I felt as if I was stealing something. The case involved a cleric who had sexually abused a number of young girls during the 1960s. The depravity of the abuse shocked me. How could anybody, let alone a person who was supposed to be minding young people, do such a thing? I felt so much revulsion that I still recall the shock, even years later.

For whatever reason the victims I met in Donegal felt they could trust me, and they also trusted John Dooley. The frankness of the responses, when finally asked what happened, sometimes stunned me. I would carefully bring the conversation around to Greene, or to childhood, finding the point to ask the question I needed: 'Were you an altar boy with Fr Greene?'

'I was, yeah.'

'What was he like?'

'Ah, he was after the lads.' Most of them, I realised, had been waiting for years to be asked, living behind stoic outer masks.

After *David Brennan* was arrested and made the first allegations, Dooley and the local superintendent, James P. Gallagher, got in contact with the Raphoe diocesan office in Letterkenny and got their hands on a copy of Greene's CV. With this they now knew every parish he had been stationed in since his returned from the missions. He spent his first ten years in the priesthood on missionary work in Africa. Since his return in 1965, he had worked in six parishes in Co. Donegal: Cnoc Fola (Bloody Foreland), Leitir Mhic an Bhaird, Gort an Choirce, Glenties, Gaoth Dobhair (Gweedore) and Cill Mhic Réanáin (Kilmacrennan). Apart from a year in Co. Cork (1969–70) and an earlier spell in Scotland, he had spent his entire career in west Donegal, mostly in the Gaeltacht parishes. Since 1994 he had lived in semi-retirement in Loch an Iúir. Armed with this information, Dooley had tracked down several men who were abused as children and we began the slow process of gathering evidence for a prosecution.

By mid-January we had spoken again to *Alan Walsh*, *David Brennan*'s best friend, and to *David*'s wife *Carol*. They provided us with formal statements confirming what they had told Dooley the day *David* was arrested. *Alan*, a 23-year-old salesman, had known *David* all his life. They became close friends when they worked together in their teens after leaving school, so much so that *David* asked *Alan* to be his best man at his wedding. A year later *Alan* returned the favour. Even though *David* had moved away since he got married, they had kept in touch and were still good friends. *Alan* told us that two years before, in the summer of 1996, they were both invited to the wedding of a mutual friend, where they got chatting over a few drinks.

'I have something wild to tell you,' *David* said.

'Go ahead, talk away,' *Alan* answered.

David hesitated for a while, and remained silent, toying with his drink. His eyes welled up and he wiped tears from his eyes. 'I was abused when I was a wee boy on the altar in Leitir Mhic an Bhaird,' he told his friend.

Alan was shocked. He asked who the priest was. *David* told him it was Eugene Greene. He explained how he was taken to the local parochial house and taken upstairs, where he was sexually abused. *David* was upset and cried a lot as he explained that the priest told him the abuse was 'God's way' and that if he went against it something bad would happen. He said he had never told anyone in his family what had happened.

A week later *Alan* met *David* again. Sober this time, he asked his friend if what he had said at the wedding was true, and if he had ever told his parents. *David* confirmed it was true but was reluctant to talk about it. *Alan* confirmed to Dooley that *David* had never spoken to anyone about what happened to him until the day he was arrested, when he was asked about the conversation by Dooley.

Carol Brennan told a similar tale. The 28-year-old factory worker said that one night between her engagement and wedding, *David* had said to her that he had something to tell her before they got married. 'When *David* was telling me this horrific story he was very emotional,' *Carol* told us. 'He stated that he had never told this to another person. I asked him why he didn't tell his parents and he said that he was ashamed to tell them and also that Fr Greene had warned him that it was a secret and that only *David*, Fr Greene and God knew about it.'

David made *Carol* promise she would not tell anyone else, and said he felt the abuse was why he drank excessively. He hadn't told her of his plan to get money from Greene. If he had, she would have stopped him. The first she knew of her husband's plan was when Dooley called to the family home and arrested *David*.

The best news *Carol* had for us was that *David* was waiting for an appointment to get professional counselling, and since he had made his statement he was greatly relieved that the Guards were taking him seriously and had begun an investigation.

Sometime later Dooley spoke to *David*'s mother *Hazel*. She told him that *David* had talked to her about what happened some months after his arrest, on the night his wife gave birth to his second child. She was able to narrow down when the abuse occurred since she remembered when *David* first became an altar boy and when he left the altar. She remembered that it was often not until 11 a.m. that *David* would arrive home after serving the early morning Mass with Greene. When she had asked him why, he told her he had to go to the parochial house to make tea for the priest as he had no housekeeper.

'*David* was a quiet boy growing up,' *Hazel* told John. 'He started drinking at 16 years of age. Every night he came home drunk he cried his eyes out. I often asked him what was troubling him. I remember I used to say to him, "*David* you are as good as the next. Did someone say something to you?"'

'Mum,' *David* would say to her, 'You don't know what's on my mind. I can't tell you.'

It bothered *Hazel* to see her son so upset, but she was unable to find out what troubled him. The night his second child was born, however, he told her about the sexual abuse he suffered as an altar boy. He had always drunk too much, but in the last few months he had become a happier person, only taking a social drink at weekends.

'I feel very hurt and angry that Eugene Greene sexually abused my son,' *Hazel* said. 'After all a priest is a person I thought I could trust. As a parent I thought it was the right thing to get my sons on the altar to serve Mass. It upsets me greatly to think that *David* felt he had to keep this abuse as a secret because Eugene Greene had warned him that he wasn't to tell and that God knew.'

The statements we gathered from *Carol* and *Hazel* and from *Alan Walsh* were critical if we wanted to build a strong case against Greene that would survive a trial. Without them, all we had were the conflicting stories of two people. With them we could prove which side was telling the truth. If we could persuade other victims to come forward, then it would show a pattern of abusive behaviour by Greene and we would have a real chance of building a case.

Chapter 4
Under the Blankets

Two weeks later John Dooley's enquiries had led us to the first person who could confirm *David Brennan*'s claims at first hand. *Andrew Kelly* had moved away to England, where he lived with his wife and young children. When the 37-year-old pipe-fitter found out that Dooley was investigating Eugene Greene, he came home to make a statement. For twenty-two years he had had to live with a terrible secret. The only person he had been able to confide in was his wife. Once he learned there was someone who would listen and act, he was determined to tell his story.

Andrew was an altar boy when Greene was moved to his parish as a curate in the mid-1970s. His duties included counting the money on the collection plates, setting up the local hall for bingo and the occasional odd job around the parochial house. When Greene decided to open a mineral bar to raise extra funds during the bingo drives, he took *Andrew* along on trips to stock up with soft drinks. *Andrew* soon realised that the priest drank a lot. His breath often smelled of alcohol on the trips.

On one of the trips Greene asked *Andrew* if he would like to steer his vw Beetle. The young teenager, who had an obsessive interest in cars at the time, was delighted. While he steered, the priest pulled *Andrew* close. The boy felt Greene's beard bristles on the side of his jaw and the stink of stale alcohol on his breath as Greene put his hand on *Andrew*'s leg.

'At first I wondered did Fr Greene realise where his hand was,' *Andrew* told Dooley. 'After a few minutes I felt extremely uncomfortable. I then jerked the steering wheel and Greene had to take over the wheel. I jumped back into my proper position in the passenger's seat and he continued driving.' *Andrew* felt 'dirty' about what had happened. He thought first that the priest was a 'poof', but the thought confused him. How could a priest be a poof? On the way home *Andrew* felt ashamed and uneasy that anyone might see him with the priest. Greene abused the boy in the parochial house that evening. Several times after that the priest abused *Andrew* on the pretence of teaching him how to drive. *Andrew* enjoyed learning how to drive but dreaded the priest's touch. He felt 'disgusted and clammy'.

'Even though I knew what he was doing was very unnatural and wrong, because he was the local priest I knew I couldn't speak about it,' *Andrew* told Dooley. 'When he would allow me to drive his car, he would be looking at me in a weird way and staring at me. He used to drink a lot of wine, although I only saw him drunk once. That was in a hotel when he took me out for a meal. He appeared a very generous man who surrounded himself with boys of 14 years and younger. He wore a very strong aftershave lotion and even to this day, twenty-two years later, if I ever smell this aftershave I immediately think back to Fr Greene and all my bad experiences with him flash through my head.'

One summer's afternoon *Andrew* and his friend *George Maguire* were working around the parochial house doing odd jobs and tidying up. When *Andrew* looked up from his work *George* had disappeared. He knew his friend hadn't gone home because he was working near the gate and he would have seen him leave, so he went looking for him. As *Andrew* searched, he met Greene, who told him he was going for a nap.

While *Andrew* continued to search, the phone rang in the parochial house and he answered the call. Someone was looking for the priest. 'I went up to his bedroom and called him,' *Andrew* remembered. 'This bedroom was upstairs with a bathroom beside it. I knocked on the bedroom door. "Fr Greene, are you awake?" When he replied I told him there was a call for him. "Just a minute," he answered. I then stepped into the bathroom and Fr Greene came out of his room wearing a red silky dressing gown. As far as I can recall his legs were bare. He did not see me in the bathroom and proceeded downstairs to answer the phone.'

When the priest went to take the call, *Andrew* looked into the bedroom. What he saw was chilling. *George* was lying in the priest's bed, trying to hide himself by pulling the blankets over his head. 'I ran down the stairs and out the door and I felt like telling the whole world that I knew for sure that Fr Greene was a poof,' *Andrew* told Dooley. When he got home he told his grandfather what had happened. The old man told him to stop telling lies about the priest. *Andrew* realised that no grown-up would believe him if he told the story of what he had seen and he would get into trouble for telling tales about the priest. His friend *George* refused to discuss what went on in the bedroom with Greene. He was 11 years old.

Andrew warned all his friends to stay away from Greene, but he was unable to tell them what the priest had done to him. There was nothing else he could do. His family were 'strong supporters of the clergy'. He did his best to avoid the priest but felt unable to tell the priest to stop. He wanted to confront him about *George* and about his own abuse, but his 'upbringing and respect for the Catholic Church prevented me from saying it to him'.

After a year, to *Andrew*'s relief, the priest was transferred to another parish. Greene made *Andrew* promise to visit him at his new posting, but the young boy had no intention of keeping the promise. One evening shortly after he had left the parish, the priest called to *Andrew*'s house. *Andrew* was working in the fields when his grandfather called him down and told him that Greene was at the house to take him to Gort an Choirce for the weekend. The boy ran out into the fields and hid until Greene eventually left.

'Sexual abuse was a taboo subject in 1975,' *Andrew* explained. 'Every time I read the papers about paedophile priests my mind always flashes back to Fr Greene. My conscience was bothering me as I always felt I should tell some person in authority about my own experience and what I witnessed in Fr Greene's bedroom. Now that I've told the full story, I feel much better and I intend discussing it fully with my doctor also.'

Andrew's palpable relief at being able to talk about what happened was typical of many of the victims. Often, once you got round to the subject, they would tell you everything that happened straight out. Too often the stories were the same — a lift down the road or a trip to get groceries. Greene would allow the boys to steer his car, sitting them on his lap. They felt great steering the car, grown up. They were groomed this way. By the time Greene first abused them, they didn't know what to do. They knew this wasn't right, but how could they stop it? This was the priest they trusted, who taught them how to drive. Afterwards, what happened was 'our little secret'. The victims of reverse psychology, they were made to feel guilty, to feel responsible for the abuse. They were trapped.

Their biggest fear was that anybody would find out because of the shame they felt. Even now, as grown men, very few victims feel able to break the anonymity. That is why some personal details in *Andrew*'s story, and those of the other victims I met, have been changed to protect their identities. But *Andrew*'s courage in coming forward to make a formal statement told Dooley he was on the right track. He now had first-hand accounts of abuse from two victims and *Andrew* had given us an eye-witness account of the abuse of a third victim. He knew he would have to talk to *George Maguire*.

Chapter 5
Is it Money They're Looking For?

Two weeks after the breakthrough with *Andrew Kelly*, John Dooley took a statement from *Ivan Sullivan*. I had no direct involvement with those first victims that John spoke to. He worked those cases along with Garda David Moore, who had been there when *David Brennan* was arrested and questioned back in December. Meanwhile I kept up my own enquiries in Gort an Choirce, still not quite able to believe that such things could happen. Not here. Not in a place so tranquil and peaceful.

Having already listened to *Andrew*'s story, what *Ivan* had to say sounded very familiar to Dooley. *Ivan* was now in his late thirties, running his own business. He was a former altar boy and though he had left the altar when he finished national school some time before Eugene Greene arrived in the area, he was still involved in parish activities like the youth club, helping with the mineral bar on Bingo nights, counting the money in the parochial house after church collections and working on the upkeep of the parochial grounds along with *Andrew Kelly* when Greene arrived in the parish.

'I can remember that there was always a strong smell of alcohol off Fr Greene. He often sent me out for drink,' *Ivan* told Dooley. 'I remember Fr Greene had a blue vw Beetle. He subsequently smashed this car while under the influence of alcohol.' Echoing what had happened with *Andrew*, *Ivan* remembered how Greene sat in the passenger seat and let him drive the Beetle on the way back from a Mass in an elderly parishioner's home. What happened next followed a by now familiar pattern, as Greene touched the boy while he drove the car.

'I felt very uncomfortable at Fr Greene's actions and I tried to move away from him,' *Ivan* remembered. 'I managed to move away from him at the start, but he kept putting his hand on my knee and his arm around my shoulder or neck.' *Ivan* managed to make an excuse and stop the car, and Greene took over driving while he sat in the passenger seat. The priest was able to persuade the boy to lean over and hold the steering wheel, which meant his hands were free while *Ivan* steered. He felt intensely uncomfortable as the priest pressed his unshaven face against his cheek, and he had a vivid memory of the smell of stale alcohol and aftershave lotion.

Ivan also told Dooley that *Andrew* had warned him about Greene and about how he saw *George Maguire* in Greene's bed, and that the priest had left the bedroom to take a phone call dressed only in a dressing gown. Far-fetched as the story sounded, *Ivan* believed it because of his own experience. The story was another piece of evidence to back up what *Andrew* had said.

Ivan never told anyone what had happened with Greene, not even *Andrew* when he warned him about the priest. Although he had since realised he was abused by the priest, he didn't know what sexual abuse was at the time. But he knew it was wrong and he never wanted it to happen again. He made sure he never got into the car with him again. Greene surrounded himself with boys in their early teens, he remembered. He felt what Greene did was 'a total betrayal of his position as a priest and the trust he held', and he promised he would give evidence in court if Greene was ever charged. *Ivan* was lucky. He didn't think his experience had affected him mentally or physically, although it caused him to question his faith in the Catholic Church. His main concern was whether Greene still had access to young boys and if he was still a practising priest.

No doubt, like many others, *Ivan* felt an immense sense of relief when Greene was moved from the parish after a year. Transferred out of Leitir Mhic an Bhaird in 1976, Greene was moved to Gort an Choirce, my bailiwick. While Dooley was speaking to the young men who had known Greene when they were boys in Leitir, I was doing the same in Gort an Choirce.

Dealing with child sexual abuse and with the hurt of the victims was one of the most gruesome tasks I ever had to deal with. I found that children were psychologically dismembered by it, even years later. Apart from being bridled with guilt and shame at the abuse, they felt they would face the disapproval of society if they ever spoke out, which made their sense of hurt and abandonment more accute. They had an unwanted friend in this enemy that was imposed on them. Their hurt, constantly haunting and hunting them, reeked of an eerie silence. Greene had intruded on their innocence and imprisoned them.

I remember one night after taking a victim's statement putting on my uniform and going out to do a routine pub inspection, and being shouted at for closing down the bar with the usual question, have you nothing better to do? I thought to myself, yes, but I have to do this too. I don't get to choose which laws to enforce. Frequently I would meet the mothers of victims in supermarkets. I couldn't but notice the tears coming into their eyes as we passed, although nothing was said. It was curiously intimate yet distant. We dealt with the hurt together yet privately. They were dealing with ghosts from the past, victims hollowed out by the sexual abuse they had suffered, and it was choking them.

I was totally confused dealing with these crimes. Nothing I had witnessed in my years as a detective in the Midlands had prepared me to deal with sexual abuse. I still saw the Church as a Christian community caring for its members, or at least I wanted to. But somewhere along the line something had gone wrong. I knew we had to bring the truth out into the open. Along with all the hidden crimes and hidden pain I was beginning to realise that the truth was also hidden. It was the victims, not the Church, that provided us with a map to the truth.

I felt we were on a blindfolded mission as far as the Church was concerned, travelling through a forest of despair while the Church took a back seat and glided gently by as if it was not their concern. Greene had abused three boys that we knew of in Leitir Mhic an Bhaird, yet he was simply moved on to Gort an Choirce after a year with no accountability.

As I entered this dark world to investigate child sexual abuse back at the beginning of 1998, nothing could have prepared me for it. I had lived with my own despair struggling with alcoholism, my shame, my guilt and inadequacies. But it was only a blip compared to what I was about to encounter. I found myself in a zone apart from the world, dealing with things most people never have to think about. My ignorance of what was going on put me to shame as I learned what happened to so many young people. John Dooley and I were coming across a catalogue of horror, but it was real — real people telling us about real events, stories of subhuman activity and horrific deeds carried out on the most innocent members of society. We were discovering a horror story that could not have been invented, a litany of abuse stories, tales of despair, anguish, guilt, horror and unimaginable degradation on blameless children.

These stories were told to us in the dark of the night, in car parks and behind walls of piers, on lonely bog roads or some other hidden location, beside beaches where abuses were carried out, in secret places where no one would see us, often the same secret places where these young men were abused as children.

Something was stolen from these boys and they didn't want anyone to know their secret. The cases were becoming far too familiar to us. Their stories were often told to us as if in a confessional, as though they were seeking forgiveness for being victims. I felt as if I was listening to their silent screams for help. They were evicted from their childhood, kidnapped by the abuse.

They weren't supposed to tell. This was our little secret, Greene told the boys, God's secret. If they told, a priest would be hurt, the Church would be hurt, the structure would collapse and it would be their fault. So they should stay silent, never dare to speak out.

Near the end of the investigation, Dooley and I travelled to meet a parish priest in whose parish Greene had worked as a curate. This man, Fr John McGlynn, we eventually discovered, had presided over a parish where two paedophiles and two serial abusers operated leaving a trail of horror as they abused at will. As we arrived at his home to interview him as prearranged, I spoke to Dooley. 'Look John,' I said, 'we will have to keep our minds pristine clear when we are interviewing this man. He will try to gloss over this as a non-event. He will try to trivialise it. We are doing our duty here. We will do our work.'

John looked at me curiously, not quite knowing what I meant. I had sensed that there was an accepted culture in place, that you did not talk about these issues, and you definitely could not confront Church management. I knew the man had pushed on in years and I had no disrespect for him, for his age or who he was, but we were dealing with heinous crimes.

The parish priest's faithful housekeeper opened the door and led us into the sitting room. The door closed behind us. It was night time and McGlynn was sitting beside a nice warm welcoming fire, sideways to where we sat on the sofa. He was aware of our mission. Before we sat down I introduced him to John Dooley. He already knew me. He leaned back and inhaled from his cigarette. 'Is it money they're looking for?' he asked me.

After all we had learned, the comment hit all the wrong buttons. I was livid. If I had met him at the beginning of the investigation or somewhere in its infancy, I could have pushed aside my own irritation and listened. But here we were coming to the end of these enquiries, having investigated three paedophiles, two of whom he presided over. As a school manager he presided over a teacher who was a serial abuser, who abused at will throughout most if not all of his career, and as a parish priest he presided over a curate, Eugene Greene, one of the most prolific rapists in the country. I knew he had told one mother that if a scandal broke she would have to leave the area. His attitude seemed to be that it would be better for an accuser to disappear than an abuser to be stopped, thus preventing scandal to the Church. Having gone through a trail of horror and destruction with these victims, listening to their stories spanning four decades, stories that no man should have to hear, and knowing young people who had taken their own lives because they could no longer live with the horror and shame, I did not need to hear the parish priest's curt remark.

As he flicked his cigarette ash into the fire, I blew my top. I had spent so much time with the victims I must have crossed over to their world and felt too much of their despair. I had vomited in disgust in toilets after listening to their stories. And having listened to mothers with broken hearts who had lost their children, I could not take his attitude. Is it money they're looking for? What money would pay for this? Is a child's dignity about money? I felt I had to try to get across some of the suffering he was dismissing so easily.

'Those lads were ruptured,' I told him. 'They were masturbated. They were sucked off. They were raped.'

He started to go pale, but I had to keep going. He had to know what had happened, what he had dismissed with his snide words about victims looking for money. 'All of that happened, and you're telling me they're looking for money? This abuse was repeated time and time again, four decades of it, and you mention money. Do you think this is what this is about, money?'

Sitting on the sofa beside me, John kept pushing his elbow into my side, indicating that I should go easy. But I felt I had to let rip. What happened to these young children was just so awful. Their tales of despair kept going through my mind. I was getting sick listening to comments about a 'compo culture'. It was sickening to hear such a comment coming from someone who should know better. How could someone think we were dealing with devious little children who could see far down the line and set themselves up for sexual abuse so they could get some money later. How sick! McGlynn was very pale by nature, but I could see his face was by now totally drained of any colour. I hadn't intended to offend or attack him, but I felt I had to call it the way it was. If he was ignorant of what really happened, it wasn't my fault. I didn't invent these crimes and neither did the victims. Coming around to take a statement from him wasn't a joyous occasion. We discovered that the abuse had been reported to him years before. We needed a statement covering what he knew, and when.

This same priest would subsequently lavish praise on another paedophile at his trial, giving him a character reference after he had pleaded guilty to dozens of offences. He became Greene's parish priest when the curate was transferred from Leitir to Gort an Choirce after only one year in that parish. No doubt, like many others, *Ivan Sullivan* felt an immense sense of relief when Greene was moved. As I was learning, while Dooley was speaking to the men who had known Greene when they were boys in Leitir, the children in Gort an Choirce felt no such relief at his arrival.

Chapter 6

Up the Fire Escape

I wasn't with John Dooley while he worked most of his side of the initial investigation further west in the county than my base. As he pieced together the stories of abuse in the mid-1970s, I was dealing with my own area doing the groundwork. We kept in touch over the phone, briefing each other on what we had found. The pattern was often depressingly the same in his area as in mine — different faces and different places, but the same stories.

I felt an overwhelming sense of duty. For most of the time that I worked on these cases I never wore the uniform, but the duty it represented was never more important. These people were taking a huge leap into the unknown, trusting us with their stories. For many of them it was the first time they had ever told their story; for many of the others, only their closest friends or wives knew. They were confused, scared, unsure if they would be believed. This was a robbery, though we weren't dealing with stolen goods but with stolen lives. Men aren't very good dealing with human emotions, doubting trust, feeling disgust, often burying themselves in a sorrowful despair. I had to abandon my Garda badge and just be a human face when dealing with the hurt and guilt, for many of them felt responsible for the abuse they had endured. We got to know them as we got to know their hurt and the terrible secret power it still held over their lives.

Along with Dooley, I took my first statement in the case three weeks after John spoke to *Ivan Sullivan*. When Greene was transferred out of Leitir Mhic an Bhaird, he was sent to Gort an Choirce, and as I made my enquiries around Gort an Choirce, one name kept cropping up — *Keith Quinn*. He had been abused horrifically and had lots of problems as a result. Everyone was concerned about him; they knew he had problems of some kind. He was also 'known to the Gardaí', though most people considered him more a danger to himself than to others. We had received several complaints about his behaviour in the past, but often people didn't want to make any statements officially. It might make the situation worse than it was. 'Guard, will you do something, please?' they would say to us. 'But I don't want my name used.' What I now suspected gave me a context for a lot that I knew about *Keith*. It explained his antisocial, self-destructive behaviour.

I spoke with *Keith* several times before we set up a time and place to take his statement. He was adamant that he wouldn't speak to us anywhere that we might be seen. We agreed we would meet in a town several miles away. We arranged a pick-up point near a well-known local landmark from which we would collect him.

It was after dark when I pulled up in my car. In the brake lights through the rear mirror I saw him emerge from the shadows behind the bushes, crouched over, hiding even though it was dark. We drove on in the night, hardly speaking. Dooley had booked a hotel room for the evening. *Keith* wouldn't walk in the front door of the hotel in case he bumped into someone he knew. We had to sneak up the fire escape ladder at the back. He was still locked in the terrors of his childhood, unable to bring himself ever to talk to girls, afraid to acknowledge his own sexuality. After we had spoken to him, we organised counselling for him.

Keith was one of a large family. He attended the local schools before going on to college, and worked in the family business. His early childhood was full of the ordinary things that should fill a young boy's days in Co. Donegal — school, homework, work around the family home, sports and friends — until he started going to secondary school.

Like many teenagers in rural Ireland he travelled to school on the bus, and at lunchtime he would wander around the town checking out shop displays after eating his packed lunch. One spring day as he wandered around the town, the local curate Eugene Greene stopped his car and offered him a lift back to school. *Keith* accepted the lift and told the priest his name. They were only about a quarter of a mile from the school, but the priest didn't take the direct route back, instead driving the longest way around along quiet country roads. Greene told *Keith* he was taking the longer route to have a chat with him and get to know him. When they had travelled a short distance he pulled over in a quiet lay-by. Although the boy tried to resist, Greene abused him despite his protests, telling him it was okay and it was normal. *Keith* kept telling him he had to go back to school but hadn't the courage to do anything else. Finally the priest relented and

drove him back. *Keith* did his best to avoid Greene after that and
rarely saw him except at Mass on Sundays.

'I didn't realise at the time that what Fr Greene had done to me was
wrong,' *Keith* told us. 'This was partly because Fr Greene had reassured
me that it was a normal thing to do. I think I was about 16 when I fully
realised that Fr Greene had sexually abused me. At that time and now,
I feel very angry about this abuse. I felt too ashamed to tell my parents
or anybody else about it. I tried to block it out of my mind, but it
would return every time I heard about sexual abuse on TV or read
about it in the newspapers.'

Quinn's body language, from his crouched appearance in the
shadows to the way he sat in the hotel room, spoke volumes about the
effect Greene's actions had on him. He sat almost in a huddle,
crouched over himself, his hands crossed over his chest to protect
himself and his head lowered. Everything about his body language
declared, 'I was abused. I can't talk about it.' But more than the need
to hide inside himself, to huddle up and protect himself from the
world, *Keith* needed to talk that night. Someone was there to listen; he
needed to tell his story.

———

A few days later Dooley called out to Greene's house to collect the
dictaphone and microphone he had given the priest back in
December to record any conversation he might have if *David Brennan*
were to show up and make good on his blackmail threat. The priest
asked how the enquiry was going. 'I informed Eugene Greene that I
could not discuss the investigation with him at that time', Dooley later
noted drily in his statement of evidence at the end of the case file he
prepared for the Director of Public Prosecutions. 'He replied that
he understood that and he informed me that he had retired on
25 February 1998 at the request of the Bishop of Raphoe, Dr Philip
Boyce.'

At the time we were so busy dealing with Greene's victims, we
barely had time to step back and think about the conversation, so it is
possible to read too much into that brief exchange with John as he
collected the electronic gear. We were totally focused on the details of
the investigation, on the victims, and on obtaining statements we

could bring to court that would stand up to cross-examination. Is it possible that Greene was fishing for information? And why, in the time since we had contacted the diocesan office for a copy of his career history and the start of our investigation, had he decided to retire? Priests don't normally retire until they reach 75. He was only 71. He had already been living in semi-retirement for several years before we began the investigation. Had someone told him the Guards were investigating a complaint? Looking back now from a wider perspective, one has to wonder. But at the time we didn't give our minds the scope to think like that. We had too many people to talk to.

I heard later that 'something had happened' in the parish of Cill Mhic Réanáin where Greene was stationed in 1994. The information was vague, as these things often are, and although a journalist also looked into the story for a while, we never managed to get a confirmation of the rumour that a family had complained about Greene and received a private settlement shortly before his retirement. Perhaps that was the catalyst that led to his withdrawal from active ministry. A priest told me later that when a senior Church official was told about this complaint, his reply was, 'He couldn't have. Sure he's cured.' Apparently Greene's behaviour, his secret abuse of children under his care, wasn't a secret to all of his bosses in the Church.

Chapter 7
Grapevine

*B*arry Hayes was an islander. Like many from the islands he was a fisherman, and like many he also did other work to supplement the precarious living he took from the sea. When I met him he was 38 years old and had quietly carried the wounds of sexual abuse inside for more than half a lifetime. *Barry* first met Eugene Greene when he was 16. As curate in the parish of Gort an Choirce, Greene often travelled out to the island to say Mass. *Barry* was one of the locals who would take the boat to the mainland each week to bring him out to the island.

About a year after he met the priest, *Barry* got a phone message from Greene, who wanted him to come to the mainland to meet him. It was a bright spring weekday and *Barry* had been working in the fields with his father. 'I asked a friend of mine, *Felix Duffy*, to come with me because I would need someone to come across with me in the boat and I had an idea that Fr Greene was fond of boys,' he told us. That *Barry Hayes* should have that notion indicated to us that Greene's behaviour was no secret. They might not have talked to adults, but in the school playgrounds and among themselves, the rumours and whispered warnings were passed along the grapevine from pupil to pupil.

When they got to the mainland *Barry* and *Felix* met Eugene Greene in a car park near a local school. Greene asked *Barry* to stay with him at his house for a few days, He had some work that he needed doing. The priest was insistent. *Barry* asked if *Felix* could come too, but the priest said no, *Felix* could go back home. *Barry* refused to go in the car unless his friend went with him. Reluctantly the priest agreed that *Felix* could come along too. 'The real reason why I didn't want to go with him on my own was because of what might happen. I was afraid he might interfere with me sexually, as I was aware of the rumours going around the school,' *Barry* explained to us.

Greene took the boys to the parochial house and made them tea, before taking *Barry* upstairs to show him the bedroom where he could spend the night. 'I had my mind made up that I wasn't going to be alone with him as I was suspicious of the reason he brought me to the house,' *Barry* said. 'He brought me to a bedroom upstairs and he showed me the bed that I would be sleeping in that night. While I was standing beside the bed, in a confined space between the bed and the wall, Fr Greene turned facing me and put his arms around my neck and held me in close. He then kept one hand around my neck and I felt his other hand moving down my body.'

Upset and close to tears, *Barry* pushed the priest away. Greene reacted angrily. 'Tá mise ag imeacht,' *Barry* told him, reverting to his native tongue. (I am going.) He walked out of the bedroom and downstairs where *Felix* was waiting. 'We're not staying. We're going now,' *Barry* said to his friend as Greene followed him down the stairs. They left. On the way back to the island *Barry* told *Felix* what had happened. Later he told some of his school friends too, but he never spoke to an adult about it. It was not until years later that he began to appreciate how much more serious the situation might have been.

I took *Barry*'s statement at his home. He was one of the few who felt comfortable talking to me at home. When we called, his wife opened the door and went to fetch her husband after nodding a smile to us. We noticed that the kitchen door was closed softly behind him when he came out, and we were ushered quietly into the sitting room where the curtains were drawn. Soon afterwards tea arrived. I remember particularly his wife closing all the doors and drawing the curtains together when I arrived with Dooley. *Barry* was the first person to confirm to us that Greene's activities were no secret in the school playground, whatever about the wider community. The boys talked to each other, warned each other about him even if they couldn't bring themselves to speak about what happened with outsiders. It helped to explain how so many of them had contacted Dooley and me once we began to investigate. The word spread from one to the other through old networks established in their schooldays: someone is taking this seriously; someone will listen; someone is finally going to do something about what happened.

We had almost become part of those old school networks; any inhibitions about talking to us were gone. While each case had to be gone through meticulously, by now we had the experience to know what information we needed to gather in each victim statement. Each story was disturbingly similar, though we couldn't tell the victims that. We had to deal with each case as if hearing it for the first time, though the stream of the abuse was becoming thoroughly familiar to us. Their words were what mattered. We could not allow ourselves to ask questions we often knew the answers to. We needed their memories. We could not allow our own preconceived ideas to influence what they might say. It was gruesome listening to these stories over and over again, but we had to bury our revulsion and deal with the victims, difficult as it may have been to stare into their hurt at times.

As policemen we realised that *Barry Hayes* had given us one critical piece of information. His friend *Felix Duffy*, if he was willing to talk, could back up everything *Barry* had told us. A few days later we spoke to *Felix*, who confirmed in detail what *Barry* had stated. He too told us that there was 'a lot of talk among the students' about Greene. He was also able to tell us about a time when he too had had a close shave with the sexual predator. The priest stopped him one day on the road and gave him a lift in his car. To no one's surprise Greene then drove on quiet side roads rather than by a direct route, before pulling the car over. Several times he made sexual advances on *Felix*, who fought him off telling him, 'I have a girlfriend. I don't want your kind.'

Felix got out of the car and walked away. He vividly described Greene at that moment, his furious face 'very red with a mad and evil look'. As *Felix* walked away, Greene shouted after him, 'I'll never forgive you.' It was the last time Greene ever spoke to him. Whenever they met after that day, there was a frosty silence between them.

Chapter 8
Weekend Visitor

I knew *Noel Campbell* before I began investigating Eugene Greene. A quiet young fellow, he kept to himself much of the time and didn't socialise much. I was on a routine rural patrol when I met him and stopped to have a chat. He asked if he could have a word with me in confidence. I arranged to meet him later along with John Dooley.

Noel told us he had been abused several times by Greene two decades earlier. He first met Greene when he was a 13-year-old altar boy and Greene was the curate in his local church. Parts of the story he told me were eerily familiar. Greene allowed him to drive his car, picking him up at his house and bringing him to a local hall to help clean up and set out the chairs before Bingo. The first few drives were uneventful as Greene worked his way into the boy's confidence. When the abuse began, *Noel* was afraid to say anything. This was a priest. What could he say? Who could he say it to?

'I would never tell at home or tell anyone what the priest Fr Greene was doing to me,' *Noel* told me. 'I just used to go into a room on my own and cry about it. I didn't have a clue at the time how to deal with it. I used to feel dirty, I was scared and annoyed, but I felt I could do nothing about it. I knew at the time what Fr Greene was doing to me was wrong, but because he was a priest I felt I could do nothing about it.'

Greene abused *Noel* on average once a week throughout that winter, in his car and at the parochial house, often getting drunk on wine and praising the boy afterwards, telling him he was a good worker and a good driver. In the spring Greene finally stopped, less willing to risk being seen by others as the days grew longer.

'I always felt so embarrassed about it that I never told anyone until today,' *Noel* told me. 'When I am drinking it haunts me and when I read about other paedophiles in the paper I go drinking to try and handle it as it brings back bad memories of Fr Greene to me.'

A few nights later, Dooley and I arranged to meet *Noel*. He told us his story again, and this time we took a formal statement of complaint from him, which we added to our investigation file.

People talk. *Noel* had a good friend, *Edward Brown*. At the time *Edward* was living and working in London. Through friends *Noel* got in touch with *Edward*, who learned what we were doing. *Edward* decided enough was enough. He too had been abused by Greene and he decided to come home and make a statement. At the time I knew nothing about any of this. Later, talking to *Edward* and others, I pieced together parts of the grapevine, who talked to whom, where and when. Some of the victims were talking and the word had gone quietly around that we were investigating complaints.

We appeared to have broken through the initial hesitation that prevented victims from coming forward. We were now welcomed. Though the investigation was still done in secret as much as possible, we felt a warmth towards us. But still an air of secrecy hung over every conversation. However word seemed to have got out that people could talk to us, which was important for both sides, the victims and us. Maybe due to the curiously intimate nature of the investigation, they got to know that it was okay to talk with us. Though often over-loaded with work, a small team, if working well together, can achieve a lot.

At the same time we also knew that if we complained that we were overworked, we might be broken up or be given outside assistance and the trust we had built up would be shattered. People would clam up. This stuff had been buried for years. The victims were comfort-able dealing with us, and our growing experience and insight into what was happening allowed us to be sensitive as we listened. We were welcomed in many of their homes, invited in and given tea. But some victims did not want us to call at their homes, and those who did sometimes asked us to do so in the dark of night.

The grapevine never ceased to amaze me. I was working on the most secretive of investigations because of the sensitivity of the allegations, but word had got around. Almost every person I spoke to knew some-one else to talk to. *Edward Brown*, for instance, who spoke to his friend on the phone about the investigation, decided he was coming home to talk to me. *Edward* eventually agreed to do a TV interview about being a victim of sexual abuse, something few of Greene's victims were able to do.

I knew *Edward* from the early nineties when I first arrived back in Donegal and before he emigrated. He was always friendly and helpful but he seemed to be carrying a cross, something I thought might be due to his drinking. While friendly he was also distant in personality. About ten weeks after I had spoken to *Noel Campbell*, I answered a knock at my door one Friday night. It was *Edward*. He looked glad to see me.

'I was talking to *Noel Campbell* on the phone,' he said. 'He was talking to you. He said it was okay to talk to you. I was abused too by Greene.' He didn't really need to finish the sentence. As soon as he mentioned that he had been talking to *Noel*, I knew he could only have come to talk to me about one thing.

He went through the whole story with me in anguish, speaking to me as if I was a long-lost best friend. He had gone through pure torture like many a victim. He seemed so relieved that at last he could talk. It must have been horrible for him.

'I just flew home for the weekend to see you,' he said.

I didn't have the heart to tell him I was off work for the weekend. I couldn't turn him away. 'Okay, *Edward*,' was all I said. He sat for several hours just talking with me. He told me he was going back to England and to his work on Monday.

'I'll take your statement tomorrow,' I told him. I knew I wasn't going to get paid for any extra work on my weekend off. There was no overtime going, but so what? I cancelled my game of golf. That was the least I could do for him and I didn't tell him; he had enough to worry about. His mother was the only one who knew why he was home. While he related his story I told him he would have to be specific about years and months and to be as clear as possible when describing what happened to him. He confided in his mother so he would be able to find out the year of his first communion and so on, details necessary for an accurate statement. He came back the next day and he went through the whole sequence of events again, a draining emotional time for him. He thanked me so much. I later contacted Dooley and kept him informed.

Later I talked to *Edward*'s mother. She couldn't keep the tears from her eyes as she spoke. Mothers seem to feel the pain most deeply. She knew there was something bothering him. As a teenager he lost interest in schoolwork, dropped out of school early, often stayed in bed until late in the day, and he began drinking early. After *Edward* came to speak to us, he also told his mother what had happened.

'I noticed a change in *Edward*'s behaviour around the age of 10 or 11, but I would never have suspected a priest was sexually abusing our son,' she told me later. 'I was totally shocked when I heard this and I didn't know where I was. I couldn't sleep that night. I feel very hurt about what Fr Greene did to my son. The hardest thing of all to accept is that Fr Greene visited this house regularly and said several Masses during the time he was abusing *Edward* unknown to me.'

Edward later spoke to a BBC documentary team and was interviewed for a *Spotlight* current affairs programme on Greene. His quiet words painted a dramatic and searing portrait of what Greene's victims endured.

'I was always number one altar boy by him,' *Edward* told *Spotlight*. 'I was always the one that had to stay behind. He would take me to the sacristy, sort of keep me to the last. That was sort of the start of it. He would say to my mum and dad, Oh, I've got to take *Edward* up to some house to visit some old person just to give holy communion or whatever. There were so many excuses. But we weren't going up to some old person; we were going out to the back of Muckish so he could have his way with me. I think Machaire Uí Robhartaigh (Magheroarty) beach was his favourite. I was only 10, maybe 11 years of age at this stage. He wanted me to fondle him, touch his penis and things like that. And I done it because he was a man of God and I had to do it. I didn't want to let my family down or let anybody down. He did rape me, which I hate to say, the word. But he did rape me. And not only once but I can't count them. I just can't. And that hurt me, and hurts me yet big time. Big time. I went to confession to the priest that was taking me to the beach, to his parochial house, to the back of mountains and raping me. I was telling him my sins, and he was forgiving me for those sins. It should have been the other way round. I should have been listening to his sins. Life has been tough. The amount of times that I stood on Tower Bridge thinking, get it over with and done with. But thank God I pulled myself together. I said to myself, that bastard's not going to beat me. He's not going to beat me.'

In his statement *Edward* described how he was raped repeatedly by Greene between 1976 and 1978, often after evening Mass. When he left altar service in 1978 he thought the abuse would end, but Greene continued to call to his home looking for the boy to help with errands. In 1980 *Edward*'s grandfather died and Greene called to his home a few

days after the funeral. After sympathising with the family, Greene
wanted *Edward* to go with him in his car.

'I refused point blank as I knew at this stage what he was doing was
wrong and I finally picked up the courage to say no to him,' *Edward*
explained to me. 'The abuse that Fr Greene carried out on me has
caused me a lot of hurt, and while I have tried to block it out, it still
seeps up. He took away my youth and the wounds are still there.'

Chapter 9

I Wish I Could Have Died

In the evenings after we had both finished our day's work, John Dooley often drove the thirty or so miles from Glenties to An Fál Carrach to see me. Since the two of us were in effect the entire investigation team, there was no one else we could talk to about what we were discovering. The very nature of our enquiries demanded discretion and silence, but we had to talk to someone about it, even if it was only to each other.

By its nature the investigation meant we worked long days. I still had my standard uniform duties to take care of, routine things like handling dole forms or traffic checkpoints, as well as BSE duty, regular border checkpoints to monitor the movement of cattle across the border from Northern Ireland and prevent the spread of bovine spongiform encephalopathy, the mad cow disease. On top of that there were the less routine parts of policing, a fatal road traffic accident, break-ins and petty thefts, sudden deaths to investigate. Dooley also had his regular work to attend to, and in the evenings we would travel to meet with a victim, to talk and listen to his story and eventually take his statement. The late evening visits became an opportunity to compare notes. I would tell John what I had found in Gort an Choirce and he would bring me up to date on what people were telling us further south in the county, before I would put on my uniform and head out to do a closing time inspection at the local pubs. Sometimes John was so exhausted after his day's work he would doze off in the armchair as we spoke. When I got back from closing the pubs I would waken him, if he hadn't already roused himself and gone home.

One of the stories John told me concerned *Philip Ryan*, a 43-year-old single farmer who had served as an altar boy in the early seventies but was no longer an altar boy when Greene arrived in his parish of

Cnoc Fola. *Philip* first met Greene when the priest called to visit the family home, and like many other young boys was called on to do odd jobs around the priest's house, cutting the grass and clearing up around the yard. In return the priest would give him a few pounds for pocket money.

The first time he went inside the priest's house, Greene put his arms around him and hugged him, pulling him close until *Philip* could feel the priest's stubble against his face. He didn't think there was anything unusual about getting a hug at first, but he became uncomfortable as it went on 'too long' as the priest held him in his embrace for over a minute. *Philip* pulled away from the embrace. He became wary of the priest, and Greene seemed to sense it. The priest hugged him on several other occasions but never did anything more, apart from putting his hand on his knee once while driving his car.

Greene was stationed in Cnoc Fola for two years, between 1970 and 1972. What Dooley learned from *Philip Ryan* showed us that Greene's behaviour had been a problem at least four years before he came to Gort an Choirce, where I was investigating his history between 1976 and 1981. The cases John had uncovered to date were in Leitir Mhic an Bhaird, where Greene spent two years between 1974 and 1976. If there had been other incidents in Cnoc Fola, then that suggested Greene had at least a decade of sexual abuse behind him, from 1970 to 1981. We wondered how long a timespan his abuse covered.

It wasn't long before Dooley found another case, a factory worker from Gaoth Dobhair called *Stan O'Donnell*. On a summer's evening while still a teenager, *Stan* had called to Greene's house for a copy of his baptismal certificate. While *Stan* stood at the front door of the presbytery explaining why he had called, Greene grabbed him by the arm and tried to pull him inside. *Stan* had been working on a building site and protested that his hands and clothes were dirty and he didn't want to make a mess of the priest's hallway. He knew the priest was drunk and told him he would come back later in the evening. He left, but as he got on his motor cycle, Greene jumped on behind him and grabbed him around the waist. Greene held on as *Stan* accelerated away, at which point he lost his seat and fell to the ground. *Stan* told his mother what had happened and made sure he never went near the priest again.

Stan thought that the bizarre incident took place in 1985, four years after the curate was transferred out of Gort an Choirce. As in *Philip*

Ryan's case, it was not among the most serious of the incidents we had uncovered. If we were to go to court with it, it would probably be on a minor charge rather than an assault charge, though it didn't bear thinking about what might have happened if Greene had managed to get *Stan* inside the house. But the report suggested that as Greene's drinking got worse over the years and his behaviour deteriorated, it expanded the extent of his problem behaviour to a decade and a half.

I told Dooley that I had come across a similar case myself. *Fabian McShane* told me that he was at a play in the local community hall in the early eighties, standing near the back because there were no seats left, when Greene came into the hall and stood in front of him. Greene pressed his backside against the young man's groin, and under the cover of his long clerical soutane, reached his hand around and touched him. *Fabian*'s companion saw what was happening and punched the priest on the shoulder, telling him to 'have manners'. *Fabian* was shocked and disgusted at what Greene did, but at the time he was too shy to report the sexual assault to the Gardaí, although years later he told his wife about the incident. A couple of years before he spoke to me, he had seen Greene again, this time giving a sermon at a funeral Mass, and he felt furious at the hypocrisy of the priest speaking about God after the indecent assault he had committed. We wondered how many other such once-off incidents there were over the years in addition to the victims we had found who were repeatedly abused by the priest.

———

George Maguire was one of the first potential victims we learned about. *Andrew Kelly* had told us how he saw *George* in Greene's bed one day when he went to tell the priest that he had a phone call, and how the scared boy had tried to hide himself by pulling the blankets over his head. *Ivan Sullivan* had also told us how *Andrew* had described to him what he saw when he warned him about Greene. Like many young Irish men, *George* had joined the trail of emigrants in the eighties and worked in construction. Because he was working away from home, it took us a while to get in contact with him, but eventually we did.

As a young boy *George* had served on the altar and along with *Andrew Kelly*, who was a few years older, did odd jobs around the church grounds and the parochial house for the priest. *George* remembered that it was on a dark evening after a function in the local community hall that Greene first asked him to walk to the parochial house with him. He didn't remember the date but he knew he was 11 years of age at the time, which fixed the year for us. When they got there, *George* didn't even ask the curate why he wanted him to go to the parochial house. Because Greene was a priest and a regular caller to his family home, *George* trusted him totally, and he had been in the parochial house several times before. He served the early morning Mass several mornings each week and one of his duties was to make tea afterwards for the priest. But this time it was different.

Immediately Greene arrived at the parochial house that night, he took *George* upstairs to his bedroom. There was a double bed in the room. Greene ordered the boy to get on to the bed and he raped him viciously. It was not until years later that *George* understood fully what had happened. At the time he was simply terrified. 'We are good friends,' Greene told *George* afterwards.

George blanked out most of the priest's small talk. He hurt terribly, but he was afraid to cry or tell Greene to stop. Afterwards Greene warned the boy not to tell anyone what had happened; it was to be their secret. *George* was in pain for a week following the abuse. Until he was transferred out of the parish a year later, Greene continued to abuse *George*, raping him on countless occasions, often after he had served the early morning Mass, usually in the bedroom in the parochial house, and each time warning him not to tell anyone, that what happened was a secret between the two of them.

Throughout the abuse Greene continued to visit *George*'s family home. *George* found this almost as difficult to endure as the abuse itself. His mother thought the world of the priest, which made it impossible for him to tell her what was happening.

The memory of the day *Andrew Kelly* and *Ivan Sullivan* had told us about was seared into *George*'s mind. It was a quiet summer's evening, a few months after the sexual abuse first began, and he was working with *Andrew* cleaning up around the parochial house when Greene told him to go up to the bedroom.

Greene locked the bedroom door so they would not be disturbed, aware that *Andrew* was still working away outside, and he again raped *George*. The priest was disturbed when *Andrew* knocked on the bedroom door, calling his name and announcing that there was a phone call for him. Greene got out of bed quickly, put on his dressing gown and went downstairs to answer the phone.

'I was still in the bed and I will never forget *Andrew Kelly* putting his head in the bedroom door and seeing me in the bed,' *George* told Dooley. 'I remember covering my head with the blankets in shame. I wished I could have died at that moment when *Andrew* saw me in Fr Greene's bed. I figured that *Andrew* knew what was going on.'

George was terrified that *Andrew* would tell others what he had seen, yet he could not bring himself to talk about what was happening with *Andrew* or indeed anyone else. The abuse continued for a full year until Greene was transferred to Gort an Choirce in the summer of 1976. Shortly after the transfer Greene arrived at the *Maguire* home and said he wanted to take *George* with him to Gort an Choirce for the night. *George* didn't remember what excuse the priest used, only that his mother thought it was nice of him to take him to his house for the night. Needless to say *George* did not enjoy his night away from home. Early the following morning Greene returned *George* to his home, again warning him not to reveal their shared secret. A few weeks later Greene called to *George*'s home again, but this time he refused to go to Gort an Choirce. After that, Greene often met the boy on the road, but *George* refused to talk to him or get into his car.

Years later, as a grown man living in another country, *George Maguire* still felt icy shivers run down his spine whenever he remembered his ordeal at Greene's hands. 'I felt I was trapped in a situation I could not handle,' he told Dooley. 'I felt very guilty and ashamed about it. I hadn't the courage to tell anyone, not even *Andrew Kelly* when he found me. I had great fear and a sense of awful shame that *Andrew* told others. When I learned the full facts of life, I felt even more ashamed about the sexual abuse inflicted on me. Greene's sexual abuse affected my life greatly. It made me a very shy person; to this day I get embarrassed very easily. My feeling of shame was one of the reasons I went to England. I was hoping to make a fresh start. You are the first person I ever told this story to. It was a part of my life that I blocked out of my mind for over twenty years. That was the only way I could deal with it, although it bothered me always.'

Having made the decision to come forward when Dooley contacted him, *George* had also made the decision to get professional counselling. He promised he would give evidence against Greene in court, but he was anxious that his elderly parents would not find out what he had endured.

Returning to Donegal after our trip to England, it was still difficult to come to terms with what we were learning. By the late nineties clerical child sexual abuse cases were being reported upon world wide, but in this north-west corner of Ireland it was still difficult to believe that it was rampant. If I had been asked about it six months earlier, I would have insisted trenchantly that it was not the case. This could not happen here. In a beautiful spot like Donegal, surely the innocence of children would be left unscathed. Several cases had already been reported in Ireland, and indeed the Brendan Smyth scandal had taken down the government of Albert Reynolds, but this was my first encounter with it. Save for a single dusty file I had seen in an office in the Midlands almost two decades earlier, I would have had no idea of the hidden dangers to which children were subjected. The abuse cases I had read about, though shocking, I thought of as isolated events. At least I hoped they were.

Chapter 10

What Am I to Do, Keep Moving Him Around?

*K*yle Carroll was a 34-year-old father of three when I spoke to him in March 1998. Twenty years earlier Eugene Greene had called to his house and asked him to go down to the church with him. When they reached the church, Greene took him up to a loft where there was a single bed. The priest ordered him to remove his trousers and underpants. It was the first time Greene abused him. *Kyle* tried to escape but Greene held him down. Afterwards the priest talked casually to the boy as if nothing had happened. He then gave *Kyle* a £5 note, told him to keep his mouth shut about what happened, and to say a few prayers for him.

'I knew what Fr Greene had done to me was wrong but I was afraid to tell anyone, especially my mother, who is a very religious person even to this day,' *Kyle* told me.

Greene called regularly to *Kyle*'s home after that, bringing the boy away with the excuse that he needed chores done around the parochial house. *Kyle*'s story included familiar elements: trips where the priest let him steer his car, the warnings to say nothing, the commands to pray. Finally the morning came when *Kyle* found the courage to refuse to go with the priest when he called to his home. Even though *Kyle*'s refusal to do chores for the priest angered his mother, he still could not bring himself to tell her what the priest had done to him.

'Greene never called for me after that and never got a chance to abuse me again,' *Kyle* told me. 'I never told anyone about this sexual abuse, only my wife.' *Kyle* also suffered from bouts of anxiety and depression because of his abuse and attended a doctor for treatment, but he never told the doctor what had happened. 'I used to feel very angry. I would get uncontrollable shakes and I would always be thinking of the abuse Fr Greene inflicted on me,' he explained. 'I still feel angry about it.'

Kyle was willing to make a statement and to give evidence in court against Greene, but he couldn't come forward publicly. His mother was a devout Catholic and he did not want to upset her. Even as we took his statement, he was still dealing with his hurt in a secret way, keeping it private, keeping it to himself.

Because *Kyle* had told his wife he had been abused, we spoke to her too to get a statement from her supporting his evidence. *Laura Carroll* confirmed that *Kyle* had told her five years earlier, whilst he was getting treatment for anxiety and depression, that he was abused by Greene. Hearing what the priest had done, *Laura* felt physically sick. Afterwards, still angry about the pain her husband had endured, she sat down and wrote a four page letter to Greene, telling him exactly what she thought of him. She told him who she was, who her husband was, that she would never forgive him and neither would God. A short time later she read in the local newspaper that Greene was retiring. He never replied to her letter.

West Donegal is a small place. It is one of the most rural Garda districts in the country. 'Ar scáth a chéile a mhaireann na daoine' (the people live in each other's shadows), as the old proverb put it. In such a small community it was impossible to ignore the interconnecting friendships and marriages that linked many of the abuse victims. A close family friend of *Kyle*, *Mark Flynn*, lived abroad, but as a young boy he too had served on the altar. When he heard about our investigation, *Mark* wrote a letter explaining what he had gone through, what Greene called 'this little secret we must keep'. *Mark* vividly remembered Greene's alcoholism, how he often drank the altar wine which he smelled on the priest's breath as he was sexually abused in the church sacristy.

Mark thereafter tried to avoid the priest by skipping Mass, but Greene went to his teacher and reported him. *Mark* was terrified in case he got into trouble with his teacher. He lied and said his mother had overslept and did not waken him. After he was abused a second time, *Mark* decided that no matter what his teacher did, he wasn't going to serve Mass again. Greene wouldn't leave him alone though and called to his home a few days later, taking the boy away on the pretext of having him do some errands and shopping. *Mark* said those 'three days of pure hell' never left his mind in the years that followed.

'I call them the lost years,' he wrote to me. 'I will, I suppose, remember them till I leave this earth. I sometimes sit alone and think of all the pain and hurt this man caused so many people. The years that followed were also terrible. I became very shy and very sensitive.'

He found it difficult to make friends and began drinking early. In his early twenties he told other members of his family what had happened. With the support of his family and his wife, he sought professional counselling. *Mark's* wife and sister-in-law were able to confirm that he had told the family about his abuse when he was in his early twenties.

———

On the same day we took a statement from *Kyle Carroll*, we also spoke to *Adrian Kennedy*, a successful local businessman. The saga of the *Kennedy* family exemplifies the instinct of the Church to cover up, the reluctance by any figure in authority to take action to stop the horror we were uncovering even when confronted with clear evidence of what was happening. We pieced together the story of what happened to the *Kennedys* over several interviews with members of the family and through other witnesses who were able to confirm parts of their story.

Adrian buried himself in his work after leaving school. He neither drank nor smoked and built up his business by hard work whilst bottling up his anger. He wasn't without emotion, but he was very quiet when we spoke to him. His wife showed more visible anger about what had happened than he did, and was more forthcoming with her feelings.

Adrian realised at the time that what Greene was doing to him was wrong, but because the curate had warned him that it was a secret between God, the priest and himself, he was afraid to tell his parents or anyone else what was going on. He started making excuses when Greene looked for him until eventually the priest gave up looking for him and the abuse stopped.

Curiously *Adrian* remembered that sometime later his father and mother asked him if Greene had ever 'interfered' with him in any way. *Adrian*, afraid to tell the truth, denied that anything unusual had ever taken place because he had been told that it was a secret with God and that it would be wrong to tell. Until we spoke to him, he had never told anyone what Greene did. Until the night we took his statement he hadn't even told *Emma*, his wife. For twenty years he had kept it secret, trying to block it out of his mind.

Adrian spoke quietly in measured, calm words as we took down his statement. He explained that his emotions were 'nulled'. It was as if he felt he had no right to feel, only to remember. Sometimes it was eerie, as people told me their stories, almost as if I could feel the coldness in their voices as they tried to keep the words they were saying away from themselves, not to look too closely at the memories. They were, as it were, almost standing back from what they endured, describing something they saw as if it had happened to a stranger. His wife sat beside him with tears in her eyes while he spoke, but he was standing back from it, completely detached, calmly telling me what he went through, what had happened to him. That detachment was the only way he could deal with it.

After a while it seems that many of the victims simply got used to the abuse. They just put up with it, accepting that being abused was part of their lives. It became one element of the accepted culture, or subculture, of their childhood. It was strange. The children knew there was abuse, but they accepted it as part of growing up. It must have been a horrible situation for them to live through.

———

Adrian had said one curious thing to us that night as we sat listening to his oddly disengaged narrative. His parents had asked him if Greene had ever done anything improper. A few weeks later we found out why. *Adrian*'s brother *Henry* lived abroad, but Dooley had spoken to him by phone. Unknown to his brother, *Henry* was also abused by Greene. But although he too was frightened of the priest, eventually he found the courage to tell his parents. 'My parents were very upset at the time and they made the parish priest aware of Fr Greene's behaviour,' *Henry* told Dooley. 'They will verify that this is true.'

The news was a bombshell. If what *Henry* said was true, it meant that Greene's behaviour had been reported over two decades ago, yet seemingly nothing had happened. We knew we had to talk to the older generation of *Kennedys*.

I cannot remember what it was that led us to contact *Henry Kennedy*. Maybe *Adrian* spoke to him on the phone; maybe another member of the family contacted him; maybe it was something we heard on the grapevine that made us think he might be worth speaking to, or even something he heard that led him to pick up the phone and call us. Whatever it was, he told us he would be back in Ireland later in the year and would make a formal statement then. In the meantime we got in touch with his parents.

Arthur, another of the *Kennedy* brothers, confirmed to us that in September 1976 his brother *Henry* had told him how Greene abused him while he drove the priest's car. He told his sister *Emer* and she in turn told her mother, who spoke to her husband *Gilbert*. Eventually, through a circuitous route, the truth had reached adult ears.

Gilbert Kennedy headed a traditional large Donegal family. Several of his sons had served as altar boys when they were growing up, some of them while Greene was curate in the parish in the mid-1970s and Hugh Bonnar was the parish priest. When we spoke to him he filled in more details on what had happened to his family. He learned from his wife *Grace* that Greene had 'interfered sexually' with his son *Henry* in the 1970s and immediately phoned the parish priest and asked him to call to his home. Within minutes of the priest arriving, *Gilbert* told him what was going on.

Bonnar just stared at *Kennedy* at first saying nothing, and said very little afterwards, but by the end of the meeting *Gilbert* had the clear impression that Greene would be expelled from the Church for his actions. Within a week of the meeting it was common knowledge that Greene had left the parish. A few weeks later the *Kennedys* got a letter in the post from Greene, mailed from a 'treatment centre or hospital where I thought he was getting treatment for his sexual problems', as *Gilbert* described it to me. Greene apologised for his behaviour towards *Gilbert's* son and thanked him for the way in which he handled the matter. He asked for forgiveness but never mentioned that he was abusing other children in addition to *Henry*. He didn't even say what he had done to *Henry*, just asked for forgiveness for an unspecified sin, and expressed the hope that he would be welcomed back into their family again. The family kept the letter for a long time, but unfortunately they no longer had it when we spoke to them. Some time later Greene returned to the parish and called to the *Kennedys'* home to again apologise for his behaviour and ask forgiveness.

'He asked me not to mention the incident with our son to anybody, which I didn't,' *Gilbert* told us. 'I spoke again to Fr Bonnar, the parish priest, a few months after Fr Greene returned to the parish. I expressed my surprise that Fr Greene was still practising as a priest.'

'What am I to do, keep moving him around?' Bonnar responded. The priest argued that shifting the problem to another parish was no solution. He assured the worried father that Greene would not interfere with his boys again. *Gilbert* said that if there was any more trouble, he would go straight to the bishop himself.

'At that time I understood that this matter was dealt with and that the bishop was made aware of it,' *Gilbert* said. 'I was still unhappy to see Fr Greene continue to perform as a priest, even though I believed there would be no further interference. At that stage I thought there was only one incident of abuse with one of my sons and I didn't want to put my son through the trauma and embarrassment of quizzing him about the incident.'

Gilbert was horrified to learn that Greene had abused more than one of his sons. He was 'utterly shocked and horrified at the collusion of the Church with such behaviour and sinning in the name of God' and 'very annoyed at the collusion and connivance of the Church authorities for covering up sexual abuse'. His family was devastated and traumatised.

There was more to come. We discovered that a third member of the *Kennedy* family, *Lorcan*, was also sexually abused several times by Greene. *Lorcan* clearly remembered that the last time Greene abused him another priest arrived at the parochial house and walked into the sitting room. Greene pushed *Lorcan* aside roughly and quickly fixed his clothing. The other priest turned his back, and *Lorcan* ran. After that, *Lorcan* successfully managed to avoid being alone with Greene. He was afraid, both as a boy and a man, to tell his parents what had happened and had only done so after our investigation began. He spoke about the emotional and psychological pain left by the abuse and the anger that it left in him over the years.

We tracked down the priest *Lorcan* thought had interrupted Greene, but he could not help us with our enquiries. He did not recall visiting the parochial house at all during 1977 and he didn't remember visiting the parochial house at any time and finding Greene 'in a compromising situation with a young boy'.

As policemen we are trained not to jump to conclusions. Add two and two together and get five, and you end up prosecuting an innocent man. You cannot rush to judgment; you can only follow the evidence. I don't know what happened the last time *Lorcan* was abused. I wasn't there. *Lorcan* may have got the priest's name wrong or misidentified the priest involved. It's hard to know. The visitor might not have been a priest. There might have been more than one occasion where visitors called to the house that were merged into a single incident by *Lorcan* in his trauma. Listening to him at the time, I got the feeling that he was telling the truth. But a feeling isn't evidence. I'm always inclined to believe the victim, but he could be wrong about which priest he saw. Or maybe Greene heard someone coming and 'fixed' himself in time to appear normal by the time the priest had reached the sitting room from the front door, and the priest could have arrived too late to see anything out of the ordinary. The situation may have been just brought under control in time. That is possible. That split second of time could make all the difference. I hate rushing to judgment. If I don't know, I don't know.

There was one more interview we would like to have carried out based on the evidence of the *Kennedys*, but we couldn't talk to Fr Hugh Bonnar. He had died several years earlier, taking to the grave whatever knowledge he had of Greene's behaviour. But even if Bonnar couldn't talk to us, at least the *Kennedys* were. After years of silence the family, three of whom were victims of sexual abuse and all of whom were hurting from it, were speaking about what happened to each other, each learning they were not alone.

The boys' mother, *Grace*, searched in vain for the letter that Greene had written during the few weeks he disappeared from the parish after they made their complaint, but she could not find it. She told us that they did not make a complaint about Greene to the Gardaí at the time because she and *Gilbert* thought what happened with *Henry* 'was a once-off incident'. It was not until much later that they would discover that Greene had sexually abused more than one of their sons. At the time the outcome wasn't perfect; they weren't happy that Greene was back in the parish, but he had been away for treatment of some sort and Bonnar had assured them that there would be no more problems.

I was more concerned about Bonnar. By 1998, when we began our enquiry, there were mandatory reporting requirements in place. There were no requirements in the mid-seventies, but even so Bonnar was the manager of the local primary school and he knew his curate had a position of trust and access to young children at the school and on the altar. Yet apparently he never even bothered to report what the *Kennedys* had told him to the school patron, the Bishop of Raphoe. At least the Raphoe diocesan office had no report in its files, even though (from what the *Kennedys* told us) Greene had apparently obtained permission from his bishop to leave the parish for several weeks and gone to a 'treatment centre or hospital'. It was hard not to sympathise with *Gilbert*'s anger at what he called the 'collusion and connivance of the Church authorities for covering up sexual abuse'. Bonnar's response to *Gilbert*, 'What do you expect me to do, keep moving him around?' sent all the wrong signals. Greene was allowed to continue sexually abusing young boys. It wasn't until over two decades later that we got a Garda complaint to investigate, even though his parish priest knew what he had allegedly done in the seventies. Even then we found out only by accident because Greene in his arrogance felt so safe that he came to us when one of his victims made a half-hearted blackmail attempt.

While 1976 was a hellish year for the *Kennedy* family, it was a special year for Brid and myself, the year our first daughter Aoife was born. On a holiday trip to Donegal we decided it would be nice to have Aoife baptised in the place where her mother was born. The curate at the time who presided at the ceremony was Eugene Greene. Little did we suspect on that day that he was one of two paedophiles who had arrived in Gort an Choirce parish in 1976 and that two decades later I would be back in Donegal investigating both of them.

Fr Hugh Bonnar may genuinely have believed that what Greene did was a once-off incident, and that whatever treatment he had received was successful. But even so, he should have notified his bishop. Common sense alone demanded that the bishop's office should know of the incident. Once off it might be, but even one more incident would have horrific consequences for some young boy. Even if the Church could live with that risk, if there was a future complaint, then the bishop's office would know Greene's misbehaviour was no longer 'once off' if they already had a report in their files. Bonnar also broke the internal law of his own Church which mandated dismissal from the clergy for any priest who sexually abused a minor. Unfortunately Bonnar was dead and we couldn't ask him what decisions he made and why, or whether he had made any report to his superiors either in writing or orally when his curate was sent away for several weeks to a treatment centre or hospital.

One thing was clear from the statements. Bonnar gave an assurance to the *Kennedy* family that Greene would not interfere with any young boys again. I had to wonder what basis Bonnar had to feel so confident that he could give such an assurance. Was it because of some treatment Greene received in the weeks he was away from the parish? Apparently the diocesan office had no record of any alleged sexual abuse complaint against Greene. I had to wonder what became of the complaint the *Kennedys* made. Why was Greene sent away for treatment, and why was there no record?

The diocesan office had to be aware that Greene was away from the parish for a time. After he returned an assurance was given that he would not interfere with boys again, not to mention that he would not drink again. The assurance was quite specific and the complaint made against him was quite specific, a complaint of a sexual nature. Greene himself wrote to the family apologising for his behaviour towards a minor, so he himself had to be confronted with the allegation, which he didn't deny, and he thanked them for the way they had dealt with it. He later admitted to us almost casually that he wrote such a letter. He admitted that he wrote to the family for forgiveness and indeed called to the family home on his return after his absence from the parish.

Though the *Kennedys* were not happy with how Bonnar had dealt with the problem, they took his assurance in good faith. Yet instead of becoming a reformed character, Greene quickly slipped into familiar patterns. The abuse escalated, so that he abused at least sixteen boys in the five years of his stay in Gort an Choirce between 1976 and 1981. And what was I supposed to make of Bonnar's rhetorical question: What do you expect me to do, keep moving him around? Had there been other complaints? Had there been previous attempts to solve the problem or at least quieten the complaints by moving Greene from parish to parish?

One other thing disturbed me as we collated the complaints from the *Kennedys*. It wasn't entirely clear looking back through twenty-year-old memories, but it seemed clear to me that whatever assurances were given, Greene not only continued abusing for years after Bonnar was told about his activities, he even abused other members of the *Kennedy* family.

It is worth looking at what the Ferns Inquiry had to say in this area. 'It is the view of this Inquiry that complaints or allegations of child sexual abuse should be properly recorded, duly preserved, and available to those who were responsible for the control of the person against whom such allegations are made', the report noted when commenting on the sparseness of records dealing with the infamous paedophile Fr Sean Fortune.

In the executive summary, the report's authors went on to say that in their view 'where a credible allegation of child sexual abuse is made against an employee (or other person acting under authority) it is the responsibility of the employer or superior to require the employee to step aside promptly from any post or position in which he has access to children'. Bishop Comiskey accepted that this principle was equally applicable in relation to priests of his diocese. Furthermore it was recognised that in the case of diocesan clergy 'stepping aside' from a position in which there is unsupervised access to children necessarily entailed 'stepping aside from the active ministry entirely pending the investigation of the allegations'.

Dealing with the question of Fr James Doyle, a priest who was sent to the treatment centre established by the Servants of the Paracletes in Stroud in England, the report noted critically that it was a 'matter of some concern that the psychiatrists treating Fr Doyle in Stroud, the Bishop of Ferns and the Archbishop of Southwark would have countenanced allowing him to work either in a parish or as a chaplain to a secondary school given their understanding that one relapse from sobriety could result in him abusing a child'.

The decisions made by the Church in the 1970s when dealing with the *Kennedy* family left us with three traumatised young men to deal with, along with their tearful mother and angry father. It was more than we could deal with at the time, so we concentrated on our jobs. Gather the evidence; take good statements, and make sure they stand up in court. Cauterise your mind; get the words down on paper in a statement for the Director of Public Prosecutions (DPP). Just do your job; think about it later. For now, concentrate on the details: clarifications, dates, times, places, years. Talk to the victims and help them check through their memories. Did this happen before or after your first communion, your confirmation? What year did those things happen? What class were you in at school? In short, look for anything that would narrow the range, allow us to formulate a specific charge. Typically we spoke to victims several times before taking the formal statements, allowing them time to think over what they knew, what they remembered. Sometimes details that did not seem important to them were often crucial to a policeman building a criminal case. All of the detail, often frustrating for the victims to remember, was vital to us since each statement had to stand up in court. A good defence barrister would go through every detail, checking the facts. If something didn't add up they would pounce. If the witness was wrong about one detail, then they could be mistaken in others, and if they found enough lines of attack then they could argue that the statement should not be allowed in front of a jury. Barristers get months to study the books of evidence before a case goes to trial. We knew we would have only one chance to get the statements down correctly.

One example in particular sticks in my mind to show how inconsistencies in the record could have landed the entire case in trouble. One of the first things we did in the investigation was to contact the Raphoe diocesan office for a copy of Greene's curriculum vitae, giving details of all the parishes he had served in during his career. From this we could work out the likely age of his victims in each area and begin discreet enquiries. There would be no point in talking to former altar boys in their twenties if the victims in a particular area were in their late thirties.

The first copy of the cv seemed to have been put together hurriedly without much attention to detail. The information was vague and, we eventually realised, inaccurate. We had collected statements from several victims in one parish, but the dates they gave us didn't match the details on the cv. It was the kind of detail a defence barrister could seize on, taking a nervous witness through his evidence, having him confirm a date several times then presenting him with an official Church document showing Greene couldn't have been there at the time. By the time a skilled barrister was finished, the jury would be looking at a witness who would be forced to admit that his memory was inaccurate. If the accuser couldn't even get the date straight, how could anything else he said be believed?

A policeman's work is made up largely of methodical thoroughness, gathering corroborating evidence, checking details, noticing discrepancies. We went back to the victims, asking them about what they remembered, asking them were they sure, could they have made a mistake anywhere. They were insistent they were right. Their dates were correct.

But something didn't add up. Either they were genuinely mistaken or they were lying and unable to change their story once we caught the lie. Dooley decided to check the official records. He contacted Fr Lorcan Sharkey, a priest appointed by the bishop to act as a liaison officer if we needed more information during the enquiry. Sharkey promised Dooley he would look into Greene's cv and get back to him. When he did, it was to confirm that the first version we had received contained inaccurate dates.

The news came as a relief to us. It explained the discrepancies and eliminated the danger of our witnesses facing a gruelling interrogation over the details of their statements in court. Just as importantly, their insistence that they were right even when we challenged them with the original written record was vindicated. The discovery proved that we were dealing with genuine witnesses who would not change what they remembered even when it was thought the official records contradicted them. When tested, their version proved to be the truth.

Chapter 11
A Sculpture in Pain

It was an early spring evening with a sting in the air. I was making my way to the Garda station to pick up my pay cheque when the car pulled up beside mine. It was an old car, worn down at the edges, looking like it had seen better days. A bit like its driver, I thought to myself. He knew me and I knew of him. He lived a few parishes away, outside my district, *Trevor Moore*. He drove eighteen miles to see me. He didn't want to go to the local Gardaí; he wanted to remain anonymous. He asked if he could have a few words. He seemed troubled. Looking at his face, it was as if it had never smiled or felt a day's sunshine spark any life into it. He was without expression, suspended somewhere between shock and suppressed terror, in a trance. His body language was a sculpture in pain.

'Martin,' he said, 'I want to talk to you. Some of your lads are investigating child abuse in my area, but I would prefer to talk to you about it.'

He waited for a positive response, his face guarded. Maybe he had more belief in me than I had in myself, I thought. Whatever the reason, he didn't want to be left abandoned and forlorn any longer. The case had opened, and while this was a relief to him, he felt as if he too was guilty of some wrongdoing, such is the power the paedophiles hold over their victims.

'I was abused too,' he said simply.

'Were you?'

'Yeah, I was badly abused.'

'That's okay, *Trevor*. Do you want to talk about it now?'

'Somebody might see us.'

'Will I call over to your house?'

'No, don't come near my house. You might be seen.'

'Do you want to make a statement about it?'

'Yeah, that's why I was looking out for you.'

'Do you want to make it now?'

'No, somebody might see me.'

'Where would suit you?'

'Could you meet me at the back of the car park at Letterkenny General Hospital?' he asked. That was another thirty miles away and he had already travelled about twenty.

'That's fine,' I said. We agreed to meet the following morning. I made my way to Letterkenny, armed with a couple of biros and a few 'half-sheets', the Garda-issued stationery used for taking formal statements. I had no idea what I was letting myself in for. We parked in different sections of the hospital car park. Secrecy was the order of the day. This subject, child sexual abuse, was taboo, a cross to be carried with shame and guilt.

The car park was about two-thirds full. *Trevor* had parked in a quiet corner facing away from the traffic so that no one would see us. I got into his car, fumbling with the sheets as I laid them on the floor. I muttered a few words of casual conversation, trying to put his mind at ease. I don't know which of us was the more nervous or anxious. I didn't want to upset him any further and this was still new territory for me. I had to tread cautiously. It was his story, not mine; it was his hurt I was dealing with. I could see and feel the pain in his face and in his words. All I could do was listen.

I had prepared him as best I could the night before, telling him that it was important to be as accurate as he could about the dates, times and places where things happened when we did out his statement. If this went to court, as we hoped it would, only the facts of the case would be dealt with. To the legal system, his emotional pain and trauma were secondary; unravelling dry facts seemed to be more important. I knew from experience that barristers would have a field day in court with any inconsistencies. I couldn't let him down, so accuracy was paramount. Dooley was the lead investigator in the Greene case. He had more experience than I had at this stage. I had spoken to several abuse victims in my area, and when we met them together, it was John who usually took the statements. He led while I followed, watched and learned. *Trevor's* statement would be the first I had taken without him. *Trevor* had come to me; he didn't want to talk to anyone else, so it was left to me to take the statement.

His words came with difficulty, halting, as if he was moving huge rocks aside. Bridled with guilt, he felt he was to blame for what happened. I found this again and again with many abuse victims. It took me a while to realise he wasn't talking about Eugene Greene. He had come to me simply because he knew me. He didn't know I was investigating child sexual abuse. He just needed to be away from home when he spoke about it to a Garda. Almost 40 years old and he had to be fifty miles from home before he felt comfortable enough to talk.

Trevor was abused by *John Reilly*, a local farmer. He was raped repeatedly. He could barely say the word 'sex'. *Reilly* would take him to his house, abuse him and make him tea afterwards. He didn't know what was happening the first time. All he remembered was that *Reilly* took him up to his house to show him some baby rabbits. When he got there, *Reilly* brought him out to a shed, but there were no rabbits. *Reilly* told him the mother rabbit had eaten the babies. *Trevor* was also sexually abused and raped in a deserted house near *Reilly*'s home, and at a deserted lake.

He unveiled to me layer upon layer of sexual abuse of incredible depravity that no child should have to endure. He didn't seem to have any feelings or emotions as he spoke; they too were stolen along with his innocence. He was not yet a teenager when he first met his assailant. As is often the case, his abuser was known to him and groomed him, earning his trust. *Reilly* also knew *Trevor*'s family. He was a respected member of society, someone they trusted. *Trevor* was led like a young lamb to the slaughter.

Trevor wanted to tell his mother what was happening, but *Reilly* was a family friend, someone who often called to his home. He told me how he could hardly move after being raped, then *Reilly* would walk him home to his house where his mother would make them both tea. *Trevor* didn't know how his mother would react. His fear held him back; he was trapped and *Reilly* seemed to cherish his control. The abuse was regular, if not weekly then a few times a month for a total of four years. *Reilly* took every opportunity he could to abuse this child, calling to the house on the pretext of doing some errand or picking him up on the road on his way home from the shops or from school. *Trevor* had no escape route. He simply obeyed adults; they always knew best. How could a child of 10 mention the word 'sex' in the Ireland of the mid-sixties? The word itself was dirty. He felt something even worse could happen to him if he told. He would not be believed. Worse, his abuser could kill him if he told.

Trevor had lived with that fear for thirty years. How could he breathe in a society incapable of taking on board what happened and removing the stigma from innocent victims. He told me how he suffered terrible nightmares in which he was abused again in his dreams.

His teenage years were a mess, as was his whole life. His marriage broke up; he broke up. His neighbours regarded him as a chronic alcoholic and a marriage wrecker, just another sad statistic, an outcast. The damage inflicted by *Reilly* followed him down the years, although he had found some help in Alcoholics Anonymous. But how could he have a normal life or a normal relationship when basic trust had been torn away from him when he was still a child, robbed of the basic tools for survival?

Trevor told me things he didn't want included in his statement. He got uncontrollable shakes at times remembering what had happened to him. He felt dirty all the time. Filled with anger, he was afraid he might kill *Reilly*, although he was just as scared that *Reilly* would kill him.

I took his statement and read it over to him. He signed it and I witnessed it. I had never heard of *Reilly* until I met *Trevor*, who only came to me because he trusted me. He had no idea I was investigating another paedophile at the time. Apart from that one day in the car park I didn't work on the *Reilly* case, although I kept in touch with *Trevor*.

I forwarded *Trevor*'s statement to Dooley for his case file. *Trevor* was just one of several victims who came forward, though no doubt there were many others. The investigation against *Reilly* was already well under way by the time I met *Trevor*. He had been arrested and questioned the previous month. By that time five victims had emerged. In total nine would eventually make statements. Thanks to their courage *Reilly* was successfully prosecuted and convicted.

Chapter 12
In the Shadows

There was a knock on the door. It must have been close to 11 p.m. one day in early summer. When I opened the door, *Craig Thompson* stood there half huddled in the corner. 'Can I see you a minute?' he asked half apologetically.

I nodded, brought him into the sitting room and sat him down by the bay window. He sat half hiding in the armchair, his head bowed, rubbing his hands together and looking at the floor. I knew what was coming. I waited while he worked out how to begin. Some things cannot be rushed. From his behaviour I had a fair idea what he was going to say before he spoke, but I waited for him to find the words. He found it so difficult to speak out. After all, how do you tell someone you were sexually abused as a child? In a way it was easier for him to confide in someone who was almost a stranger. He didn't know me but he knew about me. But how could he find the language for this? This was his secret, the wound he had carried for years. My sitting room became a surgery, a place where the wound could be exposed.

'I heard you were investigating child sexual abuse.'

'I am, yes.'

'I was abused too,' he said, almost in a whisper. 'For the last year I have thought long and hard about it.' For a while he sat motionless, staring at the floor. Suddenly he jumped forward in the chair, his eyes wide. 'Screw them all!' he shouted, his voice suddenly strong, emphatic. 'I want to come forward and make a statement.'

Craig lived in Dublin. He had come back home to Donegal for the weekend as he often did, except this time he decided to come and see me.

The policeman in me began asking questions: who, what, where, when, questions that had to be asked even if I thought I already knew the answers. I thought it must have been Eugene Greene, but I asked him anyway. 'Who was abusing you?'

'Oh,' he said, 'Denis McGinley.'

It took a few moments for that to sink in. 'Denis McGinley?' I asked him. 'The teacher?'

'Yes,' he said. 'I know you're investigating Greene. I can't really tell you anything about Greene.'

Denis McGinley, a native of Gort an Choirce, was born in 1939, the fifth of seven children born to Rose and Seamus McGinley. He received his third level education in St Patrick's College, qualified as a primary teacher and began his career in 1959 working in various schools around the county until he retired in 1996. He never married and still lived locally with his aged mother. He had always struck me as a very shy, reserved and good living man who did not take an active part in any community affairs other than supervision at local youth club sessions. He was also a committee member of Colaiste Uladh, Gort an Choirce, which catered for students learning the Irish language during the summer holidays. The McGinley family were held in high regard locally, hard-working, industrious and successful in their chosen careers. Denis McGinley had taught in Cnoc na Naomh, Derryconnor National School, for years. He taught third, fourth and fifth class, children between the ages of 9 and 12.

Craig started talking about McGinley. He hadn't been abused by the teacher at school; instead, the first incident happened when he was 14 years old. McGinley was a member of the committee that ran the local community centre, and *Craig* was a member of the local youth club during the early eighties. On winter evenings McGinley gave *Craig* lifts home in his car after youth club meetings and allowed him to steer the car on the way home. It sounded eerily familiar.

The first time *Craig* remembered anything out of the ordinary was when he was on a ladder at the community centre hanging posters advertising a disco. When McGinley passed by him, he put his hand up his trouser leg, rubbing his leg briefly. *Craig* thought it was odd and it sent a shiver down his spine, but he said nothing. That evening McGinley drove *Craig* home from the youth club again.

'I passed no remarks on this,' *Craig* told me. 'I trusted and respected this man and it also occurred to me that I might get steering the car that night.' But instead of dropping *Craig* home, McGinley drove past the *Thompson* home and headed to a local beach. There, he allowed *Craig* to steer the car as he drove along the beach, before pulling over. McGinley was nervous and uneasy at first, but it didn't stop him sexually abusing the young boy, who wasn't quite sure what was happening. Afterwards he drove *Craig* home in silence.

'I felt what had happened was wrong,' *Craig* said, 'but my greatest concern at the time was the fear of others finding out about it, so I felt it was better to say nothing about it even though it was bothering me. I continued on at school and did not have any further contact with Denis McGinley for the remainder of the school year.'

The story *Craig* told me was familiar: how he was asked to stay behind when the other boys went home from the youth club; how he was allowed to steer McGinley's car; how he was brought to isolated spots. He was taken to the beach and to McGinley's home where he was repeatedly abused. It was as if McGinley was working from the same template of abuse that Greene used.

After his first encounter *Craig* managed to avoid McGinley for about a year. But one evening the following winter he was walking home around 9 p.m. when he met McGinley's car. The teacher drove past him, turned around and came back to pick him up, suggesting they should 'go for a spin'. *Craig* was raped at least six times that winter and early spring. Afterwards McGinley would engage the boy in meaningless small talk. *Craig* didn't say much. He knew what was happening was wrong but was afraid to say anything or protest against what was happening. 'My greatest fear was that anybody would find out about it and I was beginning to feel in some way responsible for what was happening,' he said, summing up the guilt many abuse victims wrongly feel.

When the clocks went forward to summer time, McGinley eased off his contact with *Craig*. The predator preferred to hunt at night under the cover of darkness. But the following October the nightmare began again. The same pattern of abuse continued until the following spring when the dark evenings ended, and began again the following winter. By now *Craig* was 17 years old. Often McGinley gave him £10 notes after raping him. He was reluctant to take the money, but McGinley refused to take no for an answer. He also allowed *Craig* to drive his car and told him to apply for a provisional driving licence. He wanted to buy the boy a car. As the third winter of abuse drew to an end, McGinley arranged a trip to Dublin, bought a car for him shortly after he turned 18 and paid for the insurance. He took *Craig* to the Phoenix Park and taught him how to drive the car there. The following day they drove back to Donegal in their separate cars.

McGinley told *Craig* to tell his parents he was paying for the car on a hire purchase agreement.

For four years McGinley held *Craig* in his power. Shy and introverted even as he reached adulthood, the young man felt unable to tell the teacher to stop, trapped by a feeling that he was somehow to blame and haunted by the shame if anyone would find out. Ironically McGinley's decision to buy him a car gave him a way out of his dilemma. With his new-found mobility on the roads, he could avoid McGinley. Able to drive to and from work on his own, he no longer felt compelled to accept lifts from McGinley. He felt a sense of freedom and made a conscious decision to avoid his abuser. After a few weeks McGinley began phoning him at work, but *Craig* simply hung up every time. McGinley then tried writing to him, both at his work and home addresses, telling him he loved him and asking why he was being ignored. *Craig* ignored the letters, hiding them under his mattress.

It was a bright summer morning. *Craig* had gone to Letterkenny with his father *Art*. His mother *Rose* was at home. As she was making the bed in *Craig*'s room, she found McGinley's letters under the mattress. There were about half a dozen all in the same handwriting. Curious to know what girl was interested in her son, she read through the letters. They were short, little more than notes, each no more than one page long and unsigned, but one of the letters had a phone number. The content of some of the letters disturbed her, one in particular which read: 'I know where you were last night. You should have been with me.' Concerned, she decided to check the phone number. Going through the phone book she eventually discovered that the number belonged to Denis McGinley. Shocked and upset, *Rose* phoned the local curate, Fr Hugh Sweeney, and asked him to call to her house. While she waited, *Craig* and his father arrived home from Letterkenny. *Rose* told her husband what she had discovered and together they confronted *Craig*. He admitted the letters came from McGinley, who had also bought his car. *Art* was disgusted and angry to learn that his son was being sexually abused by McGinley. He couldn't bring himself to look at the letters, but *Rose* showed them to Sweeney when the priest arrived. She told him that McGinley should not be teaching children. Sweeney agreed.

Craig didn't hang around long after Sweeney arrived. He headed for the pub as he often did. A few nights later he didn't come home from the pub at all. Sick with worry, *Art* went looking for him. In the early hours of the morning, unable to find *Craig* anywhere, he called to his best friend, *Dermot Hogan*.

Dermot knew *Art* was upset as soon as he saw him. His face was wet with tears. 'What's wrong?' he asked.

'I want my son,' *Art* answered.

'What son? What's wrong?'

'*Craig*. He didn't come home last night.'

Together they headed out to look for him. They found him sitting in a pub, alone and disconsolate, and took him home. *Craig* got into *Dermot's* car, still crying. He told his father he had got another letter from McGinley. After *Dermot* drove the *Thompsons* home, he asked to speak to *Craig*. He found *Craig* in his room sitting with his back to the window.

'Oh God,' said *Craig*. 'This will kill my mammy and daddy.'

Dermot told him not to worry. He would handle things from now on. 'If you get any more letters from Denis McGinley, don't go near him. Pass them on to me or your dad,' *Dermot* said.

Craig promised he would. 'Please help me, *Dermot*,' he begged.

'I will. Me and your dad will deal with this.'

About a week later *Craig* got another letter from McGinley, asking him to meet him the following Monday night. *Craig* shook as he showed the letter to his father when he was collected from his work. He didn't go to the proposed meeting. Instead, *Dermot* and *Art* decided to confront the teacher. When they arrived at the meeting place, they found McGinley sitting in his car. *Dermot* parked his car directly behind McGinley so that he couldn't drive away, and *Art* got into the passenger seat of the teacher's car. *Art* told McGinley to stay away from his son, threatening him several times until *Dermot* calmed him down. *Dermot* told McGinley he was a disgrace to his profession and that he should seek psychiatric help. The two men then left.

A few days later *Art* took *Craig's* car to a garage and sold it. He told his wife to have McGinley call to his home. When he did, they gave him the money they received for the sale of the car. He told McGinley that if he did not leave *Craig* alone, he would make sure he lost his job in Derryconnor National School. At this McGinley pleaded: 'Please don't do that.'

Rose Thompson expected her curate Fr Hugh Sweeney to go to his parish priest, Fr John McGlynn, the chairman of the school board, and felt strongly that McGinley should be removed from his position as a teacher. She was shocked to learn the following September when schools reopened that he was still teaching there.

John Gallagher, the school principal at the time, told us he had never been told of any complaints made against McGinley. Apparently, although Sweeney reported to the school manager, his parish priest John McGlynn, the school board and the principal were never told about the complaint. Unfortunately there was no paper trail we could find that might have recorded a decision or a minute at a meeting noting a concern or a situation that might have been monitored, something that would have verified the allegations *Craig* was making against McGinley when we went to court. Small country school boards are rather informal and sometimes chaotic and don't always bother with such procedural niceties.

Craig's ordeal had traumatic long-term effects. He was almost a ghost as he sat talking to me, he looked so pale and drawn. He began drinking early — anything to numb his mind. 'I feel totally devastated and I suffer a great deal of anguish and pain that cannot be described in words', he said in his formal statement of complaint. 'This sexual abuse inflicted on me by Denis McGinley was the main reason that I left Donegal in 1990 to try and make a fresh start in Dublin. I have gone through pure hell trying to come to terms with this sexual abuse and I am having great difficulty in having intimate relationships with others. Once the sexual abuse happened I felt entrapped. I felt a great sense of shame, and even though I felt it was wrong I went along, living in fear that someone would find out. I felt at the time that allowing the abuse to continue was the lesser of two evils. If it became public knowledge, I was only a teenager and Denis McGinley was more powerful than me. He was a schoolteacher, respected in the community. I felt that I would be more likely to be blamed than him.'

Craig's statement contained several details that could be independently verified. *Rose* confirmed how she discovered the letters from McGinley, and both parents confirmed their conversations with Sweeney and McGinley afterwards. *Dermot Hogan* also confirmed the details of the meeting during which *Art* confronted McGinley, as well as his own conversation with *Craig*. We spoke to the garage owner who bought the car, and his records showed he bought a car registered to a Mr *C. Thompson* in the early 1980s.

However when we interviewed Sweeney, by now a parish priest with a parish of his own, he was of no help to us. 'I cannot recall having being told by either *Rose* or *Art Thompson* anything in relation to their son *Craig* and his involvement with Denis McGinley', he said in a formal statement. 'I have no recollection of having been shown any letters that were written by Denis McGinley. I was not aware that Denis McGinley had a problem in this area.'

It was hard not to empathise with *Craig*'s sense of helplessness. When his parents found out, they had been able to speak to McGinley and warned him to steer clear of their son in future. However, even though they had approached their local priest, McGinley was allowed to continue in his teaching job. Nobody in authority listened. Nothing happened.

Chapter 13
Coffee and Rosary Beads

By the start of June, five months after our investigation began, John Dooley and I had taken statements from twenty-five victims sexually assaulted or raped by Eugene Greene. In addition we had evidence from close to a dozen witnesses who were able to confirm what Greene's victims had told us in part or in full. It was time to make an arrest.

Dooley, Detective Garda David Moore and I called to Greene's home in the parish of Anagaire on the morning of 12 June 1998. I wasn't in uniform — we used an unmarked Garda car and I wore plain clothes. I dealt with all these cases in plain clothes. Often I feel the uniform puts up a barrier to people, whether the victims of a crime or the perpetrators. They see only the uniform. It has a silencing effect, making it harder to talk. For the victims, wearing plain clothes helped to reassure them that we would respect their anonymity. During an arrest it helped build a one-to-one relationship and made it easier to talk.

Moore waited in the car outside the house while Dooley and I went to Greene's home. His sister answered the door. John told her we would like a word with her brother. He was still in his bedroom and she went to waken him. We waited in the hallway and after a few minutes he emerged from the room. As Greene walked into the hallway, Dooley put his hand on his shoulder and told him he was arresting him under section 4(3) of the Criminal Law Act 1997 for an offence of buggery on *David Brennan* in the parochial house at Leitir Mhic an Bhaird. John delivered the standard caution to the priest as required by the Judges' Rules: 'You are not obliged to say anything unless you wish to do, but anything you do say can be taken down in writing and may be given in evidence.' Greene said nothing. He remained silent on the way to Glenties Garda Station. Calm throughout the arrest, he even appeared relieved to see us. It seemed to me that he had been expecting us.

This was still a confidential investigation. Three policemen escorting a priest under arrest to a Garda station would be sure to attract plenty of comment in a rural area. Moore drove back to Glenties over some mountainous back roads and when we arrived in the town we parked behind the Garda station and entered by the back door. We arrived at 11.20 a.m. Dooley spoke with the uniformed member in charge, explained the reasons for the arrest and Greene was processed, his details taken and his rights explained to him. He asked us to contact his solicitor, Paudge Dorrian, a well-known criminal defence lawyer in Donegal. We then took him to the interview room where we began to question him.

In a way, I think being arrested came as a relief to Greene. 'I will be truthful with you after I speak with my solicitor,' he told us. He said nothing else, but he seemed open with us, if a little shocked by his arrest, as many people are. The interview was interrupted shortly after it began when Greene went to take a phone call from his solicitor, but I felt there was a good chance he would talk to us. We weren't strangers; I had known him for years. He had after all baptised one of my own daughters in 1976, the same year he was reported by the *Kennedy* family, I realised. He had been quiet on the way to the station, but during and after his processing he seemed to relax.

We had been less than an hour with Greene when his solicitor arrived. They spoke for half an hour. The custody regulations say a prisoner is allowed 'reasonable access' to a solicitor. The solicitor felt he should be allowed more time to consult with his client. He went into the superintendent's office to complain. The super checked the logs and told him he had had ample time. When they had finished we took Greene back to the interview room and began again. But his tune had changed. Every time we put allegations from his victims to him, he responded with the same five words, 'I have nothing to say.' Occasionally he would confirm that he knew someone, or that he was stationed in a particular parish in a given year, but for the most part he just clammed up. Even his body language changed. He was on the defensive. He knew nothing any more. Whereas before he was friendly, chatting casually as we built a rapport and talking to us man to man, afterwards it was like talking to a different person. It was

frustrating, but there was nothing we could do except put the allegations to him and record his responses.

When he did have something to say, it was usually to tell us that he
could not remember. He had nothing to say when we put *George
Maguire*'s statement and allegations to him. He couldn't remember
teaching *Andrew Kelly* to drive. He said he didn't even remember who
Mark Flynn and *Keith Quinn* were — *Keith*, whom we had to sneak into
a hotel by the fire escape because he was so worried someone might see
him, and *Mark*, who although he was living abroad, wrote to us explaining what he had gone through, what Greene called 'this little secret we
must keep', and who had tried to avoid the priest by skipping Mass until
Greene went to his teacher and complained. Greene did remember who
Kyle Carroll was, but when we put *Kyle*'s allegations to him, again he had
nothing to say. There was a similar response regarding *Ivan Sullivan*.

When we asked him why his answer to almost every question was,
'I have nothing to say', his answer to that question too was, 'I have
nothing to say.' When we asked him straight out if he was denying the
allegations his victims were making against him, he refused to do so.
Once again his only answer was, 'I have nothing to say.'

While he was being processed by the member in charge at the front
of the station, Greene had effectively admitted to us that he wrote to
the *Kennedy* family apologising to them after he was sent away from
the parish for a few months in the mid-seventies. But when we asked
him about this during the interview, again his answer was, 'I have
nothing to say.'

Greene said he didn't remember who *Rory Burke* was. I had spoken
to *Rory* and taken his statement in late May, less than three weeks
before. We couldn't meet at his house. Before he would talk to us, we
arranged for a hotel room where we could meet. He would sit in the
lobby and wait until we arrived. He would go to the toilets and as we
passed we'd tell him the room number. We were to leave the door
open and he would go to that room. *Rory* was an altar boy in the mid-
seventies when Greene invited him up to the parochial house. The
priest gave him a pound note and seemed very nice, but the boy was
nervous in his presence. Priests, he told me, were treated like gods in
the parish. He took *Rory* upstairs to his bedroom, put the boy lying
down on his bed and was beginning to touch him when there was a
knock at the door. A nun had called to see Greene. As soon as she
entered the house, *Rory* left. He made sure never to go near the

parochial house again, and later when he spoke to one of his closest friends, *Mark Flynn*, about what had happened, he realised what a lucky escape he had. 'Only the nun came to the door he would probably have raped me,' he told me. When we put *Rory Burke*'s allegations to Greene, once again he had nothing to say. And he didn't remember the nun who called to the house.

Dooley asked the priest if he remembered *Gavin Floyd*. 'No I don't,' Greene answered. Dooley had interviewed *Gavin* in April. In the early 1970s *Gavin* served as an altar boy. Greene was the curate when *Gavin* started service on the altar at the age of 10. Once a week he served at 8 a.m. Mass with Greene, sometimes along with a friend, sometimes alone. His mother would waken him at 7 a.m., and he would walk to Mass before going to school. For the first six months that he knew the curate *Gavin* found Greene to be a nice man. He didn't have a housekeeper and he gave *Gavin* £5 notes for doing work around his house.

Like many teenage boys, *Gavin* was a soccer fanatic, obsessively following his favourite team's progress and consuming any information he could find on them. One early summer's morning as he carried out his chores around the priest's house, Greene came to the back door wearing a dressing gown. He told the boy he had some footballers' autographs in his bedroom. The priest took him upstairs to his bedroom. When he got to the bedroom door, Greene kissed *Gavin* on his forehead. 'I just froze. I did not know what was happening,' *Gavin* explained.

Greene continued to touch *Gavin*, saying, 'This won't hurt. You will be all right.' Greene raped the young boy, holding him down while he screamed in pain. When he finished he told him to walk up to Mass, adding that what had happened was a secret. 'Everything will be all right. I'll be right up to say Mass,' he added. *Gavin* didn't serve Mass that morning. Instead he ran to a deserted part of town and hid. Later he went to school, still in pain. At break time when he went to the toilets, he was still bleeding. When he got home in the evening he changed his bloodied underpants, hiding the ruined pair under a tree. The pain lasted for days, but he was too afraid to tell anyone what happened. The priest had said it was a secret.

Gavin's mother woke him as usual in the weeks that followed on the days he was rostered to serve at the early morning Mass. He continued to do chores around the curate's house — he was afraid not to. Greene said nothing at first, but after a couple of weeks came outside while *Gavin* tidied around the house. He asked *Gavin* to come inside, saying he wanted to explain that he was sorry for what he had done and that it wouldn't happen again. As soon as *Gavin* was inside, Greene grabbed him by the neck and threw him on the couch. *Gavin* begged him to stop, but Greene ignored him and raped him again. He then went to the chapel to serve Mass for his abuser. At school *Gavin* bled again. In the evening he again changed and hid his soiled underpants.

The following week Greene was standing outside his door when *Gavin* passed on his way to go shopping for his mother. 'Mr *Floyd*, I want to see you now.'

'I can't see you,' *Gavin* answered. 'I have to do a message for my mother and she is expecting me home straight away.'

'Do you remember our secret?' the priest asked. 'If you don't come into the house, God will get you for it.'

Gavin was terrified. He went inside out of 'pure fear'. Greene again grabbed him by the neck and dragged him to the kitchen, pushing him up against the kitchen sink, intending to rape him again. In desperation, *Gavin* grabbed the nearest thing he could lay his hands on, a saucepan, and hit him on the side of the head. Before Greene could recover, he bolted out the door.

After that *Gavin* made sure he was never near Greene again. He switched rosters with other altar boys so that he never had to serve Mass for Greene and avoided the priest's house. Eventually he stopped serving Mass, then stopped attending Mass altogether. He felt he was responsible for what happened, and after he found out the facts of life he thought he was gay for several years until he met his first girlfriend. He was barely a teenager before he began abusing alcohol, and his mother was so concerned about him that she arranged to have him assessed by a child psychologist. He got further counselling for alcohol abuse before he was 20. He was too ashamed to tell any of his counsellors that Greene had sexually abused him. He drifted from job to job, never holding down any one position for very long, and eventually he left Donegal. A few weeks before Dooley took his statement, he told his mother and father he had been abused by Greene. 'I feel like I am getting a load off my chest by telling you about the abuse,' he told Dooley. 'I thought up to this point that I was a failure in life because I thought I disappointed my parents.'

Gavin's mother remembered the change in his behaviour when he was around 10 years of age. He became withdrawn and distant and would no longer hug her. She felt an intense anger at the years her son had lost, but was relieved finally to know the root cause of his problem behaviour. Dooley dealt with *Gavin* more than I did, but I met his mother several times and got to know her very well. She was a saintly woman.

Greene's response when Dooley put *Gavin Floyd*'s allegations to him was the customary reply, 'I have nothing to say.'

Greene was arrested at 10.35 a.m. The Criminal Justice Act gave us the power to question him for six hours before releasing him. If we needed to hold him any longer we needed the permission of a senior officer. Coming up to six hours into the arrest, we were nowhere near putting all the allegations we had collected to him. During a coffee break just before Greene was due to be released, Dooley went to see Superintendent Delaney. He explained that we had only put about half the allegations to Greene and needed more time. The super agreed and filled out an extension order. At 4.30 p.m., five minutes before he was due for release, the super instructed Greene in the interview room that he would be held for another six hours.

We continued going through the questions we had to ask him as the clock ticked down to Greene's release. By 7.40 p.m. we still had a lot of allegations to put to him, but he needed a rest break. We took him to the station cell at the back of the station, a small ground-floor room with a wooden bed, while we reviewed our notes, making sure we hadn't missed anything. The cell was a small windowless room, roughly five foot wide by ten foot in length, its pallid yellow walls lit by a single light bulb in the ceiling protected behind a wire cage. The cell had no furnishings save the built-in wooden bed with a rubber mattress, a sunken toilet in the floor and an alarm button if the prisoner needed to summon help. The single exit, a reinforced steel door, had a peep hole through which the custody officer could check on the prisoner regularly. It was warm enough, but there was a cold feeling about the place. In the entire time he was under arrest Greene never ate, we noticed, although he requested and was supplied with regular cups of coffee, which he drank incessantly throughout his time in the station. Rather than sit or lie on the bed, each time he was taken back to the small room Greene knelt by its side, fumbling with his rosary beads and praying. Somehow I doubted he was praying for his victims.

Chapter 14
Nothing to Say

After about an hour in the cell, we took Greene back to the interview room. Methodically we went through the remaining questions, formally putting every allegation to him. Again and again his response was the same. 'I have nothing to say.'

Matthew McCarthy served as an altar boy in the early 1970s in north Donegal. Before he met Greene he had served Mass with two other priests and told Dooley they were both great priests. 'In the seventies you would hardly be believed if you told someone you were sexually abused by a priest,' *Matthew* told Dooley. He would not allow us to go near his home to interview him, or even meet us in the townland where he lived. We had to arrange to meet him at night by a deserted pier several miles away. It was the only place he was comfortable talking. Every time he read a newspaper report about sexual abuse, what he had endured with Greene flooded back into his mind. When we put *Matthew*'s allegations to Greene, he had nothing to say. When we asked him if he was denying the allegations, again he had nothing to say.

It was the same story with *Richard Jackson*. *Richard* had told us it was a sunny Sunday in July when he was taken to a deserted beach by Greene, who then indecently assaulted him. *Richard* was 'in a total state of shock' at what happened and on the way home Greene said to him, 'I must ask your forgiveness.' *Richard* was too distressed to answer. He was afraid to tell anyone what had happened. It was unheard of for anyone to speak against a priest or the Catholic Church. *Richard*, one of Greene's earliest victims, was abused in 1965, the same year Greene returned from his missionary work in Nigeria, where we could only imagine what he might have done.

Richard's brother *Joshua* was abused early the following year. He did odd jobs for the priest in return for extra pocket money. One day the priest told him he was going to Letterkenny and told him to come along but not to tell his parents where he was going. When the priest saw *Joshua*'s brother working as he drove through the town, he told *Joshua* to lie down and covered him with a blanket. Greene was a priest, and you did what priests told you, so *Joshua* hid as he was told. As they drove over the mountains, Greene sexually assaulted *Joshua*. The priest then drove to Letterkenny in silence, left the boy sitting in his car for half an hour while he went about his business, then drove home, again in silence.

'I didn't really know if what he was doing was right or wrong, but in my mind I thought priests never done anything wrong,' *Joshua* told Dooley. 'I knew at the time that I could never tell my parents about it. They probably wouldn't believe me, or they might have even blamed me in some way.'

Later that year Greene was transferred to Scotland where he did 'extension work' and did not return to Ireland until 1968. *Joshua* stopped going to Mass, but in the mid-seventies he went to confession. When the confessor asked him why he no longer went to Mass, he told him he was sexually abused by a priest. 'He just wasn't interested, so I felt let down by the Church again,' *Joshua* said.

In 1990 *Joshua* had a near death experience due to an accident. In the moments when he did not know if he would live or die, the thought flashed through his head that Greene would probably be on the altar at his funeral Mass, and there wasn't a damn thing he could do about it. A few years later *Joshua* sought professional help for gambling and alcohol addiction. When he told his counsellor he was abused by a priest, the counsellor urged him to go to the Bishop of Raphoe and report what had happened. He offered to go with him in support, but *Joshua* felt so much time had passed that no one would listen.

'I have nothing to say.' Greene's face was blank and emotionless. He was as silent as he had been the day he drove *Joshua* to Letterkenny, when we put *Joshua*'s allegation to him. It was the same when we asked him about *Barry Hayes, Noel Campbell, Edward Brown*, the *Kennedys* and *Kirk Buckley*.

Kirk was 11 when Greene lured him into the parochial house by promising to show him a citizen's band radio. CB was all the craze at the time. Greene indecently assaulted *Kirk* in his living room, all the while telling him, 'It'll be all right. I'm your friend.' *Kirk*'s mother had warned him to stay away from Greene, so clearly the word was spreading in Gort an Choirce about him. *Kirk* ran from the parochial house before anything worse could happen and headed straight home, distraught. His mother saw he was upset and asked if the priest had touched him, but he was too ashamed to tell her. The priest never spoke to him afterwards.

Oscar Murray was another victim. Greene called to *Oscar*'s home one evening and asked his mother if there was anyone around who could show him the way to a local landmark he wanted to see. *Oscar* was told to show him the way, and Greene abused him before driving him home in silence. When challenged on this episode with *Oscar*, he again replied, 'I have nothing to say.'

William Collins, yet another victim, was 15 when Greene offered him a lift on his way home one evening, and instead took him to the parochial house where he abused him.

'Goidé tá tú a dhéanamh?' (What are you doing?) *William* asked the priest.

'You will be all right. Nobody will know,' Greene kept repeating.

William cried and kept telling Greene he had to get home. Eventually the priest took him home, warning him to tell nobody what happened. *William* thought that if he dared tell anyone, they would think he was crazy for saying something so horrendous about a priest. Until he spoke to me he had never told a living soul.

And about *Dean Scott*, whom Greene plied with vodka until he threw up then indecently assaulted until he threw up again: 'I have nothing to say.'

Questioning Greene was an intense experience. Through our investigations Dooley and I were aware of about three decades of abuse dating from the mid-sixties to the mid-eighties. We had worked out in advance how we would approach the interviews, taking it in turns to ask questions. Dooley began with the cases he had investigated, starting with *David Brennan*. Then I'd ask him about victims I had discovered in Gort an Choirce, then back to Dooley again. The system worked well for us. When Dooley began to get frustrated at the non-answers and non-denials, I would step in and ask my questions. Dooley returned the favour when the constant negatives started to get to me.

It was hard not to get emotional during those interviews. We were dealing with horrific crimes against children, and all Greene would do was sit there, motionless, and parrot, 'Nothing to say, nothing to say' again and again, neither denying nor admitting, even in the face of so much evidence. It was the quantity of the evidence that convinced us we were right to arrest him. We had found victims from different decades, different parishes, and telling almost identical stories which illustrated the pattern of his abuse. His abuse was systematic: different places, different times, but always the same formula. By the end of the day Greene was like a stench. I wanted to puke.

As the interview drew to a close, we asked Greene when he had retired from the priesthood.

'Ash Wednesday this year,' he told us. He had been in semi-retirement since September 1994.

'Why did you retire from the priesthood?'

'Because the Bishop, Dr Philip Boyce, recommended it to me.'

'When were you in treatment in Stroud?'

He told us he had been to Stroud in 1992 getting treatment for alcoholism. Our Lady of Victory treatment centre in Stroud, Gloucestershire, England, offered 'therapy in a spiritual context' for priests with a variety of problems ranging from drug and alcohol addiction to serious sexual misconduct. The centre was run by an American order, the Servants of the Paraclete, established in New Mexico in the 1940s and specialising in treatment for priests with psychological and emotional problems. Greene signed a consent to access medical records giving 'permission to the Garda authorities to access my medical records at Our Lady of Victory'. We had no interest in any treatment Greene got for alcohol dependence in Stroud or anywhere else. He knew, and we knew, that the reason we wanted to see his medical records from the time he spent there was to see what they had to say about sexual abuse.

Our twelve hours were up. Greene was photographed and his possessions returned to him. He was released at 10.31 p.m., having made no admissions, but we felt we had enough to get a conviction in court. We had the statements of complaint against him, so many of them, and over so many years, all showing the same pattern. We had corroboration in many of the cases from family members, friends of the victims and from professional counsellors. Finally we had his own written consent and we believed it would show he received psychosexual counselling in Stroud. Perhaps Stroud was also the 'treatment centre or hospital' from which Greene wrote to the *Kennedy* family asking for forgiveness for unspecified transgressions.

Chapter 15
Evil in Our Midst

It is a defence lawyer's job to do his best to protect his client, which covers everything from advising him of his right to stay silent to picking away at the evidence we bring to court to find a reasonable doubt which will get him off. There are sound reasons for this. Over the years the courts have recognised miscarriages of justice and put up safeguards to try and make sure no innocent person goes to jail. To prove guilt it is not enough to raise a suspicion, or even to show that a suspect is more likely than not the culprit behind a crime. Guilt has to be proven beyond all reasonable doubt. The defence lawyer is an essential part of that process. If a qualified and skilled barrister does his best to keep his client out of jail, and yet the prosecution case survives all the hurdles thrown at it, then the judicial system can reassure itself that the case against the accused has been thoroughly tested and it hasn't accidentally jailed an innocent man. Lawyers call it Blackstone's Ratio, after the noted eighteenth-century English jurist William Blackstone, who defined the principle that it is 'better that ten guilty persons escape than that one innocent suffer'.

Sometimes of course the principle, and the dedication of lawyers to their clients, can be intensely frustrating to a policeman. In law, we had the power to hold Greene for a total of twelve hours, provided we could persuade the super to give us an extension to the original six hours of detention. Go over that twelve hour limit and anything we gathered during his arrest could be thrown out in court. The job of the member in charge or the custody officer in any Garda station is to keep a log of any arrests on his watch, ensure that prisoners are not abused, that they know their rights, and that they get meals and sleep if they are kept overnight. Ask anyone who has done the job and they'll tell you they're clock-watchers. Their job is to watch that clock as the detention ticks down, make sure interviews do not go on too long and make sure prisoners are not detained illegally.

Years before I moved to Donegal when I was still a uniformed Garda
in the Midlands, I had had first-hand experience of the difference a few
minutes can make. A member of the Provisional IRA was arrested after
the murder of Garda Michael Clerkin, but the case against him
collapsed because he was held too long in custody.

Michael Clerkin was a friend of mine. I was the last person to
waken him for duty before he was killed. It was a Friday, 15 October
1976. I was off for the weekend and Michael was working the weekend
night shift. My wife Brid was finished at school at 3 p.m. and we had
planned to head to Galway for the weekend when I got a call from the
station. Something had come up and the sergeant was caught short-
handed. He needed someone to come in for a couple of hours. As I
was anxious to get away for the weekend, I suggested that Michael
might do it. I thought he would appreciate the couple of hours of
overtime pay by starting a few hours early.

I can still remember calling to Michael's upstairs flat in town,
knocking to announce myself. 'Come on in,' he said. He was always
smiling beneath his waves of curly black hair. Over tea, brown bread
and cheese we spoke about the job, exchanging gossip and news, and
I bade him farewell. That was the last time I ever saw him. I went
down to Galway. Early the next morning there was an explosion. I was
told that Michael was killed. I had to come back immediately as there
was a major search on. We went through the rubble, digging out bits
of flesh and bone. Bombs don't leave much behind. We formally
identified Michael by his signet ring carrying the initials 'MC', a gift
from his girlfriend. He was just 24 years old.

We knew the bomb was no accident. It was planned, a cold barbaric
act by the IRA. The bomb was hidden in a gas container in a vacant
house in Garryhinch. The detonation coincided with the signing
into law of the Emergency Powers Act passed by the Cosgrave
government that week. No one ever claimed responsibility for the
bomb, which was specifically designed to kill detectives and uniformed Gardaí.

Some of the local Provo hotheads had decided they didn't like
some of the local Guards. They definitely didn't like the new law. They
set up the trap, a bomb specifically designed to kill Guards and made
a hoax phone call to Portlaoise Garda Station. An anonymous female
caller left a simple message: 'Armed men will be staying in Galvin's
vacant house, Garryhinch, tonight; they will attempt to do a job on

Oliver J. Flanagan.' Flanagan was the local Fine Gael TD, a noted hard-liner on law and order issues.

The patrol car went to answer the call. There were three Guards inside, Sergeant Jim Cannon, Garda Gerry Bohan and Michael Clerkin, who was driving. They were told to hold on for the armed detective branch men, and met up with Detective Tom Peters and Detective Ben Thornton before heading to the vacant house. They arrived there at 12.40 a.m. on Saturday, approached carefully in total darkness and searched quietly outside. The front door was locked. They saw nothing as they circled the house, but there was a window open at the back. Michael, the smallest of the party, decided to go in. He climbed through the window and walked to the front of the house to let Thornton in. Michael must have walked over the tripwire by the front door on his way to open it, because on opening the door and just as he turned to go back inside, the bomb went off. It brought the two-storey house tumbling down on top of him, while the four Guards outside were injured in the blast, buried under the rubble.

Cannon and Bohan were standing by the rear wall when the bomb exploded. They were buried up to their necks in rubble, their uniforms cut to shreds by flying debris. Gerry received serious injuries to his head, face, eyes and chest. Jim suffered injuries to his head, back, eyes, hands and both legs. Gerry managed to free himself but couldn't free Cannon, whose legs were trapped in the debris. Bohan ran to a nearby house to get assistance while Cannon slowly managed to free himself. As he did, he heard sounds coming from the centre of the rubble and crawled towards it. He found Peters, his head sticking up from a mound of rubble. He was at the front of the house and the roof slates hit him full in the face. Peters was blinded and lost most of his hearing. His face was badly disfigured by the blast. Ben suffered injuries to his head, ears and eyes. Unable to shift the rocks from Peters, Cannon then stumbled through several fields to a nearby cottage for help. Thornton's life was saved by the work of local men who dug him out after an hour underneath the rubble. Michael Clerkin, who took the full force of the blast, never stood a chance.

The forensics people estimated afterwards that up to 100 pounds of explosive was used in the bomb. They also found a live hand grenade in the rubble; somehow it hadn't gone off in the blast. We made twelve arrests afterwards, in Dublin and Laois, but there was never enough evidence to bring any charges in court. In one case a suspect was questioned for a handful of minutes more than the legal maximum, and because he was questioned illegally, the legal advice was that all the evidence was tainted because of that breach and no charges could be filed.

Some time later I was on patrol when I noticed some kids playing cowboys and Indians, but something struck me as odd. I called over one of the boys and asked him to show me the gun he was playing with. It wasn't a toy gun. It was the real thing, with a bullet in the breech. When I asked the youngster where he got the gun, he told me he had found it.

I asked him where, and he told me. We organised a search of the area, an old dilapidated building. We recovered trip wire of the same sort used in the bomb that killed Michael Clerkin, ordinary items like clothes pegs and a child's school copybook with directions on how to use them in assembling a home-made bomb, along with .303 rifles and ammunition.

There was something chilling about knowing there was such evil in our midst, coldly planning death and destruction. Nowadays thankfully those days are fading into history, but at the time we felt as if we were at the edge of chaos. When I moved to Donegal, the first cease-fire was in sight and things were changing. But it was devastating to learn what had been going on unknown to me there. There was another evil in our midst, another chaos to fight.

Chapter 16

Getting the Full Story

John Dooley, the lead investigator in the Eugene Greene case who had received the first complaint from *David Brennan* back in December, now busied himself preparing the file for the Director of Public Prosecutions (DPP). Except for minor cases taken before the district courts, the decision to launch a prosecution is not up to the Guards. We are solely investigators. When we finish, we send a file containing all the evidence we've gathered to the DPP who examines it and makes the decision on where to go from there.

Although Greene never admitted anything when we arrested him, we were pretty confident we had a strong case against him. The twenty-six complaints we knew of, ranging over decades, all showed a consistent pattern of behaviour, and in many cases we had independent support for the victims' stories from family members or friends. There is no such thing as an open and shut case, but we were pretty sure we had enough evidence to get the case to court. After that it was up to the jury.

After Greene's release we went over what we had, doing our best to divorce ourselves from the emotions of the case and concentrate on the facts. There was still a lot to be done, the tidying up that's essential before the file goes to the DPP. Everything has to be cross-checked, any loose ends tied up. Sometimes you realise you need more information about a specific allegation and you have to go back to the victim and take another statement, maybe specifying a year when something happened or the type of car Greene was driving — any detail that might help the DPP in framing the charge. Sometimes you spot something you missed the first time that leaves an ambiguity, so you take a statement to clarify what was meant originally. Sometimes you realise there are other people you can speak to, a friend, a neighbour, a relative, someone who may not even realise they can help with a detail but who often provide a small but critical piece of evidence.

Then there's the simple clerical work. Preparing a file for the DPP sounds routine, a minor part of the investigation, but cases have been won or lost in the preparation of a file. There are a thousand years of common law and statute involved in every criminal case, a thousand years of rules of evidence and reasonable doubt, of due process and fair procedure for barristers to test before judge and jury. Get a step wrong and the accused walks. An original signed statement is evidence which has to be kept securely. The DPP doesn't get those handwritten statements, but typed copies. Those copies have to be typed accurately, proofread and double checked. Then we have to prepare our own statements. Any Garda involved in the investigation, however tangentially, has to provide a statement, from Superintendent Joseph Delaney who gave permission to allow an extension to Greene's arrest for a further six hours and later to take his fingerprints and photographs, to Garda John McGroary who as member in charge of Glenties station that morning booked the prisoner and explained his rights to him before we questioned him. In addition the interview notes we took while questioning Greene had to be typed up. Then there were the Gardaí who were involved back when *David Brennan* was arrested in December, the superintendent and two officers who were members in charge at different times that day, and Detective Garda David Moore who questioned *David Brennan* along with Dooley. Every piece of paper in the file then has to be checked and rechecked along with other correspondence, and a final report prepared for the DPP outlining the case. The Gardaí do have access to clerical staff, both civilian employees and officers who specialise in preparing the paperwork, but given the need for confidentiality in the case, John did the work on the file himself. There was no need for any more people than were absolutely necessary to know the identity of the victims, who wanted their names kept confidential.

While Dooley set aside a few hours each week to work on the file along with his other duties, I had a second case to investigate. A few weeks before we arrested Greene, *Craig Thompson* had told me about Denis McGinley, the teacher who abused him, but I hadn't taken a statement at the time. 'There's no point in me starting until we have all the facts,' I told him. 'You have to get everything straight in your mind, the complete story from start to finish.'

After that I chatted to him on the phone several times in the weeks that followed before we sat down to do out the statement of evidence.

Growing up in Connemara: (*Left to right*) Back row: Caitlin, Liam and Maureen Ridge. Middle row: Treasa, Martin, their mother Kate, Paddy (with a puppy) and Colm Ridge. Front row: Tomas and Brid Ridge. Missing from the photo, taken for Treasa's confirmation, are their oldest brother Michael, and their father who was working in England at the time. (*Author's Private Collection*)

Garda Recruit Martin Ridge during his student days at the Garda Training College in Templemore, the first time in his life that the Gaeltacht native had to speak English full time. (*Author's Personal Collection*)

Martin and Brid Ridge on their wedding day in 1974. The couple met when Martin was transferred to his first posting in Co. Donegal in 1967, and kept in touch by letter while Brid studied in England, spending summers and holidays together. (*Author's Private Collection*)

The funeral of Garda Michael Clerkin, killed by an IRA bomb planted in a vacant house near the Laois/Offaly border in October 1976. Garda Martin Ridge is third from the right in the front row of the guard of honour. (*Irish Press Archive*)

Glenties Garda Station, where the investigation into Fr Eugene Greene began when Detective Garda John Dooley arrested a young man accused of blackmail. Six months later, the investigation ended in the same building with Greene's arrest. (*Gerard Cunningham*)

Detective Garda John Dooley, now retired, without whose hard work Eugene Greene would never have been brought to justice. It was John who asked that Garda Martin Ridge should work on the investigation. The two knew each other from previous cases and Greene had worked in Ridge's subdistrict for several years. (*Gerard Cunningham*)

Retired Garda Martin Ridge, sitting at the venerable Gateway computer he bought out of his own pocket in order to prepare the prosecution file against schoolteacher Denis McGinley, rather than wait for a replacement for the ancient Remington manual typewriter in the local Garda station. (*Gerard Cunningham*)

A more recent picture of Martin Ridge with his brothers and sisters. (*Left to right*) Back row: Tom, Colm and Martin. Middle row: Michael, Brid, Caitlin, Maureen and Paddy. Front row: Treasa and Liam. (*Author's Private Collection*)

Martin Ridge on a trip to Inis Bó Finne (Inishbofin) Island, with the Donegal coastline of Gort an Choirce (Gortahork) in the background. The island was inhabited year-round for many years, but is now empty of people for most of the year. (*Gerard Cunningham*)

The small church on Inis Bó Finne (Inishbofin) Island, part of the parish of Gort an Choirce (Gortahork) where Eugene Greene abused some of his victims. The priest spent several years as a curate in the parish, which also includes Toraigh (Tory Island). (*Gerard Cunningham*)

Most Reverend Dr Anthony McFeely, Bishop of Raphoe from 1965, the year Eugene Greene arrived in Co. Donegal, until his resignation in 1982. Gardaí were told that a search of the diocesan archives from the time McFeely took over until Greene's arrest found 'no records of any allegation being filed' against the priest. (*The Irish Times*)

The parochial house in Gort an Choirce (Gortahork) where Eugene Greene was stationed between 1976 and 1981, and where he abused several of his victims. The white door to the side of the building led to Greene's private rooms. (*Gerard Cunningham*)

We spoke about what happened and I explained to him what we should do, how he needed to think about everything and tie down as many specific incidents as he could. In the meantime we could concentrate on finishing the investigation phase of the Greene case. By early July, *Craig* was ready. I travelled to Dublin with Dooley to speak to him on 7 July 1998.

We knew where we stood with Greene. We had the witness statements and we had made an arrest. But suddenly I had two child sexual abuse cases to investigate, not one. Dooley was in the same boat. He had the *John Reilly* case to complete, one that I had had a marginal involvement in, taking a single statement from *Trevor Moore.*

We took *Craig's* statement in a quiet house in the Dublin suburb of Blackrock. My brother, who owned a house there, was on holidays and had given me the keys. It would be ideal, and to be frank we had no other facility. Like all of the sexual abuse victims, *Craig* didn't want to go anywhere near a Garda station. The last thing they want to see is a uniform or a Garda station. They need a safe environment in which to talk.

We had thought of booking a hotel room in Dublin for a day, but when I spoke to my brother about the problem he told me not to worry. I'll leave the key with the next door neighbour, he told me. When we got to Blackrock I collected the house keys. We settled down, drinking tea and coffee all day while we spoke with *Craig.* It worked perfectly. We had privacy in which to talk, no anxiety about who might see him arrive at a hotel or wonder why he was there.

Craig was living in Dublin in a flat on the north side of the city at the time. He was clearly shaken. Coming forward hadn't been an easy decision for him, but he had reached the point where he knew he had to speak out. He was still in the throes of abuse, trying to bury the bitter memories in alcohol and addiction, trying to deal with different traumas, different layers of pain. His whole life was upside down. He told me afterwards it was a good job he was living in Dublin; he had feared what he might have done if he still lived in Donegal. 'I was afraid I might kill the bastard,' he told me bluntly.

We spoke with *Craig* from around midday until after seven in the evening. At the end of the session we had a comprehensive thirteen page statement. Crucially it contained several points which could be backed up by talking to other people. It wasn't an easy session; seven hours is a long time to talk about anything, never mind something so painful, but *Craig* wanted to do it. More than that, he needed to do it. It was very harrowing, all the things to be gone through, the years of abuse reduced to mere written words on a page while *Craig* relived memories that were still fresh. Afterwards he thanked us for spending so much time with him. We took him out, brought him to a restaurant and bought him a steak. I think it was the best meal he'd had in days.

What disturbed us most was that *Craig* had received no support from those in authority who had responsibility in this matter. In 1984 when his parents found out what was going on, they had approached the curate in the parish, Fr Hugh Sweeney. When I spoke to them, they told us how they had shown Sweeney the letters McGinley had written to *Craig*. Yet nothing had happened. Even though the parish priest was told that a teacher in his school had raped a 14-year-old boy, there was no investigation, no report, no attempt to keep him away from children.

Chapter 17
Brothers

I first met *Craig Thompson* towards the end of spring 1998 while we were preparing to arrest Eugene Greene. Before he knocked on my door I had hardly ever spoken to him although I had got to know some of his family over the years. I took his statement in July the same year, a few weeks after Greene's arrest. One bizarre element of his formal statement stayed with me, his reference to daylight time. The abuse began in winter, stopped when the clocks went forward for the summer, and began again when the clocks went back in the autumn. In the long evenings McGinley didn't want to be seen. He worked under the cover of darkness.

It wasn't until May 1999, pretty much a year after I met *Craig*, that Dooley and I took the next statement for the file on McGinley. The delay puzzled a lot of people. Even the office of the DPP asked us about it when we handed in the file. There were several reasons. We wanted to finish the Greene file, get it out of the way, and Dooley (along with other detectives) was busy with the *John Reilly* case too. Mostly though it was down to the time it took to talk to people, the conversations necessary to build trust, and after that the time victims needed to think about what had happened, trying to remember details that would be critical for their statements.

The time wasn't wasted. While we took no statements for nine months, we built a profile on McGinley and spoke to several of his victims. The dates on official statements didn't tell the full story. They were the result of the investigation, not its entirety.

Gordon Regan was the first to make a formal statement in May 1999. The abuse he suffered affected him badly. He got panic attacks as a child. Like many victims he moved away from Donegal and lived in Dublin. He moved to Dublin because he couldn't trust himself in Donegal. Too many times he had gone for a few drinks and afterwards thought about going to McGinley's house, breaking in and killing him. Instead, he moved away from the area and rarely returned home.

Gordon was just over 4 years old when he started his schooling in Derryconnor National School. His first two teachers were women, one while he was in junior infants and senior infants and then a second for first class and second class. Four years into his primary schooling McGinley became his teacher. The teacher gave the children spelling assignments each evening and tested them the following morning on what they had memorised overnight. 'I was not very good at my spellings,' *Gordon* explained to me. 'When I got my spellings wrong in front of the class, McGinley would tell the girls in the classroom to put their heads down on the desks. He would open my belt first, he would then ask me another spelling and if I got that wrong he would open the zip of my trousers. I used to get upset and I would start to cry. I can remember looking down at the class and the girls would be looking up at me and they would be laughing.'

Gordon endured this treatment for two years. His spelling skills deteriorated as he grew tense and nervous before each morning test. At lunchtime he had to face the mercilessly cruel teasing of his class-mates. Every morning he went to school knowing he had to face into the same ordeal again. Occasionally McGinley took the boy behind a large map of Ireland in the corner of the room, where he would abuse him. At night *Gordon* suffered from horrible nightmares, dreaming that the teacher was in his house or lurking outside in the yard. He remembered one night in particular when he became so agitated his mother had to hold him down in his bed. 'I told my mother that Denis McGinley used to take down the trousers off me,' *Gordon* explained. 'But I was small at the time and I think that my mother did not believe me, or maybe she thought I was looking for excuses for not going to school.'

At school *Gordon* was teased and slagged by the other children: 'Teacher's pet! Teacher's pet!' Whether he grew immune to it or the teasing eased off, it wasn't as bad in fourth class as in third, and he survived the second year of abuse, where McGinley used to make him sit on a convection radiation heater in the classroom while he abused him. He remembered seeing a fourth class boy often sitting on the heater back when he was in third class. McGinley had a conveyor belt of victims at his disposal. *Gordon* learned that the older pupils had a nickname for McGinley: Poofy Den. The teacher's behaviour was no secret, at least in the schoolyard.

The abuse had a profound effect on *Gordon*'s education. He remembered his mother telling him several years before that he was a good speller until he began third class. He lost interest in school, felt awkward in front of the other pupils and dropped out early. He felt angry all the time, drank too much and frequently got into fights. When he drank, it was then that he thought about going to McGinley's house with a baseball bat or other weapon and assaulting the teacher. Instead, he left Donegal altogether.

Gordon's mother *Helen* confirmed that he had nightmares during the years he was taught by McGinley, often waking shouting and screaming at night. When *Gordon* told her that the teacher put his hand down his trousers, she couldn't believe it; it simply couldn't be true. *Gordon* had to be making it up to get out of going to school. 'I thought that the school was the next safest place to home for a child,' she explained. *Helen* felt an intense sense of guilt for not believing her son when he tried to tell her as a child what was going on at school every day. McGinley had also abused another of her sons, *Eric*.

Gordon's nightmares ended when he moved from McGinley to the next teacher at school. He had little confidence in himself and told his mother that everyone thought he was stupid. Shortly before his 20th birthday he told her he was abused as a boy by McGinley. Around the same time *Helen* had heard other rumours around the town. Pupils had written graffiti on the school walls: 'Poofy Den'. But it would be another six years before *Craig* came to me with the statement that would initiate the investigation.

Eric Regan, who was two years older than his brother *Gordon*, also confirmed that McGinley was known on the schoolyard grapevine as Poofy Den. He was abused by McGinley several times while he was in fourth class, but resisted as best he could. The teacher put him sitting in a corner after that, isolating and largely ignoring him in the classroom. McGinley's inappropriate behaviour was 'common knowledge' among the children, he confirmed.

Eric named four other boys whom he thought were abused by McGinley. Two of them made statements; the other two declined. He never saw the teacher interfering with the girls in the class. Two other boys confirmed that they saw *Gordon* abused by his teacher.

Again and again I would come across similar patterns in the complaints from McGinley's victims, just as I had with Greene. Paedophiles find a pattern of behaviour that works, then stick to it compulsively. But the recurring pattern that stunned me most was the 'common knowledge' in the schoolyard. All the children knew about Poofy Den. There was a subculture in the schoolyard, things children knew and accepted, something that was virtually part of the school curriculum because no one ever told them any different. Trapped inside their own shame, most never even dared speak about what was happening. Poofy Den was simply a gauntlet to be survived during their childhood, an obstacle to be passed on the way to growing up.

Chapter 18
Part of Growing Up

Speaking to McGinley's next victim involved a trip to Dublin. *Raymond Graham* was about the same age as *Gordon Regan*, and like *Gordon* he lived in Dublin. I travelled to Dublin along with Dooley in early June 1999 to meet with *Raymond*.

I had first gone to see *Raymond* one weekend when he was home from Dublin. His father had told me before then that he had heard we were investigating Greene and had mentioned it to *Raymond*. When *Raymond* heard this, he broke down in tears saying, 'Thank God this is coming out.'

A few weeks later *Raymond*'s father rang and told me his son was coming down for the weekend if I wanted to call round and have a word with him. When I got there I told *Raymond* we were investigating what was going on, and not just with Eugene Greene, although I kept it in fairly vague and general terms. He cried with relief. He knew immediately what I wanted to talk to him about.

'Yes, Denis McGinley abused me,' he said. It was like a weight had been lifted off his shoulders. *Raymond* told me that McGinley began organising daily quizzes in the classroom shortly after he began third class. He ran two or three quizzes a day and gave the winner a 5p or 10p prize. *Raymond* was a bright boy and often did well in the quizzes. His reward was the 5p or 10p piece and to be allowed to sit on the convection heater beside the teacher.

'At first he would put his arm around me; then that gradually led on to a cuddle which I would have taken to be a compliment at the time,' *Raymond* explained. 'I felt good getting the answers right.'

Raymond was brought up to respect and look up to teachers and didn't feel uncomfortable with McGinley's actions at first. Over time the teacher had him sit on the heater regularly, and when he ran a class quiz he would help *Raymond* with the answers, for instance tracing the shape of a number on his back in answer to an arithmetic question. *Raymond* didn't mind; it meant he won the quiz and got his prize money. He felt flattered that the teacher liked him and helped him win.

But as time went by McGinley stepped up his misbehaviour. Instead of tracing an answer over *Raymond*'s shirt, he would place his hand under the boy's shirt. Looking back, *Raymond* realised McGinley was gaining his confidence with each step by allowing him to win the quizzes. Eventually McGinley escalated to full-scale abuse, touching the boy indecently, often in full view of other pupils. *Raymond* 'had total respect for Denis McGinley' and did not realise at that time that what he was doing was wrong until he graduated to fifth class, when the older boys teased him for being Poofy Den's pet. When *Raymond* learned the facts of life, he felt dirty, used and ashamed by what McGinley had done to him for the previous two years. He endured the teasing and slagging from the other students until he finished in national school, his embarrassment so great he was too ashamed to tell anyone what happened, either his parents or anybody else. He did his best to block out what happened. When other child sexual abuse cases came to light in the early nineties, they reawakened *Raymond*'s memory of what happened.

'Every time I read about sexual abuse in the newspapers or saw an item about it on television, I was constantly reminded of my own abuse, which caused me enormous upset and stress,' he told us. 'I felt I was reliving the trauma of it. This trauma finally forced me to come forward. I now realise that the only way to deal with the pain and hurt is to come forward and make a complaint and have the matter finally dealt with.'

Two other pupils gave us information which supported what *Raymond* told us. His father *Harry* told us that his son became a virtual recluse as a teenager, withdrawing from his family and friends, rarely leaving his bedroom, while his friends played football outside. *Harry* couldn't figure out what was wrong with his son but was relieved when after about a year he seemed to finally come out of his shell and began a training course. He never suspected his son had been sexually abused until *Raymond* told him shortly before he made his statement to us.

'Looking back now, I have no doubt but that it was the sexual abuse on him by Denis McGinley that caused him to withdraw from the family and his friends,' *Harry* told us. 'He got very emotional and cried his heart out. I feel very hurt that a child of that age was sexually abused by his teacher while I was thinking it was the safest place for him to be.'

Harry assured *Raymond* he would support him when he went to the Guards. He was convinced McGinley's actions had long-term effects on his son, who was quite bright at school but lost all interest in his education and did not finish the course in his secondary school.

Douglas Ferguson told me a similar story. He was a couple of years ahead of *Raymond Graham*, but his experience was virtually identical. McGinley had abused him in front of the class in the prefab behind the main school building on at least four specific occasions that he could remember. He too remembered McGinley's distinctive and politically incorrect schoolyard nickname.

'I knew at the time what Denis McGinley was doing was wrong and I felt embarrassed as I knew the class was looking at me,' *Douglas* told me. He also said that he saw the teacher abuse two brothers, *Simon* and *Kevin Lynch*. Even after *Douglas* moved into fifth class, he still felt a deep anger at what had happened and did his best to avoid McGinley. However, one day he remembered McGinley passing a comment to him in the yard during a break between classes. He couldn't remember what McGinley had said, but the throwaway remark infuriated him and he made a well-known obscene gesture, the two-finger salute or V-sign. As a result, the boy was reprimanded by the school principal.

Corroboration, always critical in any investigation, was helped by McGinley's own sense of invincibility. So arrogant was he, so certain that he was untouchable, that he had frequently abused children in front of his class, taking no greater precaution than to order the pupils to put their heads down (Ceann síos!) before abusing his chosen victims. One of the boys' former classmates, *Ronan Hughes*, gave us a witness statement describing what he saw, and his account was plain, straightforward and objective. In starkly simple language he outlined what happened at school, explaining how it was virtually a daily occurrence, a part of the routine, just another part of growing up.

McGinley's classroom, *Ronan* explained, was in a prefab, a temporary schoolroom behind the main school building. McGinley had his young charges to himself, away from adult eyes. Several times *Ronan* saw the teacher touching other boys inappropriately, so often that it was routine. When he first moved into third class he found McGinley's behaviour embarrassing, but he soon realised it was common practice. The boys McGinley picked on were often quite popular with their classmates, but they all got the nickname of teacher's pet, while McGinley was nicknamed Poofy Den. McGinley never touched *Ronan*, but for the two years he spent in third and fourth class, he felt anxious and uncomfortable with his teacher's behaviour towards the other boys. He also remembered the regular class quizzes. Although it was a mixed class, he could not remember a single occasion when a girl won a quiz. McGinley pretty much ignored the girls in his class. Listening to *Ronan*, I realised there were more victims than just the boys McGinley abused sexually. The abuse affected everyone in the class, as other pupils worried they might be next, while half his pupils were virtually ignored.

A policeman is supposed to stay objective. Get too close to a case, lose objectivity, allow your emotions in and you lose sight of the evidence. If instead of following the facts a policeman follows his feelings, cases fall apart. Emotions cloud judgment and investigations can get sidetracked to what the investigator wants to believe instead of what the facts state.

While investigating sexual abuse, I found it very difficult to stand back and be utterly objective. I found myself in what I thought of as 'the zone'. Whenever I showed up, people knew what I was there for, what I was investigating, why I was calling. No amount of official secrecy could keep our investigation under wraps completely. Confidentiality was important to the victims and the wider community was unaware of our work, but within the still surviving grapevines from their schooldays word spread quietly.

The victims' reactions varied, but however they reacted when we spoke, I was in the zone. Part of me had to sit back, concentrate on dates, times, years and other details. Part of me listened, talked to them, explained at first in general terms, and in detail if they opened up exactly what we were looking into. Another part of me watched, trying to assess how the young man in front of me would handle getting into a witness box and taking the oath, how good a witness he would make, how he would stand up to an aggressive cross-examination. And part of me was just plain furious at what I was hearing.

Some victims were emotional. But for others it was as if they were trapped in psychic ice, as if frozen inside their own fog of memories, words tumbling out of the fog for me to write down. Emotionless, locked down, it was the only way they could deal with this. For two years they woke up every morning and they knew they were going to be sexually abused before the end of the day. They had accepted they were going to be abused. Battening the hatches and locking down their emotions was the only way they had to deal with it. They talked about it in a measured way, detached, unemotional, almost as if they were describing something that happened to a stranger. Listening, I knew they were hurting, but it was contained, wrapped up tight and hidden away.

For years it was a secret, yet everybody in the place seemed to know. Poofy Den was a fact of life, something you survived growing up and tried to forget. I did my best to hold my anger back, stay in the zone and do the job. When it was over, then I could get angry.

Chapter 19
No Written Record

While I worked on the Denis McGinley investigation, there was still work to do on Eugene Greene. John Dooley's superintendent, Jim Gallagher, had first contacted the office of the Bishop of Raphoe in early January 1998 following the first complaint from *David Brennan*. We had requested, and were given, a cv listing all the parishes in the Raphoe diocese where Greene had served during his career. The bishop's office also contacted the St Patrick's Missionary Society in Kiltegan, Co. Wicklow, about Greene's service in Africa. In late February the vicar general of the order wrote back to tell us he had examined the society's files and found 'no reports in them of any form of misbehaviour by Fr Greene during the years he spent in St Patrick's Missionary Society — or indeed subsequently'.

In March, Gallagher wrote again to the bishop's office, informing them that we now had several more complaints in addition to *David Brennan*. The super informed the bishop that he understood Greene might have received psychosexual counselling at the Our Lady of Victory treatment centre in Stroud. He asked the bishop to confirm this. Ten days later the bishop's office wrote back to confirm that Greene had been in Stroud from September to December 1992, but this was 'in connection with alcoholism which had damaged his health and impaired his ability to function as a priest'. According to the bishop's office, Greene had returned to Stroud 'in the spring of 1993' for a follow-up visit. As a result of his visit Stroud provided a report saying the priest 'had gained a good quality of sobriety', but given his 'fragility and his inability to cope with the stress of parish ministry', he resigned as parish priest of Cill Mhic Réanáin in September 1994. After that, Greene 'had no official position in the diocese'. He lived 'in semi-retirement' in Loch an Iúir and 'helped the local priest whenever needed'. Things rested there until the day we arrested Greene. Before his release he gave us written permission 'to have access to my medical records at Our Lady of Victory, Stroud' where he was a patient in the early nineties.

We were not sure what to make of the dates. Greene could have been to Stroud several times and we suspected he might have been there in the mid-seventies when he disappeared for several weeks after the *Kennedy* family had complained to Fr Hugh Bonnar. In August, Superintendent Joseph Delaney wrote to the director of care programmes at Stroud, asking for Greene's medical records. Specifically the super asked the director if Greene 'underwent psychosexual therapy while under your care'. Enclosing Greene's consent to release his medical records, the super asked for written details covering the extent of the therapy and Greene's progress. Within a few weeks Benedict Livingstone, the programme director and Father Servant at Stroud, wrote back to say that he had discussed the matter with Greene and with Greene's legal advisers, and 'as a result of these discussions I regret that I can be of no further assistance to you in this matter'.

We had hit a dead end. The gates were shut. We were not going to get any records. Greene's medical records could have provided valuable evidence to corroborate the charges against him, but he had had a change of heart and probably legal advice since his release from custody and withdrawn his consent to release those records.

But the refusal was puzzling. According to the information we had from the bishop's office, Greene and his lawyers were refusing us access to any records Greene had in Stroud for treatment for his drink problem. But we were investigating child sexual abuse. We only needed his records from his psychosexual therapy and counselling; we weren't interested in any other problems he had, whether it was alcoholism or anything else. When we had asked Greene for access, he had simply nodded and told us he would give us access to the files, so we assumed there was no problem releasing the files for psychosexual therapy while he was in Stroud. But it didn't work out like that. Whether because of legal advice, or the Church hierarchy, Greene had changed his mind, restricting our access to his medical files and what they might tell us. The shutters were down. There were times when I felt it was easier to put an echo in a frame than get the truth out of the Catholic Church.

I often wondered why the legal teams, whether on behalf of the Church or Greene himself, blocked our access to his medical files. If the files dealt only with his reported alcoholism and were not relevant to the investigation, they simply would not, could not, have been used by the DPP. So why block them? And if the records showed that he was only treated for alcoholism, his legal defence might even be able to use that as a point in his favour. The Church of course did not categorically deny that Greene had received psychosexual therapy and counselling in Stroud or anywhere else. Instead they stated that he was treated for his alcohol problem there, although we were not investigating his alcohol history. They gave us information we never looked for.

Any alcohol-related problems Greene might have had were of no interest to the Gardaí or the DPP, and alcoholism was not introduced at his trial by the defence lawyers as a mitigating factor. However Greene's lawyers later appealed the severity of his sentence, and at that point they did argue for a reduction in his sentence, pointing to their client's alcohol-related problems in mitigation. With the lawyers making that argument, I would have expected them to introduce his medical files as further evidence to bolster their appeal to the court for leniency. Unfortunately, although the prosecution would still have been anxious to throw an eye over the elusive medical records, they were never placed before the appeal judge. The absence of the records at that point astonished us. Any decent lawyer knows that an argument, no matter how persuasive, is always bolstered by independent evidence. Appeal courts are wary of reversing the decisions of their colleagues, and judges are reassured if they can point in their judgment to fresh evidence to justify their decisions, particularly from an impartial source like an independent medical expert.

Astonishingly the appeal judge saw no such file. The decision was an odd one. If the medical files backed up their argument for leniency on the grounds of alcoholism, surely the lawyers would have seized on them. Yet no files appeared. Alcoholism was not a huge mystery. Most families in Ireland know that such problems exist. I could see no reason why any shame due to alcoholism, already acknowledged by Greene's own barristers, would prevent the release of the files at that point. But the curious culture of secrecy I had come across before within the Church was again evident during the appeal. I couldn't help but wonder if there was something in those files they did not want us to see. After the appeal we were left with still more questions unanswered. Why the secrecy surrounding the medical files? What did they contain that was so sensitive? I wonder if we will ever know.

Whatever the files might have said, though, I suspected Greene had been sent off for psychosexual counselling at some point in his career, if not in Stroud then somewhere else. I had spoken to other priests. None of them would go on the record, but they had passed things on to me. One priest I heard of who was in Stroud with Greene had been sent there after having a gay affair. While he was there he phoned a friend back home in Ireland to tell him Eugene Greene was there too, also receiving psychosexual counselling. In some circles, apparently, it was open knowledge that Greene had been to Stroud, and why.

When we arrested Greene in June 1998, we had put the allegations of twenty-five victims to him, all of which he denied. A twenty-sixth victim, *Lorcan Kennedy*, lived abroad and had not returned to make a statement by the time we arrested Greene. Later that summer, though, when he came home on his holidays, he too made a statement of complaint to us. So in the middle of the groundwork on the McGinley case, we had to go and see Greene one more time to put one more allegation to him.

We had two options. We could have arrested Greene for a second time and brought him in for questioning again. *Lorcan*'s statement was new information and section 10 of the 1984 Criminal Justice Act allowed us to rearrest a suspect if new information came to light, provided we could satisfy a district justice that we had sufficient grounds. However from our first arrest we had a fair idea of how a further interrogation would go, and Greene wasn't a flight risk. We knew where he lived. It was simpler just to call to his home first.

Just after 11 a.m. on 15 September 1998, Dooley and I called to Greene's home in Anagaire. He invited both of us into his house and took us into an office. Dooley cautioned Greene. Policemen deliver the caution so many times in our career we can virtually recite it backwards. Dooley told him that *Lorcan Kennedy* had made a written statement alleging that he was sexually abused in the parochial house in the summer of 1977. Greene told us he would prefer to deal with the allegation there and then, and we explained that he wasn't under arrest and that we would leave any time he wanted. We went through *Lorcan Kennedy*'s statement, as Dooley kept a note of the questions and answers.

Greene's responses echoed those he gave us in custody in June. He remembered *Lorcan* had served as an altar boy and that the young boy often did odd jobs around the parochial house in Gort an Choirce, but when it came to the substance of our visit, he was back to the same old refrain: 'I have nothing to say. I have absolutely no recollection of that.' Dooley read over the memo; Greene agreed it was accurate and signed it. It was a frustrating exercise, taking almost an hour, but it was necessary to complete the book of evidence Dooley was working on.

A few days later Dooley took a formal statement from Róisin McBride, a substance abuse counsellor with the North Western Health Board, confirming that *Joshua Jackson* told her during a counselling session in 1993 that he was sexually abused by a priest when he was a child. It was one more piece of corroboration for the file to the DPP, bringing us one step closer to a conviction.

A couple of weeks later Dooley spoke to Fr Lorcan Sharkey, the parish priest in Killybegs. The Bishop of Raphoe had set up a committee to deal with allegations of sexual abuse against clergy in the diocese, and as a delegate to the committee Sharkey was asked to find out if the diocese had any record of allegations of sexual abuse made against Greene. There was nothing to report. Sharkey told us that an 'investigation of the current file' from the parish of Gort an Choirce showed that 'there were no records of any allegation being filed against Fr Eugene Greene', and a search of the archives of all the parishes Greene ever worked in found 'no record of any allegation being made against Fr Eugene Greene'.

It was another dead end. I found it disturbing to learn that no written record existed of the complaints from the *Kennedys* in the seventies.

Chapter 20
He Will Never Make Much of Himself

There may have been no Church records on what was happening in their national school in Gort an Choirce, but other people noticed something was wrong. Poofy Den was an open secret as far as the children were concerned, one of those open secrets they accepted as one of the hazards of life to be endured and overcome. Children live in their own enclosed culture a lot of the time. There are things they assume adults know and don't talk to them about, and things they don't talk to adults about because, well, you just don't talk to grown-ups about some things. Some things stay in the schoolyard. Most of the time McGinley fell somewhere within that hazy category of things children only spoke of among themselves for one reason or another, but even so there were grown-ups who noticed strange things.

Sandra Nolan couldn't understand what was wrong with her oldest son. *Lee* had been such a happy-go-lucky boy all his life. He loved school, but he had changed since he turned 8. Normally outgoing, he had withdrawn into himself, his usual smiling face almost a memory as he became irritable, impatient and scowling. He had difficulty concentrating on tasks for any length of time, but when she asked him if anything was wrong, the only thing he would say was that he hated Denis McGinley, his new teacher.

Sandra worried but she didn't think there was much she could do. One of the younger children was ill, which took up a lot of time with trips to hospital, medications and tests. A new class in school was a big adjustment and she hoped that in time *Lee* would adjust to the new teacher and that his lessons and homework would improve. But when *Lee* showed little progress by the end of the school year, *Sandra* learned that he would be put into a remedial class the following autumn. At the next parent-teacher meeting *Sandra* raised *Lee*'s poor performance with his teacher, McGinley. 'Tá an Rang sin lag' (That class is weak) he told her. *Sandra* pressed him, but all McGinley would say about *Lee* was 'Ní dhéanfaidh sé a dhath choíce dó.' (He will never make much of himself.) McGinley seemed distant and distracted when *Sandra* spoke to him, staring out the window and never meeting her eyes. He told her that her son was a 'mammy's boy', easily upset over little things.

But it was no little thing that was upsetting *Lee*. Since he had transferred to McGinley's class he had become the sexual predator's latest victim. Somewhere between September and Christmas of third class, the teacher targeted *Lee*. 'It started during drama classes when he would have the whole of third class up around the desk,' *Lee* remembered. 'Denis McGinley would be sitting at his desk and he would put me standing beside him, on his left-hand side. He would put his arm around my shoulder and during the class he would put his hand up under my jumper.'

Over time the abuse intensified and by the end of the year McGinley regularly called *Lee* up to his desk and put him sitting on his knee on the pretence of revising his spelling or arithmetic, touching him sexually while his classmates concentrated on their work. While his friends enjoyed two months of freedom at the end of the school year, *Lee* hated that summer, knowing that at the end of it he would have to go back to McGinley.

Lee rebelled, inasmuch as a 9-year-old boy can. He refused to do any work for McGinley's class — no more homework, no more spelling exercises or sums in class. He shut down. He couldn't think of anything else to do except not co-operate. If he did nothing, maybe the teacher would leave him alone. McGinley bullied him, gave him a cruel nickname and used it in front of the other pupils to demean him.

Lee was terrified of McGinley. When you are 8 or 9 years old your teacher holds the power of life and death over you. He had tried to resist the teacher, pushing him away whenever he came near. But he was only a small boy; McGinley was a grown man. He knew the teacher could overpower him in an instant, and every day he went to school McGinley bullied him, punishing him for his impudence. *Lee* couldn't bring himself to tell his mother or father about the horrible things the teacher was doing, but he desperately wanted to tell somebody about it, someone who would make him stop. But how could he tell anybody?

Finally, *Lee* saw his chance. McGinley told the class he had a special assignment for them. He had written a series of essay topics on the blackboard and the boys and girls were free to write anything they wanted on the topic they chose. It was a creative exercise; they were free to write anything they wanted from the starting point of the titles he had suggested. Because this was a special test, they were to spend the afternoon quietly working on their compositions. There would be prizes for the best efforts which would be shown to the headmaster.

Nine-year-old boys don't always operate on adult logic. They are still living in a world of childhood magic, still half believing in Santa Claus and the tooth fairy, or wanting to believe in them despite rumours to the contrary. They still accept what someone in authority says and does. The headmaster is in charge, *Lee* thought to himself. The headmaster would stop what Denis McGinley is doing if I could tell him. *Lee* couldn't bring himself to approach someone as imposing and distant as a headmaster on his own, but if he wrote the best essay ever, the headmaster would surely read it.

'You can write anything you want,' McGinley had said. *Lee* knew what subject he wanted to write about. One of the suggested composition titles was 'Bullying'. He would write about how his teacher bullied him. Concentrating furiously, making sure his handwriting was perfect and his spelling the best it could be, he wrote about what McGinley was doing. His would be the best essay in the class and the headmaster would read it. McGinley had promised, and a teacher wouldn't lie about something that important. After he handed in the paper, *Lee* waited anxiously for the results of the composition test. He knew it was the best essay he had ever written. It had to win a prize. The headmaster would get to see it.

———

Denis McGinley smiled. 'There are lots of good essays here,' he told the class. 'The headmaster will be very pleased.' He worked his way through the papers, reading each one aloud to the class, praising the pupil who wrote it and telling them how well they had done. *Lee* sat in his seat waiting until McGinley got to 'Bullying'.

McGinley paused and frowned. 'These are all very good essays,' he told the children. 'Everyone has done very well — almost everyone, that is. But there is one very bold boy in this classroom. I'm not going to say his name or read out his essay, but I will be having a word with the headmaster. I will have to tell him what a bold boy this is. I'll have to report him.'

Lee cringed. The teacher had read out every essay except his. He was close to tears. Everyone would know he was the bold boy and the headmaster would be told he was bold too. McGinley tore his composition into shreds, crumpled it into a ball in his hands and tossed it into the wastepaper basket. No one would ever read it, certainly not the headmaster. McGinley had lied. For the 9-year-old boy it was a cruel introduction to the duplicity of adults. Before he knew it, he wasn't just a bold boy, he was a slow boy too. A few weeks after he tried to tell in writing what was happening to him, *Lee* was told he would be held back in the remedial class. He just wasn't good enough.

Lee didn't know what to think. He believed what he was told, that he wasn't good enough, but he also knew deep down that being sent to the remedial class was a punishment for being a bold boy because he tried to tell on what McGinley did. Trying to fight back didn't work; it only made things worse. If he kept his head down, then it would have to end sometime. The teacher couldn't hold him back for ever. Eventually he would have to move up to the higher classes. If he kept quiet, he would get through this. When he moved up, it would be over.

Eventually *Lee* did move up to fifth class. The punishment of being sent to the remedial class was a blessing in disguise. He got on well with his new teacher, his work improved and at the end of the year he moved up to fifth class along with the rest of his friends.

His mother noticed the change in his behaviour once he began fifth class. He started doing his homework again and seemed much happier in school. The old *Lee* was back. Whatever phase he had gone through, he had come out the other side. He just concentrated on getting on with life but made sure to avoid his former teacher. He hated McGinley and fantasised about getting a gun and shooting him for what he had done to him.

Sandra Nolan didn't find out what was bothering her son until our investigation began. She was furious when she learned what happened. She had always blamed herself for *Lee*'s difficulties. She was distracted with another child's illness at the time and felt she had neg-lected *Lee*. If she had spent more time with him, she thought, maybe he would not have been so moody and impatient. Maybe he would have been able to concentrate on his homework; maybe he wouldn't have been held back. At least now that she knew what really happened, she knew she shouldn't be angry at herself. McGinley deserved her anger for his deceitful betrayal and his abuse of trust. And *Lee* was a changed boy since he had spoken out. He told her he was glad he told her, and seemed generally happier and more content. At night when her thoughts turned back to what her son must have suffered, she often cried, but she felt an intense relief that everything was out in the open. She knew we would not stop our investigation until McGinley was brought to justice and made to pay for what he had done.

Unlike most of the victims I had interviewed, *Lee* was still a minor when I met him. He was abused in the early nineties. His abuse wasn't a memory he had lived with from the sixties or seventies; it was still raw and recent. The wounds never heal, even for victims who have lived with the knowledge of abuse for decades, but somehow this was different. I realised it had happened on my watch. Before, I had spoken to men ranging in age from their twenties to their fifties. Speaking to them I could imagine the young boy inside who had suf-fered unspeakable horrors at his abuser's hand. This time I didn't have to imagine. The young teenager who told me what he had lived through, and his futile attempt to report it, was sitting in front of me.

Chapter 21
Permission to Talk

*L*inda Murphy was doing the after-dinner washing up while her son *Dylan* and one of his friends chatted away among themselves outside the kitchen window, when she realised she should pay more attention to what they were saying. The pair were talking about teacher's pets and how their teacher, Denis McGinley, liked to hold young boys on his lap during class, when the young boy's comment caught her ear: '*Dylan*, what are you laughing at? Doesn't he do the same thing to you?'

It was already late in the evening and although taken aback by what she had overheard, *Linda* decided it was too late to talk to *Dylan* about what she had overheard when his friend went home. But the following morning she brought the conversation round to what she had overheard the previous evening. *Dylan* had just begun third class the previous month and *Linda* had noticed a change in his behaviour that September. Before, he had loved going to school, but now he was reluctant to get up in the mornings and often cried and refused to go. She asked *Dylan* if his sudden dislike of school had anything to do with his new teacher, Denis McGinley.

For *Dylan*, it was like the floodgates had opened. He had permission to talk. '*Dylan* told me that Denis McGinley used to have him sitting on his knee during class and that he put his hand on his trousers over his private parts while he was correcting his homework,' she recalled later. 'He told me that Denis McGinley's behaviour made him feel bad and dirty.' *Dylan* couldn't bring himself to tell his mother everything McGinley did on that November morning, but he also told her the nickname the children had for their teacher, Poofy Den. He also told her he didn't want to be known as McGinley's pet. *Linda* didn't doubt her son for an instant. She knew he was telling the truth. Her first instinct was to take him out of school for his own safety.

Dylan was still a minor when we spoke to *Linda* in the early autumn of 1999. In her presence and with her consent, Dooley and I took a statement from *Dylan* outlining what had happened when he started third class in school. He had McGinley as his teacher for two years, in third and fourth class. Within days of starting third class, McGinley had adopted the habit of calling *Dylan* up to his desk, sitting him on his knee while he asked him English spellings or tested him on arithmetic. The pattern progressed rapidly and within a few weeks McGinley was finding excuses to call the boy up to his desk several times a day.

'The first few days that Denis McGinley put me sitting on his knee he put his hand up under my jumper,' *Dylan* told us. 'He then started rubbing my leg with his hand outside my trousers. He carried on doing this for about a week. He then progressed to putting his hand down the front of my trousers and rubbing my penis and testicles with his hand outside my underpants.' Every time *Dylan* missed a spelling or got a sum wrong, McGinley would say to him: 'You poor pet, there is light at the end of the tunnel.'

Behind the minimal cover of his desk, out of the direct gaze of the other pupils in the classroom, McGinley's abuse continued from the start of the school term in September until the middle of November, when *Linda* spoke to her son. 'I hated going to school because of what my teacher was doing to me. The more Denis McGinley fondled my privates, the more disgusted I felt about what he was doing as I knew it was wrong and I didn't know why he was doing it. I used to feel sick about it and I started making excuses to my mother in order to avoid going to school,' *Dylan* said. 'I hate Denis McGinley because I realised that he was sexually abusing me when I was an innocent boy in third class under 9 years of age.'

Eventually *Dylan* was able to talk to his mother about what was happening once she asked him about his teacher, but he told us he was 'too ashamed and embarrassed to tell my mother the full extent of what McGinley was doing to me or how often it was happening'. Immediately he told her what happened, *Linda* kept him away from school. He spent the next week at home.

I received confidential information letting me know that the *Murphy* family had made a complaint at some point about McGinley. I went to speak to *Linda* along with Dooley, following up on the lead. When we interviewed *Dylan*, he also told us the names of two other boys who were regularly called up to the teacher's desk and held on his knee. One of those was *Lee Nolan*, the boy who had finally rebelled by writing an essay on his teacher, the bully, and found himself placed in a remedial learning class without any good reason as a result. It was that which led me to approach the *Nolan* family. But not everyone was as willing to make a statement to us, and it was hard to blame them. The other boy that *Dylan* mentioned who had been selected by McGinley never made a formal complaint.

Dylan also told us that McGinley took another older boy up the slope behind the school two or three times a week, to the whin bushes about 200 yards away. At the end of the break this young boy was often seen crying as he walked back to class. When we approached his family, they too declined to make any statement. As policemen we knew that each complaint on record was one more example of the consistent pattern of abuse typical of a paedophile, one more piece of evidence to help secure a conviction, but it was understandable that a parent or a victim, who simply wanted to move on and forget, might not want to relive the past. Dooley and I had discussed it and agreed that we would approach every victim, or their parents where they were still minors, and offer them the chance to tell their stories. We would only have one shot at a criminal trial and we didn't want any story left untold because we hadn't followed a lead. If they wanted to talk to us, that was fair enough, and if they didn't want to talk, that was fair enough too, but at least we had given them the opportunity.

Chapter 22
Teacher's Pet

I had known *Frank O'Neill* since I had moved back to Donegal in the early 1990s. One of nature's gentlemen, in the true sense of the word, he was one of the gentlest men I had ever met. Quiet and reserved, often hesitant to speak out of a deep public shyness, he did his own thing in his diffident, mannerly way. *Frank* had qualified as a tradesman after leaving school and had a reputation locally as an excellent worker, reliable to a fault though quite withdrawn into himself.

Listening to *Frank* talk when I approached him in the autumn of 1999, it was easy to trace the source of his shyness. He was affected quite badly by the sexual abuse inflicted on him by Denis McGinley, but what really hurt was the teasing, 'Teacher's pet!' Every day since McGinley first turned his attention to him, playtime was a nightmare for *Frank*. He hoped it would end when he graduated from McGinley's class to the senior years, but the taunting followed him until the day he left school.

Even now as an adult, I felt that *Frank*'s quietness came from the schoolyard taunts he could still hear. If anyone remembered, if anyone repeated the sing-song taunt even today, the shame and embarrassment would flood back. It was easier to stay quiet, make sure not to draw any attention to yourself and hope others forgot or at least said nothing. Avoid large groups, find solitary hobbies and interests, don't get involved in team sports. Better to keep quiet and do your own thing. Two decades later as an adult his biggest fear was still that somebody would find out and talk about what he had endured.

Frank was able to back up what I had already been told by *Raymond Graham* and *Gordon Regan*. When he first moved into McGinley's class, the teacher was in the habit of making *Raymond Graham* sit on his lap, and often called *Gordon Regan* up to sit beside him on the convection heater. He remembered that *Gordon* in particular loathed the teacher, and in the playground referred to him as 'Poofy Den'.

In his second year under McGinley's tutelage, the teacher targeted *Frank*. At first McGinley simply positioned himself during the day on a stool by the heater close to *Frank*'s desk. He organised class quizzes, asking questions on arithmetic or spelling, with a 10p prize to the winner. He would trace the answers to questions on *Frank*'s back with his hand and the boy felt good, winning quizzes and extra pocket money regularly. He felt important, the teacher liked him and helped him win prizes, and he trusted his teacher as a result. Having established that position of trust, McGinley progressed to leaning over and placing his arm around the young boy's body, and from there to slipping his hand inside the waistband of *Frank*'s pants, assaulting him indecently as he had so many others I had spoken to. *Frank* endured this abuse two or three times each day, each time lasting up to twenty minutes, hating every moment that seemed to stretch into an eternity of torment. Just as bad were the breaks in the school day when he would have to go outside and endure the taunts of the other children.

I couldn't help but think of the numbers. Each McGinley victim I spoke to was able to name two or three others in the same predicament. At any given time McGinley seemed to have three or four children he identified as potential pets. As he had taught in Derryconnor National School for twenty years, that gave me a total of about forty potential victims. Eventually eleven came forward, which meant there were others out there still hurting. I doubted McGinley suddenly began abusing children the day he arrived in Gort an Choirce. He had been a teacher for seventeen years by then, which meant there could be up to seventy victims throughout Donegal damaged by just one paedophile. All those damaged lives, all those men living with quiet shame, blaming themselves for what their abuser had done to them — it didn't bear thinking about.

Frank felt uncomfortable every time McGinley came near him. 'I felt scared telling anybody about it,' he told me. 'I didn't tell my parents either as I was scared to tell them as I thought I might not be believed. I never had the courage to stop Denis McGinley as he was the teacher and was in total control.'

Frank was abused virtually every schoolday for two years in the early eighties, and afterwards he had to face the taunts in the playground, 'Poofy Den's teacher's pet!' He remembered once a pupil scrawled 'Poofy Den' on the wall outside McGinley's classroom which the teacher had to clean off, but nothing seemed to stop his abuse. McGinley acted on compulsion and behaved as if he was untouchable, protected by the authority of his position in the classroom and society.

Chapter 23
Teachers and Priests

The same morning that *Dylan Murphy* told his mother what was happening at school with Denis McGinley, his mother *Linda* called twice to the parochial house to see the local parish priest and school manager, Fr John McGlynn. There was no sign of the parish priest, but on the second visit she met his curate, Fr Denis Quinn. *Linda* explained to Quinn what her son had told her that morning.

Quinn contacted the school principal, Teresa Doohan, made an appointment for her to see *Linda* and promised to talk to the parish priest. This was the first definitive record we had of a complaint about McGinley's behaviour.

That evening *Linda* called to see Teresa Doohan at her home and again told *Dylan*'s story. Teresa told *Linda* that McGinley 'was already warned not to touch the pupils or put them on his knee'. The principal had not waited to speak to *Linda* before acting. Even before finding out the details of the complaint, she had gone to McGinley and spoken to him about inappropriate behaviour. She asked *Linda* to take *Dylan* to the school to meet her. The following day *Linda* did as she was asked and Doohan interviewed *Dylan* in his mother's presence. He again told the story of what was happening.

Teresa Doohan was appointed principal teacher in Derryconnor National School in 1993. She later confirmed to me that she had received a phone call from Quinn outlining a complaint from the parent of a pupil at the school about McGinley and 'inappropriate touching'. She asked the curate to arrange a meeting, but even before the meeting took place she confronted McGinley with the allegation the curate had passed on to her. The teacher 'totally denied' any improper conduct. Later Teresa met with *Linda* and *Dylan* and listened as the boy explained what happened to him in McGinley's class.

Later when the parish priest returned from his holidays, Teresa discussed the complaint with him. Being a Catholic primary school run under the patronage of the Bishop of Raphoe, as parish priest Fr John McGlynn was the school manager and chairman of the school board of management. McGlynn told Doohan that he too would confront McGinley about the complaint. She also contacted Ann McHugh, the local public health nurse, about the complaint. McHugh later called to the school and took a written statement recording the allegation. Later again a social worker called to the school to follow up on the complaint, and a second social worker called to the *Murphy* home sometime after, but she could not remember their names.

Within a couple of years of the complaint McGinley had retired. Although she had not contacted An Garda Síochána about the complaint, Doohan had discussed it with the teacher concerned, reported it to her school manager and made a report to the health board. She was satisfied that she had reported the complaint through the appropriate channels.

Doohan told me that the complaint from *Linda Murphy* was the only one she had ever received about McGinley, but I wondered if there had been earlier complaints about him to others. Unfortunately it was a thread we never followed up on. Doohan's statement provided us with the evidence we needed to corroborate *Dylan Murphy*'s story and, more importantly, she told us the public health nurse had made a written report. That contemporary report could provide valuable evidence in court. We focused on getting the health board report.

Fr Denis Quinn also told me that *Linda Murphy*'s was the only complaint he ever received about McGinley while a curate in Gort an Choirce parish, but as he also pointed out, he was not on the school's board of management. His parish priest was. As curate he had passed the complaint on to his parish priest and school manager Fr John McGlynn and to the school principal. He also said that he told *Linda* it was important for her to make a complaint in writing to the school board.

To his credit, Quinn had approached the school principal and his parish priest, and he was helpful and informative when we spoke to him, while other priests seemed to be afraid to speak out in fear of authority. But I wondered why he never made a report to the bishop's office. Was it an oversight based on the assumption that his parish priest would do so? Every cleric I met seemed to be allergic to ink.

John McGlynn turned 75 in 1999 and was recently retired when we interviewed him about the *Murphys*. (He died at the end of July 2007 while this book was in preparation.) A native of Letterbrack, he was ordained in Maynooth in 1949 and served for eight years in the archdiocese of Seattle in the United States before returning to Ireland in 1957. The following year he came to Gort an Choirce as curate and spent two years there before moving on to Baile na Finne and Gaoth Dobhair, before returning to Gort an Choirce as parish priest in 1977, one year after McGinley had moved to Derryconnor National School. He spent the rest of his career there until his retirement in early 1999. When we spoke to him he confirmed that he had visited *Linda Murphy's* home and spoken to her about her complaint that McGinley 'was interfering with her son during school hours'. The following day McGlynn called to the school to speak to McGinley. McGlynn timed his visit to coincide with a break in the school day and found McGinley in the schoolyard. When he told the teacher he wanted to speak to him, McGinley replied, 'I know what it is about.' The priest told McGinley about the complaint from *Dylan Murphy*. 'Denis McGinley did not deny this and it was obvious from his reaction that he was doing this. I warned Denis McGinley not to take any children on his knee in the classroom,' McGlynn recalled. 'Apart from this complaint from Mrs *Murphy* I got no other specific complaint regarding Denis McGinley's behaviour towards pupils in the school.'

McGlynn claimed that when he went back to *Linda* to tell her that he had spoken to McGinley, 'she then informed me that her son had told her that nothing had happened and that he made up the story himself. In view of Mrs *Murphy's* attitude I saw no reason to take the matter any further and in the absence of any specific complaint I felt it was not appropriate to take the matter any further.'

Linda told me that McGlynn only visited her home once, a few days after she spoke to the school principal Teresa Doohan. She made it clear to him that she believed her son and was taking his complaint very seriously. 'He was very dismissive of my complaint,' *Linda* remembered. 'He was making me feel guilty for any subsequent scandal that might arise out of my complaint.' The priest more or less implied that if a scandal broke, she would have to leave the area. After the visit *Linda* felt it was useless talking to the priest. 'I felt at the time that I wasn't going to get anywhere with my complaint,' she recalled in a statement she made to the court.

Linda thought about taking *Dylan* out of the school altogether but decided he would miss his friends and let him go back after a week. She was unhappy that McGinley was still allowed to teach, but she had reported what *Dylan* told her. McGlynn had promised to carry out his own investigation (though he would never call her back to let her know the result of this 'investigation'), and she kept a close eye on *Dylan* afterwards.

'When I returned to school Denis McGinley sort of ignored me and did not take me up on his knee or touch me after that,' *Dylan* told me.

Chapter 24

I Could Do Nothing About It

P eople deal with the legacy of abuse in different ways. Some bury themselves in their work; some bury themselves in alcohol or drug abuse to numb the pain; some withdraw from the world, becoming quiet, solitary figures, barely registering in the consciousness of their friends and neighbours, quiet, peaceable fellows like *Frank O'Neill.* Diligent in their work habits and modest in every aspect of their lives, they keep to themselves to avoid the social contact that might bring painful memories back to the surface. Some learn to wear a mask of amiable sociability, until sometimes the mask becomes almost real, a familiar face, a nice young fellow, always a welcoming, cheerful smile, almost the definition of happy-go-lucky.

To the outside world *Gary Daly* defined success. Happily married and with a successful business to his name, he was a role model for the new confident Ireland of the nineties, brimming with entrepreneurial spirit, ready to take on the world and win. Before I spoke to him in late 1999, the only person he had ever told about the hellish memories of his youth was his wife. Although I spoke to him several times, during which he talked freely about his experiences, it took him a long time to decide to make a criminal complaint. The very success he had achieved in his life, and which everyone admired, held him back, made him hesitate. He worried about his good name. Deep inside he still felt somehow responsible for what had happened and fretted that others would view it the same way. If it became common knowledge, how would it affect his business?

When he spoke about the abuse, *Gary* changed. His voice dropped a register, he withdrew into himself, all colour and emotion left his voice. Usually well spoken and eloquent, he became awkward and tongue-tied. After a while when he found the distance within himself to stand back from his own memories, the words would come, slow and measured. Matter-of-fact, almost robotic, emotionless, it was as if the only way he could talk about it was to look at it from the outside. At times it felt as if *Gary* was describing events that happened to someone else.

Gary was one of the earliest victims of Denis McGinley after his arrival in Gort an Choirce. He was in his thirties when I spoke to him, an intelligent, articulate adult, yet somehow the guilt still twisted his gut so that he couldn't shake the feeling that somehow he did something wrong. He felt stigmatised, wounded to the core, afraid that if anyone knew what had happened, he would somehow be looked upon as less than a full man, though the fault was never his.

McGinley was *Gary Daly*'s teacher for two years in the late 1970s. His experience was at once singular and yet familiar. Shortly after he started in third class, McGinley took to sitting on the desk beside him, putting his arm around his waist, then his hand under his waistband. The abuse, open and brazen, could happen at any time during the day while children studied or read from their lesson books, even while *Gary* himself was reading to the class. The abuse was constant, two or three times a day, every day, all through third and fourth class. 'I felt at the time what Denis McGinley was doing to me was wrong, but I felt I could do nothing about it. I was embarrassed to tell my parents about it,' he explained.

Gary wasn't the only victim in those years. While he was in McGinley's class other boys were also abused: *Adam Maher*, *Simon* and *Kevin Lynch*. *Gary Daly* and *Adam Maher* were good friends, but they never spoke to each other about what was happening. Maybe if you didn't speak about it outside the classroom, it made it a little less real. Once you walked out that door, you could pretend it hadn't really happened. *Gary* told me that *Simon* and *Kevin* were brought up to the heater to sit beside McGinley while he abused them. The rest of the class might be told to put their heads down and read. Maybe McGinley really believed that no one dared look up, that no one noticed what was going on. Maybe he simply didn't care.

Gary's younger brother *Darren* was luckier. Two years his brother's junior, the overlap in classes meant that he witnessed McGinley sexually abuse *Frank O'Neill*, *Raymond Graham* (often while *Raymond* had to stand in front of the heater reading to the class who listened with their heads down) and *Gordon Regan*, but he himself was never targeted by the paedophile.

Darren remembered that McGinley was particularly cruel to *Gordon Regan*, a nervous and hesitant student, forcing him to stand in front of the class during spelling tests and ridiculing him publicly when he made a mistake. Finally *Gordon* could take no more and called his teacher 'Poofy Den' to his face. In a rage McGinley lifted his foot and kicked the desk in front of him, breaking it with the force of the blow.

There was little conventional learning in McGinley's classroom. Lessons were an excuse for the teacher to tell the majority of the pupils to put their heads down and read while he abused his victims, and the rest of the pupils, ignored for the most part, learned little. Because there was nothing to learn, *Darren* lost all interest in school and studies, and the lack of interest stayed with him even after he moved on from McGinley's class. He blamed McGinley for the apathy that led him to drop out of secondary school early.

To *Darren* and many others, two years of abuse and apathy in McGinley's classroom became the norm. It was part of growing up, and he spoke about it bluntly and honestly. Like others who were not abused themselves but who witnessed the sexual assaults on their classmates, he spoke about it almost casually, as if telling a mere anecdote. They got used to it. This was just the story of what happened every day. What could they do? They were trapped. It was part of the culture in the school.

Gary hated Poofy Den. The anger burned inside and refused to go away, even after he reached fifth class and a new teacher, and even after he finished national school and finally escaped the paedophile's clutches.

A few years into his secondary education, he was heading home from school one day when McGinley's car passed him on the road. *Gary* couldn't stop himself. In a rage he shouted 'Poofy Den' as the car passed. McGinley stopped, reversed his car, got out and warned him never to use that name again or he would go to his father. Scared by the encounter, *Gary* bit his lip after that whenever he saw his abuser. As an adult he had considered going up to McGinley's house and confronting him about the sexual abuse he had endured as a child. He abandoned the idea when he reached the decision to make a formal criminal complaint in his statement to me. The law would take care of Denis McGinley.

In a way, *Gary* with his calm, measured voice and emotionless narrative reflected what I had come to think of in my own case as 'the zone'. Dealing with so many people living with the trauma of child sexual abuse, it was easy for my own mind to become fogged with their pain. To deal with it I had to place myself in the zone, otherwise you became numb, desensitised by the anaesthetic of abuse. At one and the same time you had to listen and yet stand back, or else the person in front of you became 'just another victim, just another story'. *Gary* was clinical and emotionless as he spoke to me, a state I realised I too inhabited much of the time as I processed the case files for Greene and McGinley. I couldn't afford to think too much about what they were telling me or it would overwhelm me and I wouldn't be able to do my job. I simply had to concentrate on getting these words into a statement, process what I was hearing as evidence, and deal with the emotions. When this comes out, when trials are held in public, there will be outrage in society, there will be calls for a tribunal of inquiry, and I can deal with it then. For now, I just needed to put my emotions on hold. Later I could afford to be angry along with the rest of society.

Sadly I discovered later that society often dealt with the pain hidden in its midst by ignoring it too. Don't say anything about that; let them talk about it in Dublin or Cork, but not here. Society had little appetite for pain and none of our leaders was willing to take responsibility for raising a topic that needed to be discussed. Abuse is still something whispered about in Ireland. It should be a scream of outrage.

Chapter 25
The Health Services

Until our investigation began *Dylan Murphy* told no one the full story of what he endured with Denis McGinley. Embarrassed and ashamed, until then he had told only his mother and the school principal that McGinley made him sit on his knee and made him feel uncomfortable, touching his back, stomach and legs. Speaking to us some years later, older and more confident, he was able finally to tell the full story both to us and to his mother. At the time the full brunt of what happened was just too much to talk about, and *Dylan* never received any counselling or therapy that might have revealed the full scale of the abuse.

Linda Murphy kept a diary which proved invaluable when our investigation began. Any contemporary note, no matter how small, is always significant in a court case as it provides details from the past which can confirm what is said in evidence. *Linda's* diary contained brief notes of meetings, starting from the day she spoke to *Dylan* after overhearing the conversation that disturbed her so much as he played at home with his friend one evening. Even before that day the diary makes it clear that *Dylan* was having problems, recording several Monday mornings in the first two months of the new school term when he missed school due to a sore tummy or headache, before she learned what was bothering her son and went to see Fr Denis Quinn and Teresa Doohan. The diary also noted *Linda's* visit to her doctor a few days later, and how she went to Mass in a different town the following Sunday, as well as the visit to her home by Fr John McGlynn. Things got worse before they got better, and in one diary entry *Linda* wrote that *Dylan* stayed at home all day: 'tummy sore, lay on settee for most of day, very down' before his spirits rose and a few days later the relieved mother was able to write: '*Dylan* back to school. Everything ok thank God.'

Linda's diary provided the first piece of contemporaneous documentation to support her evidence, but not the last. Anne McHugh, the public health nurse, confirmed that she spoke to school principal Teresa Doohan about the complaint from *Linda Murphy* that her son's teacher 'rubbed her son's back, tummy and legs and that the child missed school for one week'. After the meeting she sent a report to her boss, the superintendent based in the North Western Health Board office in Ballybofey.

Meanwhile during a routine health check-up, a local GP, Dr Nicola O'Brien, asked *Linda* how things were with the rest of the family. She told her doctor how worried she was about her son who 'was having problems at school and had become very quiet', before going into greater detail about what *Dylan* had told her, that his 'teacher had put his hands on his trousers over his private parts and had rubbed his upper legs while correcting his homework'. She also mentioned that she had noticed other children teasing her son and was considering changing her son to a different school. Dr O'Brien discussed what she had learned with her colleagues in the practice that evening and asked *Linda* to come into the surgery again.

When *Linda* returned, she told the doctor she had discussed what was happening to *Dylan* with the local priest and the school principal, and they had assured her they would 'monitor the situation'. Since he had spoken out, *Dylan* seemed a lot less worried and happier with himself. O'Brien told *Linda* she might have to report the incident to the director of community care. *Linda* told her that if anything else happened she would tell everybody about the teacher. O'Brien again discussed the case with her partners in the practice. Bound by patient confidentiality and aware of *Linda*'s clearly expressed reluctance to go any further, now that *Dylan* was improving and that the head teacher had told her she would keep an eye on McGinley, the doctor postponed contact with the director of community care, and towards the end of the year O'Brien wrote up the case for the practice files.

After we began our investigation, *Linda Murphy* signed a consent form in September 1999 allowing the Gardaí access to confidential medical and health records. Her consent form granted me 'access to all files relating to my complaint' including 'any files in the possession of doctors, social workers and the North Western Health Board . . . in relation to my son *Dylan Murphy*, with regard to the behaviour of Denis McGinley, his teacher'. That evening I spoke to Dr Lochlann McGill, one of the senior doctors in the practice, and the next morning he handed over O'Brien's report to me. He explained that because of *Linda*'s reluctance to take the case any further at the time, they felt their hands were tied under the rules of medical professional ethics. Nevertheless he himself had gone to McGlynn at the time and 'spoke quite firmly' to him, telling him that 'something should be done about Mr McGinley'. Worryingly, he said he had been aware of rumours about McGinley since his arrival in Gort an Choirce in 1976, although until *Linda* came to the attention of the practice he had no proof. McGlynn told McGill he would 'look into the matter', and he subsequently learned that the principal teacher had made a report to the public health nurse and 'would keep a close eye on Mr McGinley'. McGill felt it was an 'unsatisfactory conclusion', but without a complaint from *Linda* he couldn't take it any further.

We could now build a documentary profile of the *Murphy* case to demonstrate the difficulties encountered by the victims in coming forward or discussing what was happening, something which was prevalent and made it easier for them to hold back due to their shame.

The medical records handed over by McGill and O'Brien confirmed that the public health nurse had called to the school and spoken to the principal. This supported what Teresa Doohan had already told us. The next step was to obtain the report she had filed as a result of that visit, something that was unlikely to present a problem since we had written consent from *Linda* to access all her records.

I contacted the public health nurse concerned, Ann McHugh, and explained the situation. 'No problem,' she told me. 'Call down to the office and you can pick up the file.' I made the appointment for the following Friday morning. She told me to call at around five past eleven, that she should be free for a cup of tea and I could collect the file. In and out, I thought. This won't take much time. It was my day off so I could be sure I would not be distracted by any other duties that might crop up. There would be no overtime of course, but I didn't mind sacrificing half an hour of my time off for the trip. It was the least I could do for McGinley's victims. I called at 11.05 as arranged and at about 11.25 she called me into her office. But somehow, between setting up the appointment and meeting the public health nurse, the goal posts had moved, or rather I had run into an obstacle.

Ann McHugh told me that her advice from the health board was that she could not release confidential information until I contacted their solicitors, even though I had written consent allowing her to do so. Did I have to get a court order, I wondered. It was doubly frustrating after I had obtained the records from Dr McGill's practice just days before with no fuss, but I decided not to mention that. The original contact, though cordial, had suddenly become very official. I would now have to choose my words carefully. 'Okay,' I said, 'I will be back to you next week when I am working to take a statement from you.'

'Take a statement from me?' she exclaimed.

'Yes, we are conducting a criminal investigation into alleged child sexual abuse on young children. I'll need a statement about your report.' I left on that note.

So much for a quick stop to pick up a file on my day off, I thought. Things were not going as smoothly as I thought. I got home shortly after midday and phoned Noreen Mee, the health board solicitor. An easy-going woman, she was dismayed when I explained to her the reason for my call and more or less told me the health board had no reason to block access when consent was given by a patient. She promised to double check and get back to me, and I forwarded her a copy of the written consent from *Linda Murphy* for her records.

The following Monday morning Noreen phoned me back. She confirmed there was no reason for the health board not to release any documents since they were needed as part of an official criminal invest-igation and the Gardaí had the required written consent. I thanked her for her quick response. Now I could make contact with Ann McHugh again, armed with the go ahead from the health board's solicitor. That should simplify things, I thought. This time, when I got on the phone to McHugh, she told me that it was her superintendent who had advised her not to hand over the files. I left a message with the nursing superintendent and spoke to her on the phone the following day. She seemed very pleasant and told me that by coincidence she was meeting McHugh on that very day. 'Leave it with me,' she assured me.

Ann McHugh seemed to be getting conflicting signals from her superiors about what she was or was not entitled to do, caught between her duty to protect patient confidentiality and the need to aid a police investigation.

The next day was Wednesday. When I got on to McHugh this time, she told me her superintendent was off work on a holiday break and she couldn't hand over the file unless the superintendent was present. All I could do was wait. I could see why victims so often became frustrated at the slow pace of an investigation. The simple act of picking up a file was turning into a bureaucratic saga. I kept in contact and eventually the file was handed over to me by the superintendent in the presence of McHugh. What should have been a ten minute chat over a cup of tea while I picked up a file on my day off had taken twelve days.

Public health nurse Ann McHugh's brief report to her supervisors was the only record of any complaint against McGinley located in the child community care offices of the North Western Health Board. The power of official titles in Ireland sometimes amazes me. We are a republic with a constitutional bar on titles and nobilities, yet our society is filled with them — Minister, Doctor, Father, and I suppose in some instances, even Garda. Throughout the report McGinley was referred to deferentially as 'Master Denis McGinley'. The handwritten report marked 'Confidential' recounted *Linda Murphy*'s complaint, as reported by principal teacher Teresa Doohan, that the class teacher 'rubbed the child's back, tummy and legs'. It wasn't much, but it was the beginning of a paper trail, and it demonstrated that *Dylan*'s complaint existed in the early 1990s and caused his mother enough concern to report it to priests, a senior teacher and her doctor.

Linda was later able to confirm to me that as a result of the public health nurse's report, she got a phone call from a social worker about her son, asking if she would like a social worker to visit. *Linda* had mixed feelings when she got the phone call. While she was still upset about what had happened, she didn't want to upset *Dylan* any more. He seemed to be coping well since he had told her, even though she didn't realise he wasn't able to tell her all that had happened. Doohan had spoken to McGinley, and McGlynn had promised to conduct his own investigation. She turned down the offer.

A senior social worker at the North Western Health Board wrote to me when I looked into the visit and noted briefly that 'a social worker did call with the principal of the school, however the parents would not co-operate and therefore we were unable to progress the matter any further'. In follow-up correspondence the same senior social worker wrote to confirm that '*Dylan*'s mother was contacted . . . and declined social work intervention at that time'. Something about the phrasing of those brief letters annoyed me. Using a word like 'con-tacted' gives the impression that someone called to *Linda*'s home and sat and talked with her, something quite different to a single phone call. I thought that social services might have tried just a little harder. Perhaps someone could have called to *Linda*, sat down over a cup of tea and teased out the options available. If she had still refused help from a social worker after hearing what was available, fair enough. But at least she would have had time to consider all the options, rather than make a hasty decision after only a brief phone call.

Chapter 26
A Strong Case

Once I spoke to *Gary Daly*, I knew I had to speak to the *Lynch* brothers, *Simon* and *Kevin*. His stark testimony made it inevitable. Some deal with the pain by hiding behind quiet lives, withdrawing from the community in which they live and keeping to themselves. The *Lynch* brothers dealt with it, as many did, by getting out, leaving Donegal behind them along with its painful memories. The sexual abuse they endured as children had taken too much out of them to stay in Donegal. It was easier to just go away, to start over again somewhere else. The abuse had gone on too long and it was easier just to leave, find work somewhere else away from home, away from the past, somewhere to switch off. Most of those who go away don't want to come back, though some do return eventually.

What sticks in my mind most about the *Lynch* family is their mother. *Hilary Lynch* was very open and supportive, a wonderfully strong woman. Most mothers were not afraid to talk about what happened to their sons. Fathers were more reticent, reluctant and sometimes unable to face what had happened. But *Hilary* was relieved that someone was taking the complaints seriously, grateful that someone had launched a full criminal investigation. Caring and concerned for her sons, she told me to call any time and often contacted me to ask how the lads were doing, as did many of the mothers of victims that I grew to know. Meanwhile I discovered that in many cases their fathers found it difficult to face their pain and were more likely to head out to the pub for a pint than sit and chat if I called to their homes. It was easier to walk away from the carnage and let someone else deal with it.

The *Lynch* brothers themselves seemed to be well-mannered lads. They didn't come home to Donegal very often, but when I spoke to them they came across as good characters. Like *Gary Daly*, they didn't let their emotions flow too freely.

Simon Lynch, the older of the two brothers, worked in a Dublin factory. I spoke to him in early January 2000 along with Dooley. He was one of the last of McGinley's victims to make a formal criminal complaint while we planned the arrest. *Simon*, like many victims, was taught by McGinley for two years during third and fourth class, in his case in the late 1970s. *Kevin*, a year younger, was in the class behind him.

Simon was not sexually abused in third class. He was able to tell me that he remembered the first time he was brought up to sit on the heater, his brother was then in third class and was at school that day. Time seemed to stand still and stretch out to infinity while his teacher abused him that first time, but he thought the entire ordeal might have lasted ten or fifteen minutes, although at the time it seemed much longer. McGinley began by touching the boy around the neck, then inside his shirt. From there it progressed to a more serious sexual assault. 'I felt very embarrassed about this as the whole class was looking at me,' *Simon* told us. 'I can recall that Denis McGinley had me on the heater a good few times. I feel angry at what Denis McGinley did to me and I would feel embarrassed if other people would know about it.'

After a gap of twenty years not every detail was clear in *Simon*'s mind, but the first time was etched vividly in his memory. Like *Gary Daly*, he also mentioned *Adam Maher* as someone who was potentially one of McGinley's victims, and like many others he confirmed that McGinley was known as Poofy Den. He also remembered that McGinley frequently 'had his hand down inside his own trousers' in class.

Simon's younger brother *Kevin* worked in construction. He made a formal statement of complaint around the same time. In his early thirties, he too had left Donegal and seldom returned home. McGinley began sexually abusing him, bringing him up to his favoured spot on the heater at the side of the room 'on the pretence to warm myself or up to read' shortly after he began third class, which Dooley and I realised meant that the teacher began sexually abusing both brothers in the same year.

The abuse usually lasted about twenty minutes at a time, often several times in one day, and as well as the familiar spot on the room heater McGinley also had *Kevin* sit on his knee. The teacher also held impromptu class quizzes during the time *Kevin* was one of his pupils, tracing answers on his back and rewarding him as the quiz champion with sweets, coloured pens or small amounts of pocket money to gain his trust. *Kevin* was sexually assaulted on a regular basis almost every day for two years. Still too young to know the facts of life, the young boy wasn't quite sure what was happening at the time.

'It was when I moved out of his classroom and started to learn the facts of life that I realised that Denis McGinley was manipulating me in order to abuse me,' *Kevin* told us. 'The sexual abuse on me by Denis McGinley went on on a daily basis and sometimes more than once a day while I was in both third and fourth class. He was also known in school as Poofy Den and sometimes there would be some things written on the walls of the school and the blackboard about him.'

Once he learned the facts of life, *Kevin* held a deep anger against the teacher. 'I knew then what Denis McGinley was doing to me while I was in both third and fourth class was wrong.' In common with many of the teacher's other victims, he told us that our investigation, belated as it was, came as a relief. Justice, he hoped, would finally be done.

Kevin also remembered that McGinley had his brother *Simon* up on the room heater, and although he was not certain at the time, he felt that *Simon* was also abused by the teacher. Each brother confirmed the other's statements. Like *Simon*, *Kevin* named a third boy, *Adam Maher*, as another classmate who might have been abused on an almost daily basis.

Adam Maher was one of those who decided not to make a statement. It wasn't something we pushed. Whenever a name came up, we approached people, offered them the chance to speak out, but ultimately it was their own choice whether to do so or not. Some were delighted to finally find someone who would listen and spoke to us straightaway. Some preferred to stay in the background, occasionally speaking to us confidentially but without making a formal statement, sometimes not speaking at all. Some refused to speak to us altogether, though after thinking about it again, some of these changed their minds and eventually came back to me to make criminal complaints. All we could do was offer each victim the opportunity to tell his story. We hoped as many as possible would take the opportunity we offered them, but if they didn't, at least we knew we had tried. No story would be ignored. In the end, eleven of McGinley's victims came forward and spoke to us on the record, making statements which illustrated his abusive behaviour pattern. Along with documentation from other sources, from the health board to *Linda Murphy*'s diary, and corroborating evidence from parents, relatives and friends, we knew we had built a strong case.

Chapter 27
The Bureaucrat

I got a very strange phone call one evening towards the end of 1999. The caller introduced himself, rattling off his name and job title at the North Western Health Board by way of explanation. Another bureaucrat, I thought to myself.

I felt uneasy at the way the bureaucrat brandished his title like a badge. I had dealt with other people at the Health Board who didn't find it necessary to put tags after their names and got on well with them. As I listened to him it became clear he was one of the mid-level bureaucrats dealing with the referral forms I had sent to the North Western Health Board.

The health boards and An Garda Síochána had agreed a protocol on child protection a few years previously where we had to notify all cases involving minors at risk to the health authorities, and they were required to notify us in cases of sexual abuse, physical abuse and wilful neglect. Since beginning the investigation into Denis McGinley, I had made five referrals to the health board. Out of the five suspected cases I forwarded, only two of the minors would make statements, although the information we had gathered from our enquiries suggested that there was a strong case in all five instances. John Dooley and I got on with our work gathering statements from both minors and adults where people felt able to come forward, and left the health board to do their own work in cases involving those who were still minors. Occasionally I had contact with social workers and found them helpful, often arranging for counselling for victims and their families.

While John and I got on with the investigation, the health board I am sure were doing their own thing — they were notified that minors were now involved, or suspected at any rate. Of course I was not privy to their work. Social workers operated in teams led by team leaders — a bit like the Guards, I thought, where our units were headed by sergeants.

Mostly when social workers contacted me — or when we got in touch with them — they would make the normal polite enquiries as to how things were going and the progress being made with the case. This bureaucrat was different. He more or less said that the Gardaí should not interview anyone without his approval until the health board and social workers had gone in first. They were the professionals; they had the specialised training; we were mere amateurs.

I knew several excellent social workers who were dealing with the victims, but I wasn't prepared to create a situation where I would have to tell someone who wanted to make a statement that they had to talk to a social worker first. I was already all too aware of the courage it took for a victim to come forward and how easy it would be for them to slip back into silence and hide in the shadows if they weren't listened to. This stuff had been left buried for years. If someone wanted to talk to me now, I wasn't about to stop them.

I had got on very well with every social worker I had met so far, but this bureaucrat was different. I told him I had no problem with who went in first, but I could not stop people talking to me and I believed it was my duty to deal with their complaints and investigate them as soon as they came to me. The investigation wasn't about me or him; it was about the victims. I felt like saying if you are so good, why did the response to the 1994 *Dylan Murphy* complaint hit a dead end, but I decided it was best not to venture down that avenue. I bit my tongue.

I was involved in my third child sexual abuse investigation by then, all three cases overlapping. John Dooley and I along with a handful of other colleagues had uncovered some of the most horrific abuse cases in the land. I had not seen the bureaucrat's name come up in any investigation as a team leader, social worker or investigator, and now I had to take a lecture from him. I told him that I did not draft the policies on child protection. To myself, all I could think was, there is one very self-important little boy like you in every department.

Because some of McGinley's victims were still minors, a Child Protection Case Conference was called and took place at the local nursing unit a few months after I first crossed swords with the bureaucrat. In attendance was a team of social workers along with myself and the principal of the secondary school some of the victims were now attending. It went well, but the bureaucrat wasn't present. We exchanged views, discussed what was happening and what had still to be done. I felt we should all be working as a team and I described the difficulty I was having in getting files from a certain section of the health board, without mentioning names, and the frustration the delay caused. I mentioned that I got a phone call from a bureaucrat and said I had no objection to who went in first, and if they wished, social workers could come with us when we were taking police statements. That said, I mentioned that a crowd of social workers and policemen descending on a house together might scare the victims, though I was no expert.

There was another case conference called shortly after this, chaired by the bureaucrat. The principal of the secondary school asked if something urgent had come up that we needed such a meeting so close to the last one. The bureaucrat said he wanted to know if the Garda file for the DPP was ready. I had to contain myself. I knew that the file for the DPP had absolutely nothing to do with him; that was my responsibility and that of my super. He went on at length, adding nothing new as he summarised the case, though he wasn't able to tell us anything he had done. He shuffled paperwork; that seemed to be the extent of his involvement.

As he kept on talking, I realised he wasn't aware that the *Murphy* case was reported to the health board back in 1994. Surely he would have some referral form on this? Eventually I had to ask about the case. The health board was aware that some concern was raised previously about the abuser, I told him. Wasn't there any mention of this in his records?

The bureaucrat began protesting. There were no earlier complaints about Denis McGinley. They were not aware of it. As he spoke I searched through my own files and handed him a copy of the 1994 report from the public health nurse. He didn't know what to say. I wondered exactly what kind of bureaucratic chaos the health board was in if he wasn't aware of this report.

The bureaucrat was speechless, but only for a moment before demanding from me copies of the statements that I took. That I could not do. A Garda statement is not just another piece of data; it is evidence gathered for a criminal trial. I had already referred every minor we encountered to the health board, even where we had no statement, but I could not hand over evidence.

I told him I had no authority to hand those documents over to anyone, but if he felt he was entitled to them, then he should apply through the proper channels. Since after all he was so desperate to be 'first in', he should already have their stories on file.

This bureaucrat was an exception. The social workers and team leaders I met in Donegal were generally among the most professional and capable people I ever worked with. But his pointless phone calls and meetings and bickering were an example of how a single individual can disrupt the work of dozens of others.

Fr Hugh Bonner, now deceased, who received a report of misconduct about his curate, Eugene Greene, in the mid 1970s. Greene disappeared from the parish for a few weeks after the report, but apart from that, nothing happened as a result of the report. (*Author's Private Collection*)

Most Reverend Dr Seamus Hegarty, former Bishop of Raphoe, and at time of writing the Bishop of Derry. In 2002 he told a BBC *Spotlight* documentary team that Eugene Greene 'was handled very professionally, very responsibly' despite evidence of complaints dating back to the 1970s. (*Donegal News*)

The striking parish church of St Connell in Glenties, designed by Liam McCormack, which won a European Award for its design in 1974. Eugene Greene was stationed there between 1981 and 1983. Ironically, the Garda station where Greene was taken following his arrest is less than five minutes walk from this building. (*Gerard Cunningham*)

Our Lady of Victory treatment centre in Stroud, where Eugene Greene was treated for alcoholism in the early 1990s. Gardaí were unable to find out if Greene had ever been treated there on other occasions for sexual misconduct. Stroud was the only residential treatment centre working with paedophile priests in the UK when it closed in 2005. (*Mark Watkins Photography*)

Most Reverend Dr Philip Boyce, who told the BBC *Spotlight* documentary that 'there were rumours going around' concerning Eugene Greene when he [Boyce] was appointed Bishop of Raphoe in 1995, but added that 'nothing substantial could be found'. (*Donegal News*)

Fr Michael Sweeney, who gave the court a glowing reference for schoolteacher Denis McGinley. The *Donegal News* report on the sentencing hearing after McGinley pleaded guilty to sexually abusing pupils in his care, quoted the priest's character reference describing him as 'a kind, caring person and a good teacher'. (*Donegal News*)

Darragh MacIntyre, the award-winning investigative reporter who produced a BBC *Spotlight* documentary on Eugene Greene. Darragh got to know the priest's victims during the time he spent on a career break from journalism, running a pub in Gort an Choirce. (BBC *Northern Ireland*)

April 2000: Eugene Greene is led away in handcuffs after he was sentenced to twelve years in prison, one of the longest sentences ever handed down to a paedophile in Ireland. Gardaí uncovered a trail of abuse dating back at least to 1965. (*Donegal News*)

Cnoc na Naomh, the hill of saints, also known as Derryconnor National School, where Denis McGinley preyed on young boys from the 1970s until the 1990s. McGinley also had pornographic videos delivered to him at the school, bought through a mail-order company. (*Gerard Cunningham*)

Circuit Court Judge Matthew Deery, the trial judge in both the Greene and McGinley cases. During Greene's trial, he was forced to adjourn the hearing, so gruelling were the details he had to hear. Sentencing McGinley, he noted with concern that when the mother of one victim made a complaint, 'it would seem her complaints were not taken and explored the way they should have been at the time'. (*Donegal News*)

Denis McGinley shields his face and hands from waiting photographers as he is led from Letterkenny courthouse after sentencing in April 2002. He had shown little remorse when he was arrested in February 2000, seeking to minimise his crimes and only expressing regret towards the end of his time in custody. (*Donegal News*)

Colm O'Gorman, founder of One in Four, an organisation set up to offer a voice to and support for women and men who have experienced sexual abuse and/or sexual violence and also to their family and friends. (*The Irish Times*)

Chapter 28
Museum Pieces

Resources are always a problem in any government-run organisation, and An Garda Síochána is no different. When I was transferred to Donegal in the early nineties, the four uniformed Gardaí working out of the station in An Fál Carrach had one dilapidated old manual typewriter to deal with paperwork. In fact the station I first worked in when I moved there was itself a relic of a bygone age, an old barracks first built to house the Royal Irish Constabulary in the days before Irish independence. I thought it hadn't seen a lick of paint since then, although the Gardaí have since moved into a new modern station. The Sean Bheairic felt like a museum piece when we worked there, and now it truly is one — it was renovated and opened to the public with a visitors' centre, café and crafts shop after the Gardaí moved out. At the time when the McGinley investigation began, we were still working with carbon copies when paperwork had to be submitted in duplicate. I doubt most people nowadays even know what a carbon copy is any more. They are more familiar with changing ink cartridges than typewriter ribbons.

The Garda station's battered Remington typewriter had served us well over the years, but it had seen better days and, truth be told, it probably belonged in a museum too. Some of the keys were almost completely worn away. We were far from being skilled typists, but we often touch typed from memory simply because we had no choice. Around the time I began the McGinley investigation, the Remington finally gave up the ghost and we had to put in a request for a new typewriter, or with luck a computer.

To get a new typewriter, we had to go through the engineering support section. That meant more paperwork. In order to get a new machine, engineering support had to certify that the old one was beyond use. After the usual wait I got a letter asking for an engineer's report to certify that the Remington was worn out beyond repair. I remember being so angry at the bureaucracy at the time. Or maybe it was just the anger I felt at the cases I was dealing with, anger I couldn't face yet because I had to stay focused, and the triplicate forms and paperwork allowed me an outlet to vent the frustration and rage inside. Every office in town was computerised, and here we were still using a relic from another age. Yet the paperwork travelled at a snail's pace as paperwork always did.

I was the lead investigator on the McGinley investigation. It was my job to make sure every document was filed correctly and every statement was typed up for eventual submission to the DPP. Normally a job like that can be delegated, these days often to a civilian clerical worker. But given what we were dealing with, I wasn't comfortable doing that. In any investigation there is a need for confidentiality; in this case even more so, given the need to protect the identities of the victims. The fewer people who knew who the victims were, the easier it was to respect their wish for anonymity. I would type the statements myself.

I decided that if Garda management was not going to give us a new typewriter or computer in An Fál Carrach station, that was up to them, but I couldn't wait around for one any longer. I would do something myself in the meantime, I told my sergeant. I ordered a computer from Gateway out of my own pocket. Confidentiality had become very important to me as I worked with the victims. I could set up the computer at home under lock and key and do the statements there. It would be one extra layer of security.

The computer arrived within a week and I set it up in a spare room. Thankfully it wasn't too complicated. The instructions were pretty straightforward and the various wires and cables were colour coded. But then I had to do a course to learn how to use it. It drove me crazy at first. I would lose files by accident, or think I had lost them, even though they were still there and I just didn't know where to look because I had 'minimised' them. I would hit 'preview' by mistake and I couldn't figure out how to bring the file back to 'edit' mode. When I had finished a file, I didn't know how to save it properly and often lost it and had to start over again. Fortunately I found an evening computer course locally, an hour and a half for a few evenings every week, and taught myself the basics: starting up, opening files, saving and printing, everything I needed to work a simple word processing programme, type up the statements we had taken and submit regular progress reports on the investigation to my super, Jim Gallagher.

Halfway through my investigation my superintendent changed. Complaints from the McBrearty family in Raphoe had led to a high-level investigation headed by assistant commissioner Kevin Carty, what came to be called the Carty Inquiry. The inquiry involving dozens of detectives was based in the Co. Donegal divisional Garda headquarters in Letterkenny Garda Station. Shortly after it began the Letterkenny district superintendent Kevin Lennon was transferred to Milford, replacing Jim Gallagher, while the Carty team investigated allegations made against Lennon.

Between transfers and senior officers taking holidays and arranging temporary replacements, there was a while when it seemed that a new super or inspector was in charge at the district office in Milford every other week, so that I was never quite sure whom I would have to deal with if I called into the district HQ. Meanwhile Lennon was fully occupied with the Carty Inquiry, which was going over his handling of the McBrearty case with a fine tooth comb. Among other things he was accused of planting evidence, creating bogus IRA explosives dumps which he would then 'find', taking the credit and boosting his career until he rose to the rank of superintendent. Incredibly the allegations would turn out to be true, but in 1999 they seemed bizarre beyond belief. True or false, though, the investigation was obviously a major distraction for Lennon.

Something else crossed my mind. While it was no harm for assistant commissioner Carty and his team to clean up a Garda investigation that had clearly lost the run of itself, it was amazing how much money could be found to fund thousands of hours of overtime, transferring dozens of detectives into the division to work on the case, while at the same time there seemed to be none available to buy a single computer to finish a child sexual abuse case which probably involved close to a hundred unknown victims. I think that as far as Garda HQ was concerned, Donegal was far away, a neglected corner of the State, and as for An Fál Carrach or Gort an Choirce, they were remote even within Donegal. We were simply not a priority.

I worked unlimited hours on the cases, much of it unpaid, something that was often unavoidable because of the nature of the work. The victims were understandably protective of their anonymity, often insisting on meetings after dark and in other towns where they were less likely to be recognised. There was no overtime available, I was told, at least not in Milford, whatever about the Carty Inquiry's resources in Letterkenny. It felt as if I was being paid for a tenth of the hours I was working, between late night encounters and the hours spent preparing documentation on the computer. But it was important work. I wasn't about to let the victims down by telling them I couldn't meet them because I was off the clock, but it made for long days and nights carrying out a major investigation in the hours left over after my regular duties.

We could have asked for more help on the case, of course, but we felt there was a benefit in working in a small team. The victims grew to know us, they knew they could trust us, they weren't dealing with an organisation but with individuals. They got to see the same people each time so that a relationship developed, not simply whoever happened to be on duty on any given day. The system seemed to be working and the old adage applied: if it ain't broke, don't fix it. What frustrated us was that even with the unorthodox hours we sometimes kept, we couldn't work full time on the cases.

Had we been able to do so, perhaps we could have gone further, found victims in other schools where McGinley had worked, other parishes where Greene was stationed. To this day I know there are victims out there who have never come forward, never got the counselling they need to heal. With more time we could have done more, but always it was a question of resources. For us to work full time someone else would have had to be found to take over the other duties on our rosters. The small team worked well; we didn't really want any more people working on the case. But we could have done with counselling and support to help us deal with what we uncovered.

Some rosters provided a few hours of overtime. On one occasion I claimed for thirty-three hours and it was questioned by the super. We worked a twenty-eight day roster, so it averaged out at a little over eight hours a week. I knew there were detectives in the division working sixteen hours a week overtime, maybe twenty hours if they worked on their day off. My thirty-three hours covered an entire month. I knew I had worked for far more hours than I had claimed and I complained to the super, accounting for each hour.

Every statement on file represented hours of work, meetings with the victims as they told me their stories, time spent explaining the importance of dates, times, any details that might possibly be corroborated by someone else, all the things they would need before we took the formal complaint. It meant hours spent on my own before we took a statement, double checking details to satisfy myself, knowing what I needed to cover in the statement so that nothing was left out.

I felt a sense of obligation towards these people who had waited so long to tell their stories. I couldn't shut the doors on them now. I wouldn't have turned down money if there was money going, but that wasn't why I was doing it. Yet I knew the hours I had claimed for were a fraction of those I had worked. If somebody had come to me and said, 'I am hurt, will you take me to hospital?' I could hardly refuse because I was off duty. The psychological pain the victims felt was every bit as real and cut every bit as deep as a physical wound. To his credit, the super listened patiently while I let rip, then told me to tear up the memo he had sent me querying my work hours.

I found I was feeling angry all the time and grew short tempered and frustrated easily. I never knew that I possessed so many buttons for anger and revulsion. It was very traumatic dealing with all those cases with no psychological back-up — meeting victims in car parks, on country roads, on piers. The sense of isolation, anger, betrayal and shame was contagious. I nearly had to shut out my own family. I found myself walking round the house fuming. I felt like a contained lunatic for a while, I was so angry dealing with this tank of corruption. The anger had to come out, be displaced, and too often I vented at the wrong people.

I don't think An Garda Síochána has come to terms with the impact of child sexual abuse cases on investigators yet. The force offered no support to myself and the handful of other officers involved in the west Donegal cases. In contrast to police forces in the UK including the PSNI in Northern Ireland, there was virtually no logistical support, to the point where I had had to buy my own computer and teach myself how to use it.

There was no Garda liaison officer to work with the victims and their families during the investigation, so by default I became the liaison officer. It was a difficult position to be in. Although I was the lead investigator, often I knew little more than they did once I had submitted the investigation files to the super's office and the DPP. Some of the mothers got together and set up support groups, and in other cases Dooley and I were able to refer victims to professional counsellors. One Letterkenny-based counsellor in particular was a very good sex therapist, and I found her wonderful to deal with.

Once she rang me up and asked me if I was getting much back-up, psychological back-up. None, I told her. She found it difficult to believe that we were dealing with so much sexual violence and getting no therapeutic help. I can arrange someone for you, she told me. She arranged a few sessions with a colleague, but I never received any counselling through the force in the years I worked on the sexual abuse cases. Dr John Wallace, a clinical psychologist, later told me he had spent sixteen years dealing with sexual abuse in London. He told me he dealt with only one victim a week, and afterwards he in turn got counselling. After a while the pain eats inside you, almost as if you have been raped yourself. You get into the victims' minds, trapped in their trauma. We spent years on the cases dealing with multiple victims and we were never debriefed, never provided with the profes- sional and counselling support that would help us deal with the horrors we met and their long-term effects. An Garda Síochána still has a long way to go in this respect.

Chapter 29
Trip to Britain

By the beginning of 1999, John Dooley had prepared a file on Eugene Greene for the office of the Director of Public Prosecutions. It was a huge amount of work. In little over a year a small team of two Gardaí had uncovered the unbelievable, exposing what children in this quiet corner of Ireland were subjected to, an unimaginable depravity. The investigation had started on John's patch. He took responsibility for the prosecution file. He typed all the victim statements and witness statements, and collected the corroborative and other relevant data that was required for the file. The file was excellently prepared. This work was done by John in a spare room in his own home, just as I would prepare the file on Denis McGinley. The victims wanted, and needed, anonymity. There was no way he could risk leaving a mountain of sensitive paperwork lying around an office that was shared with other people.

Working with John, I expected nothing less from him than the professionalism he had shown previously on undercover operations. He was attentive to the most minute of details; nothing was overlooked. He was the best Garda I ever worked with. His sensitivity towards people as he dealt with their grave hurt amazed me. There was never a flippant comment from him; he always listened patiently. Victims at last could talk about things they had kept buried for years, and though it was gruesome and hard to listen to, it had to be done. His approach was always professional. It was a pleasure to work with him, though the work itself, trying to make sense of the sordid stories the victims had to share with us, was far from a pleasure. When John came into my area to work with me, he was welcomed as one of the family. Sixteen of Greene's victims had now come forward in my area out of the total of twenty-six that we dealt with. And of course I knew there were more who would never come forward.

Words could not describe what we were coming across, but I

wondered why they had kept silent for so long. Fear was holding them back, I guessed. Encased in their hurt and with their dignity obliterated, they were fearful, controlled people. Generations of respect had been instilled over the years in their minds: respect for the Church, for the collar, for the schoolmaster. They feared they could not talk. Who would listen? Who wanted to listen? This fear belonged to them and owned them. I got the sense that these children were pawns in a system, through no fault of their parents, and were seen by the abuser as no more than items of abuse. It was horrible, a total betrayal of trust. Even when I was away from the victims, I could not get what happened out of my mind. I could not make sense of it. At times I could barely breathe.

As the Greene file came back from the office of the DPP, they looked for clarifications as they often do in these cases. Everything seemed clear to us, and to the victims, but the legal system operates to its own rules. Things that might seem self-evident must be spelled out in minute detail or a defence lawyer will have a field day. Why didn't you include this or that in your statement? I put it to you that you are making this up. If a defence barrister can raise enough doubts, evidence is thrown out. Enough doubts and a case can be lost. Any loopholes had to be closed. The director's requests for clarifications took Dooley and me overseas to tie up the loose ends. Dooley contacted most of those we had to speak to in advance, while I got in touch with *Edward Brown*, the young man who had travelled home to Donegal from London one weekend to talk to me.

We arranged the schedule and booked our flights in March 1999. We had a busy schedule ahead with several meetings arranged and flights to different parts of Britain. On 8 March we boarded a mid-morning flight from Carrickfinn Airport, then waited a few hours in Dublin to catch a connection to London Heathrow, arriving just after 6 p.m. *Edward Brown* had told me he would meet us there. That was a relief. We had barely walked into the arrival bay when his smile embraced us. He was glad to see us. It was his first meeting with Dooley but he felt at home immediately with him. John was already busy on his mobile phone. A London CID officer was to meet us at the airport, but Heathrow of course was as packed and chaotic as ever. After a couple of minutes John made contact on the mobile and we followed him as he set off in search of a landmark where our contact was stationed, under a large illuminated sign. In the chaos and crowds we kept missing each other, until John and his contact almost walked into each other, each still talking on their mobiles.

John's contact from the CID turned out to be a young blonde officer in her early twenties, perfect for undercover surveillance work. We exchanged greetings and she shook hands with *Edward*, though we didn't tell her who he was, and we made our way to her car. She was alone. We sat into a black VW Golf GTI, not exactly what I was used to thinking of as a standard police car. We asked if the car was official issue. 'In a way, yes,' she said, 'and in a way, no. Every few weeks we hire out a fleet of vehicles from different companies. It's a VW at the moment; it could be a Rover the next time or a Toyota or Ford. It makes us harder to spot. We can do better surveillance than before.'

We could learn from that, I thought to myself. She eased her way through the hectic London traffic as if it was second nature to her, which I suppose it was. Eventually we arrived at Catford Police Station. 'I hope I meet you again,' our escort told us, but we never did. As she disappeared into the night we were ushered upstairs to a small conference room where we were left undisturbed for our meeting with *Edward*.

By now it was 8 p.m. and we hadn't had time to eat. However we sat down and discussed the case with *Edward* and cleared up the outstanding issues for the lawyers back home by taking an additional statement. By the time we were finished it was close to midnight.

Edward insisted on making his own way back to his digs. We thanked him and bade him goodnight. Through the CID John had arranged a B&B for us close by. As my mind wandered, it dawned on me that we were getting less money for accommodation overseas than if we were on an overnight trip back home, a difference of about two quid on the allowance of about £45 to cover food and board. But if we happened to have a senior officer along with us, we could have claimed about £90 a night, almost double our usual rate. Sleep is more expensive if you have brass on your shoulder, I thought. It was almost 2 a.m. before we stopped talking and went to bed.

The second day started early. We were picked up by a different CID officer and driven to the airport. The contrast with the young officer the night before could not have been more marked. It soon became apparent that we had a blabbermouth with us. All he could talk about was women. He told us he had been married five times. God help those women, I thought.

Our destination was the north of England. We had arranged to meet Greene's victims in the evening, so we had some time to spare when we arrived. We had something to eat and walked around a bit. When we met the victims as arranged, they brought us to their homes. They were noticeably more friendly and relaxed around us than they had been back in Donegal. The local football team was playing at home that night under floodlights and we were offered a pair of tickets to the match. We would love to have gone, but our pre-booked flight was leaving that night. Though practically strangers to us, there was a growing bond beyond friendship between us. Having to go back over the hurt with them that night was not pleasant, their memories of childhood back home full of misery. At least they were away from that scene now, coping the best they could and glad to be away.

We bade farewell and made our way back to the police station. From there we were taken to the airport by a sensible middle-aged man, and on to another northern English city. Unfortunately Greene's victims were dispersed all over the globe, some as far away as America. But they had arranged to come home to see us. For now, though, we had to travel to see those in Britain. We arrived at night time and settled down for the night at another B&B which was a wee bit drab, but it would do. We had half of the next day free with no meeting scheduled until the afternoon, but it was damp and raining. We spent the time in the local police station playing pool. There we met several constables, some of whom couldn't wait to get out, disgruntled with their job, and some young and bristling with energy. In the afternoon we dealt with another victim, gruesome details revisited again, but at least we had each other for support. We stayed in the same B&B that night again, chatting and drinking coffee into the small hours.

Our next destination was Scotland. Again we were left at the airport by the local police. We were booked first class this time, though not by design. It was the only available connection at the time. We got to spend some time in the VIP lounge before our departure seeing how the other half lives. A second connecting flight and we reached our destination. Our appointment wasn't until late afternoon the next day, so we headed to the police station where we were staying. It was cheaper than the local B&Bs, a huge building. We were upstairs in neatly kept rooms, but smoking was prohibited. That didn't suit John or myself so we went outside if we wanted to smoke. There was a canteen attached where we had breakfast. The architecture of the town was wonderful. I had spent some time there in 1974 on my honeymoon, never envisaging that I would be back decades later on an investigation. We walked around the town that night sightseeing. It seemed so quiet and peaceful, so clean, nothing much stirring in the streets.

We spoke to a policeman on duty when we arrived back at the station. We told him that it must be easy to police the area. It seemed too good to be true. 'Don't be taken in by what you see,' he said. 'There are drugs and a lot of domestic violence in the estates that you cannot see.'

Our final appointment was the next day. Unfortunately the abuse was very much alive with him. He never fully dealt with or came to terms with it. He was one of the saddest people we met. We had to bring him through the trauma of the events again to clarify the statements that the court would see in evidence. We brought him for a meal that night and made sure we waited with him until he boarded a bus home. He was so fragile. When he got off the bus he went missing for a few days as he buried himself in alcohol, we discovered the next day. But by that time we had taken our flight back to Dublin, and on from there to Carrickfinn and home.

After seven flights in five days it was good to be home, to be back in peaceful Donegal again. But like the town in Scotland, what appeared peaceful and tranquil to the eye did not reveal all that was happening. The file was updated with the additional statements along with other clarifications we were asked for. This time they met with the standards of the office of the DPP. The case could go ahead.

Chapter 30

The Damage Done to Those Lads is Terrible

I was on my way home from a day spent following up on a break-in at the local golf club. Someone had broken a window at the back of the clubhouse and stolen some drinks and cigarettes from the bar. I was close to home when I met *Norma Healy* on the road a little way outside the town. 'I'm glad you're investigating that fellow McGinley,' she told me.

It didn't surprise me that *Norma* knew about our investigation. I had first met her because of a tragedy in her own family. She was the same age as many of Denis McGinley's victims, and I knew already of the schoolyard grapevine that often went ahead of me as I investigated the teacher, so that many of his victims knew what I was doing before I spoke to them. Some, I knew, had confided in others, in wives or girlfriends, and in many cases his abusive behaviour was no secret. His nickname, Poofy Den, was too widely known, the schoolyard taunts and jeers too widespread. I asked her why she was so glad.

She named one of McGinley's victims. 'I was doing a line with him,' she told me. 'The damage he did to all of them is terrible. We went out for two years together. He's a lovely quiet lad, but it's like his emotions are frozen. He could hardly hug me. He just froze up. He never even put his hand on my knee, he was so damaged by what happened to him at school. The damage done to those lads is terrible. They cannot handle a relationship. It's good that somebody is looking after them now, that somebody is looking into it. What you're doing is helping him so much.'

Norma's concern for her childhood friends struck a chord with me. Time and time again during the investigation one thing hit me quite strongly, the strength and dignity of the women faced with the damage sexual abuse inflicted on their sons, brothers and husbands, both the maternal caring instinct of their mothers and in women of a younger generation. I came across this too with the victims' support group which was set up later by the mothers of several victims.

Norma had to deal with the emotional scars from her own childhood, I was to discover. McGinley ignored most of the girls in his class, but he isolated *Norma* and bullied her in third and fourth class. Something sparked a particular dislike for *Norma* in him. She was never quite sure why he had such a set against her. The only thing she could think of was that she played football with the boys during play breaks and this somehow offended him. She was very friendly with the boys she played with and McGinley resented her for it. Purposefully he set about turning the boys in the class against her.

The memory of the first time McGinley singled her out for special treatment was still raw in *Norma*'s mind. She was in third class and McGinley was checking arithmetic homework. All her answers were correct, but that wasn't enough to satisfy McGinley. The teacher showed her the work of another girl, who had written out her work in blue ink, underlining the result of each calculation in red ink with the words 'An Freagra' (the answer) while *Norma*'s work was done in pencil. Although every calculation was done correctly, the teacher told her that her work was 'sloppy' as he hit her in the face with her copybook and threw it on the floor. She didn't know why, but she sensed that McGinley took pleasure in humiliating her in front of her classmates.

Norma played football a lot, both with the boys during school and afterwards at home. McGinley seized on her tanned skin and dark brown hair and christened her with a racist nickname. In the classroom, rather than using her given name, he referred to her exclusively by this nickname and encouraged the other pupils to do the same. One day in particular, as the classroom windows steamed up, he wrote her name and her nickname on the glass with his finger, encouraging the boys to laugh at her.

The name stuck and the pupils followed their teacher's lead, making *Norma*'s life a misery. Things got so bad that she went to another teacher and complained how the boys were bullying her. The teacher put a stop to it, but *Norma* was afraid to tell her that the bullying was started by a teacher.

'The two years I spent in Denis McGinley's class were the worst years of my childhood,' *Norma* told me. 'It was a very lonely time for me. I felt I was mentally tortured at the instigation of my teacher. I started questioning my own identity and wondered if I was adopted because everyone called me a racist nickname. I even asked my mother if I was adopted because Denis McGinley made me feel so different from everybody else.'

McGinley's cruel streak wasn't confined to *Norma*. She told me how he also picked on some of the slower boys in the class, notably *Eric* and *Gordon Regan*, whom he also abused sexually. Both boys were frequently brought up to the blackboard to do arithmetic exercises and ridiculed if they got into difficulty. McGinley also cultivated favourites, and *Norma* remembered how he often invited *Simon* and *Kevin Lynch* up to sit on the heater, but she knew that being a favourite was not something to be envied. Like every other pupil she had to watch as her less fortunate classmates were routinely sexually abused, often several times a day. The memory that stayed with her was of the boys having to tuck their shirts back inside their trousers as they returned to their seats after McGinley sat with them on the heater.

'At the time I knew what Denis McGinley was doing to the boys was wrong, but I was not aware of the seriousness of it,' she explained. 'I remember once Denis McGinley took some of his favourites, boys only, on a school outing. I can't remember any other school trips ever.'

Norma was still angry at the hell she went through for two years at her teacher's hands. She eventually made a witness statement, outlining McGinley's mental cruelty to her and providing corroboration of the sexual abuse he inflicted on other pupils.

But no statement, no matter how much time we put into it, could adequately convey the anger, hurt and emotional carnage McGinley left behind in his wake. No statement could convey the lives wasted in alcoholism and drugs or destroyed by depression. Young men are killed on our roads every week in this country and we regard it as a national scandal, but the damage caused by abusers like Greene, McGinley and *John Reilly* is largely invisible, except, I suspect, in our suicide statistics. We switch off as a nation when a new story of sexual abuse emerges. It's easier to reach for the remote control and switch stations.

McGinley's arrogance, his innumerable sexual assaults, the way he ordered the girls and boys in the class to keep their heads down while he sexually assaulted their friends and his casual bullying of young girls like *Norma* infuriated me. It was hard to believe what I was hearing every day. McGinley had not only abused dozens of boys but did so openly. The children became so accustomed to sexual abuse that nobody blinked an eye any more — this was just another part of growing up. There was no point in complaining because when complaints were made, nothing happened.

Thinking about it, all I could do was clench my fists and keep my anger in check. Dooley and I had a job to do. We couldn't allow our anger to cloud our judgment. We had to focus on hard evidence. Cold statements of fact would bring justice for the victims. I don't think I could do it again without going out and kicking down a few doors. The legal system looks on the criminal process as purely prosecutorial, the gathering of statements and forensic evidence, the compilation of files, the serving of papers, legal arguments to be made before judges, precedents to be dissected. But we were dealing with people's lives, and that was often forgotten in the process. The law focuses on proof. The human aspect is never taken on board.

Chapter 31

Operation Alpha

It was a cold winter's morning towards the end of 1999, insistently wet as only an Irish winter's day can be, not raining hard but with that light half mist drizzle that soaks you quietly before you even notice it. When I got to work, lying on my desk, thick with paperwork, was a plain brown envelope marked 'secret and confidential' and forwarded to me from the district superintendent's office. More paperwork, I thought to myself, probably a memorandum on something trivial marked secret by an overenthusiastic clerk in the district office.

I slit open the envelope and began to read. What I saw stunned me. This was no pointless circular reminding every Garda of the importance of submitting crime reports in triplicate, or the need for cutbacks in the photocopying budget by using both sides of a sheet of paper. The file described *Operation Alpha*, a major investigation headed by British police into the distribution of homosexual and child pornography.

Operation Alpha (not its real name) ran over several years and involved the police in several European countries and the United States. At its heart was an elusive British criminal still at large in continental Europe, who made his fortune distributing paedophile pornography. This criminal had fled British justice in 1994, skipping bail while awaiting trial on charges under the Obscene Publications Act, and since then the police in England had continued to pursue him, uncovering his distribution networks and tracking his complex web of financial records, often involving false names. One of the false accounts, I noticed ironically, used an overseas branch of an Irish bank.

Over the years the police had broken up several of this criminal's distribution rings, arresting several of his accomplices although he himself continued to evade their reach. During these investigations they had secured several convictions, seizing pornographic material and lists of his customers. I was reading the file because those lists contained a name from my area. My heart almost stopped when I read it. 'D. McFionnaile, Cnoc Na Naomh'. I recognised it immediately. Cnoc na Naomh (Hill of the Saints) was the formal name of Derryconnor National School. 'D. McFionnaile' could only be Denis McGinley, Donchadh Mac Fhionnlaoich as he was officially known in Irish on the service records of the Department of Education. The same name appeared on two of the mailing lists.

After everything I had heard in the last two years I thought nothing further could shock me, but the descriptions of the videos sold to people on these mailing lists made for stomach-churning reading. The arrogance of these men astounded me. I first got involved in this investigation because Greene had felt so untouchable that he expected us to arrest a blackmailer and not wonder what the blackmail was about. Now I discovered McGinley had been ordering the most graphic pornography, which he had delivered to the remote country school where the innocent were attending and being taught.

I could not get over the coincidence. As I was investigating McGinley, further evidence had landed on my desk, thanks to a British investigation which began while I was still stationed in the Midlands. Mark Twain once wrote that 'truth is stranger than fiction, but it is because fiction is obliged to stick to possibilities. Truth isn't.' If a detective novel contained a coincidence like that, the author would be laughed at as a desperate hack who had run out of ideas and was reduced to *deus ex machina*, introducing last minute surprises to dig himself out of a hole in the plot. Yet here it was right in front of my eyes. The information from *Operation Alpha* was incredibly important. It gave us impartial, independent evidence against McGinley, and if we presented it to a judge, reasonable grounds to obtain a search warrant.

I added the information from *Operation Alpha* to the file on McGinley, now almost complete, and sat down to compose a reply to my British colleagues, confirming that I could identify the potential purchaser in my area and explaining that he was already the subject of an ongoing Garda investigation for alleged child sexual abuse and that I would report on future developments. Then I phoned Dooley and told him the news.

We were ready to move against McGinley. We had complaints from a total of eleven victims, witness statements corroborating much of what they told us in detail and even documentary evidence from the health board about a previous complaint. Now we also had evidence that McGinley not only sexually abused children, but that he might have bought paedophile pornography. We double checked everything we had collected, made sure we had not overlooked anything and prepared for the arrest. The search warrant would be issued under section 7 of the 1998 Child Trafficking and Pornography Act, which required an officer of at least the rank of sergeant to swear an 'information' before a district court judge and satisfy him that there were reasonable grounds for suspecting that evidence of the possession of child pornography would be found.

On Friday, 11 February 2000, one of my colleagues appeared before Judge John O'Donnell, and after explaining the evidence we had collected, got the signed search warrant 'to search dwellinghouse and out-offices of Denis McGinley otherwise D. McFionnaile'. The final piece was in place. The raid would take place on Monday morning.

That weekend I considered the two Donegals I knew. On the one hand there is the Donegal that tourists and sightseers know, the place I thought would be a quiet tour of duty after the hectic years in detective branch. From my home I can look out on a landscape bathed in beauty, protected by the landmarks of Muckish and Errigal Mountains lording over the area with Glenveagh National Park sheltering behind them, while to the west lies the proud parish of Gaoth Dobhair. The glens and valleys between the mountains and the isolated beaches lie still as if undisturbed. Further out at sea are the islands of Inis Bó Finne and Toraigh gracing the mind — innocence personified. You could easily believe these quiet glens were the safest places in the world.

To the south of Gort an Choirce in the beautifully stunning parish of Dún Lúiche (Dunlewy) with its wonderful churches, there's a spot called 'the poisoned glen', a haunting and mysterious place, its strange name the starting point for several local folktales, among them that an English cartographer mistook 'neamh' (heaven) for 'nimhe' (poison) and renamed the heavenly glen as the poisoned glen. Maybe the cartographer was closer to the truth than we realised, I thought. There was a second Donegal beneath the beauty of the mountains and the gentleness of their inhabitants, a place where lonely mountain roads, beaches and islands had witnessed the appalling degradation of innocent children. While the valleys were protected from the elements by the mountains of Errigal and Muckish, no one had been able to protect the innocence of those children.

Two different worlds existed together, one of beauty and one of horror. Evil collided with innocence and consumed it on a scale that was unimaginable. It was a cruel world, and I wished I knew less about it.

Chapter 32
I Was Expecting You

There were three of us in the search party. John Dooley, myself and a sergeant served the search warrant. The sergeant knocked on the front door, and when Denis McGinley answered, we explained briefly why we were there, showing him the signed search warrant we got three days previously based on the information from *Operation Alpha*. McGinley nodded his understanding, opening the door to usher us inside.

McGinley looked strangely relieved. 'I'm glad to see you, lads. I was expecting you,' he told me. 'I've been waiting for you to call for the past two weeks.'

'What?'

'Fr Hughie Sweeney was here last week, and he told me that you were investigating me. I could hardly sleep since.'

On questioning him further he told me that two weeks earlier Fr Hugh Sweeney had called to his home. There, the priest told him that the Gardaí were investigating him for alleged sexual abuse. 'He called me out to his car and said something to the effect that Fr Greene did wrong and that he had his chance to get lost and that he didn't, but you can't do that because of your mother,' McGinley told me, adding that he had slept little since the visit because he was 'anxiously awaiting the arrival of the Gardaí every day'.

It wasn't the first time I had come across Sweeney's name, of course. In 1984, when *Craig Thompson*'s mother discovered letters from McGinley in her son's bedroom, she and her husband approached Sweeney, at that time the local curate in the parish. The *Thompsons* expected that Sweeney would go to his parish priest John McGlynn, and that McGinley would be removed from his position. They were shocked when the following September they discovered he was back in his position as a teacher in the school. Police work is all about confirmation, cross-checking details in one statement against what others have said. After speaking to the *Thompsons*, we had gone to Sweeney to see if he would corroborate what the family had told us.

It was not a productive interview. In his statement he told us he could not 'recall having been told by either *Rose* or *Art Thompson* anything in relation to their son *Craig* and his involvement with Denis McGinley'. He had 'no recollection of having been shown any letters that were written by Denis McGinley' and 'was not aware that Denis McGinley had a problem in this area'.

I was dumbfounded when McGinley told us he was expecting us. The teacher's victims knew we were investigating him; it's impossible to carry out an enquiry of that sort without some people finding out what's going on, but we had taken care to keep our enquiries discreet. There was always a risk that McGinley would find out in advance that we were investigating him, but I hadn't expected this. The schoolyard grapevine was one thing; there was little we could do to stop the victims talking about it among themselves, and it even helped us. The fact that people heard from each other that we were investigating, and that people had come forward, encouraged others in turn to come forward, confident that we would listen to them and take them seriously, creating the momentum for yet others to come forward. But this we had not seen coming. This wasn't a slip of the tongue, an overheard conversation that tipped off our target. Sweeney had specifically warned McGinley that he was under investigation. The priest, who had apparently done little or nothing when the *Thompson* family went to him fifteen years earlier, had alerted a paedophile that he was under investigation. How sad, I thought. I wondered why paedophiles were afforded protection and innocent children were not.

Even within the force, only a few Gardaí who were not directly involved in the investigation knew what we were doing. It wasn't something we talked about openly for obvious reasons. The investigation was kept so confidential that I had only briefed the sergeant who applied for the search warrant days earlier, just before he applied to the judge for the warrant, as one more step in making sure there was no danger of information leaking. The fewer people who knew what we were working on the better. Now, with a single conversation, Sweeney had jeopardised months of work with his meddling. McGinley knew we were coming for two weeks. To say the very least Sweeney's interference was unprofessional and unhelpful, giving

McGinley the chance to get rid of any child pornography he might have in his possession.

McGinley denied he had ever bought or owned any child pornography, and I doubted we would find anything incriminating, but we searched anyway. Police work is often about following rules and procedures methodically. Never assume you know something. Look. Verify. Double check. Unless you look, you won't know if there's anything there or not. I found fifteen video tapes in McGinley's bedroom. We later established that the tapes contained soft porn, though they mostly consisted of recordings from late night Channel 4 programmes. None of them contained child pornography.

At 9.55 a.m. on the morning of 14 February 2000 I arrested Denis McGinley under section 4(3) of the Criminal Law Act 1997 on suspicion of having sexually assaulted *Dylan Murphy*. There was a large amount of corroboration in the *Murphy* case from statements and records from social workers to his mother's diary. Even if other cases didn't make it to court, we were confident this one would and we would get a conviction. McGinley was cautioned. He was taken to Milford Garda Station where we arrived at 10.45 a.m. and booked by Garda Sean Tolan, the member in charge and station orderly, who took his details, explained his rights to him in detail and gave him a written copy of his rights, form C72. McGinley waived his right to a solicitor before he was searched and then taken to the cells.

McGinley said little during our first interview as we went through the evidence we had collected against him. The interview began as usual with the official caution that he was not obliged to make any statement, but if he did it would be taken down in writing and could be given in evidence. The Judges' Rules are nothing if not persistent. McGinley told us he wouldn't make a written statement. He was casual, almost dismissive of the complaints we laid out before him, as if he was thinking, is that all you are bothered about? We went through the statements covering an eighteen year period from 1976 to 1994. I wondered how many other victims still suffering in silence he had left behind in the seventeen years before he arrived in Derryconnor National School, and how many we had failed to find since then.

The interview was interrupted several times, mostly regular checks by the custody officer to make sure everything was going all right and if McGinley had any complaints or wanted a cup of tea or coffee. I was aware of the clock running down as we went through the questions.

Every Garda always is. He was arrested at 9.55 a.m. and between one thing and another we didn't sit down to interview him until after 11.30 a.m. Ninety minutes out of our six hours were taken up with transport and paperwork. Two hours of questioning, and then we had to stop. McGinley's brother Seamus had arrived at the station and wanted to see him. We needed a break anyway. It was a handy coincidence. Dooley and I left to compare notes in the station canteen while McGinley and his brother spoke in private.

The brothers spoke for about half an hour, and by the time Seamus left Dooley and I were ready to go in again. Within a quarter of an hour we made a breakthrough. In a brief statement McGinley said he would deal with each allegation made against him individually and, critically, made at least a limited admission of guilt, saying that 'some of the allegations are true and some are untrue'.

Meanwhile out at the front of the station a 'changing of the guard' was taking place. Sean Tolan had been on duty since 6 a.m. His shift was over and he was replaced by Garda Orla Filan as station orderly and member in charge. Sean updated her on the investigation, bringing her up to date on the arrest. Shortly after McGinley made his statement, Orla called down to the interview room. She introduced herself, explained to McGinley that she was the new member in charge if he had any complaints and reminded him that he had a right to change his mind if he wanted to see a solicitor at any time. He told her he was fine and he didn't need to see a solicitor. Orla checked in on him several more times during the day. Each time he assured her things were fine. Although he had the right to do so at any time, he never asked to see a solicitor.

McGinley was talking but the clock was still running. His six hours were up at 3.55 p.m., but we still had a lot of questions to put to him. The super, Kevin Lennon, was briefed on our progress and he agreed to extend McGinley's detention for a further six hours. After that we would have to let him go. We took a break at 3.20 p.m. A meal had been ordered and McGinley was taken to the dayroom while Dooley and I took the chance to grab a cup of tea and review our notes again. The meal break was uneventful save that McGinley made a phone call home. Afterwards he was taken down to the cells again.

At 4.20 p.m. Garda Barry Mulligan escorted McGinley back from the cells to the interview room where John and I waited. We were now into extended time. Six more hours to count down, and that was it.

There would be no more extensions, no more chances. We settled down to work, moving steadily over the ground we needed to cover, our work punctuated by the occasional visit by Orla to check that everything was okay.

We questioned McGinley together while I took notes. John and I were the only Gardaí to question him. We knew the evidence best. The investigation had been kept small partly because we simply didn't have the budget resources for a larger team, and partly to protect the identities of the victims. Some of the allegations we put to him he accepted, others he denied outright. A few times he said he simply couldn't remember. Always, he tried to minimise what he had done. It was as though he had no idea of the damage he had caused over the years.

McGinley worked as a teacher from 1959 to 1996, retiring after thirty-seven years, three years short of a full pension under a scheme which allowed public servants to take early retirement after thirty-five years' service on a reduced pension. When I asked him why he retired early, he told me it was because his mother could not cope on her own at home. I had to wonder if there were any other factors that had pushed him to that decision. In the early 1990s the *Murphy* family had complained about his behaviour. Could there have been other complaints we didn't know about?

McGinley denied that he had sexually molested *Dylan Murphy* and *Lee Nolan*, both of whom were still minors, and described the allegations as lies. He admitted using a cruel nickname for *Lee Nolan* but denied he had ever heard his own nickname, Poofy Den, used by his pupils. He denied sexually assaulting *Gary Daly* but did concede that he had once stopped his car and got out of it after *Gary* shouted abuse at him as he drove past. *Gary Daly* said he had shouted 'Poofy Den' as the teacher drove past. McGinley said he had not heard what the boy said and stopped the car only because he heard the teenager shouting but hadn't caught the words.

He quibbled over details of when and where, but admitted that he had sexually assaulted *Craig Thompson* while he was still a schoolboy in a local secondary school. He accepted that he bought a car for *Craig* at a cost of £3,000 and paid £1,000 insurance, and that he wrote letters to him when he started ignoring him. He confirmed that he was confronted by *Craig*'s parents about the letters he wrote, and that they sold the car and gave him back the money they made on the sale.

McGinley denied abusing *Gordon Regan* who he said was 'a very slow learner and didn't like school', but accepted that he sexually assaulted or molested *Raymond Graham, Eric Regan, Frank O'Neill, Douglas Ferguson* and *Simon Lynch*. When we asked him about *Kevin Lynch*, he answered: 'It may have happened but I don't remember.' When we asked him why he abused so many young boys, his answer was, 'I thought nothing of it at the time; it was curiosity more than anything else.' Throughout the day he minimised the sexual abuse and the seriousness of the allegations did not seem to register with him at first, but towards the end of the day he seemed to realise the gravity of his situation and expressed some remorse, telling us that he 'now regretted everything that happened. Listening to the extracts and allegations during the day, they are very sad stories and I am sorry I caused trouble and distress to so many young people.'

McGinley told us he had stopped sexually abusing young boys after *Dylan Murphy*'s mother made a complaint in the early nineties. 'I learned my lesson that time,' he explained. 'I knew I was being watched by everybody.' When we asked him why his name was on a mailing list from a child pornography distributor, he said he answered a newspaper advertisement about a decade earlier when he first bought a video machine and received pornographic videos featuring adult men. He told us he watched the videos a couple of times, then destroyed them, but he continued to receive brochures from the company after that although he never made any other purchases.

With about an hour to go, I read over the notes I had taken to McGinley. He agreed they were accurate and he signed them. We took him from the interview room to the custody officer, his property was returned to him and he was released from custody at 9.45 p.m. Later that night I updated the DPP on the case. It would be some time before the files were completed and sent to the director's office, but I already knew how they would conclude. McGinley had abused the trust given to him in his position as a primary schoolteacher, molesting children at will in his classroom on a daily basis. There were clear patterns and similarities in ten statements of complaint from his former pupils, even though the victims were of different ages as the abuse was spread over two decades. On top of that there was the well-documented complaint from *Craig Thompson*. In some cases there was corroboration from independent witnesses, and although McGinley tried at every opportunity to downplay what he did, he had admitted when we

questioned him to sexually abusing at least some of his victims. I was
determined for their sake that he would face the full rigours of the
law. My report would end with a recommendation to prosecute him.

Chapter 33
Guilty

'Father Eugene Greene, 71, was sentenced to twelve years in prison after pleading guilty to sexually abusing altar boys. He admitted to more than forty charges of indecent assault, buggery and gross indecency in Donegal, Ireland. Most of the offences took place between 1965 and 1982.'

The brief three-line report went out on the Reuters news wire service on 6 April 2000. Behind it lay months of delays, adjournments and legal applications. Greene had pleaded guilty to forty sample charges out of a total of 115 originally brought by the DPP.

John Reilly had already been sentenced to twelve years in July 1999, after pleading guilty to forty-one sample charges of sexual assault, indecent assault, buggery and acts of gross indecency covering the years between 1980 and 1995. Among the victims were two sets of brothers. Unlike Greene and McGinley, the farmer from west Donegal was never named in open court. His identity was shielded in order to protect the identities of his victims. I had learned about him almost by accident when *Trevor Moore* decided to come to me about what had happened to him at *Reilly*'s hands. Apart from dealing with *Trevor Moore*, I had little to do with *Reilly*'s prosecution, but John Dooley was deeply involved in the case and did an incredible amount of work to make sure that the state prosecutor was able to bring in a successful verdict. As I write in the spring of 2008, *Reilly* is still in jail, a tribute to the Trojan work that Dooley, Gerry Curran, David Moore and other Gardaí put into these cases.

The DPP decided early on not to prosecute *David Brennan* for blackmail. Since he had suffered so much at Greene's hands, and given that he never followed up on his half-hearted demands by showing up to collect the money, it was a humane decision and it allowed us to focus on the real criminal, but it still took some time for the legal system to finally convict Greene. Statements had to be clarified before the director's office was happy to go ahead, and then the usual delays began as legal teams exchanged papers, arguing about the details of the case, and psychiatric evaluations were arranged and then they too were argued over. Finally the victims were given their day in court when Greene decided to plead guilty to forty-one sample charges in December 1999.

There was still one more step in the legal process. The judge accepted the plea and adjourned the court until April 2000. Before a judge passes sentence he has to hear evidence. A guilty plea means there is no trial before a jury since there is no need for one. The charges are not denied. But the evidence we collected still has to be presented to the judge in court. Then barristers for both the State and the guilty person argue before the judge about what sentence he should impose. Dooley as the lead investigator had to formally detail the allegations against Greene for the record that April morning in the cramped, drab courthouse in Donegal town. It took him three and a half hours.

Dooley's professionalism shone through in the preparation of the investigation file for the DPP. After she had completed the case file, when everything was checked and double checked and we were satisfied that all the charges were in order for the trial, Liz Howlin, the professional officer in the director's office who dealt with Greene's case, wrote in September 1999: 'The Guards should be complimented on the preparation of this file and their subsequent reports.' The compliment was endorsed and relayed to us through the State solicitor's office and was deeply appreciated by all of us, particularly John.

Those forty-one sample charges of course only scratched the surface of what had happened. The DPP had eventually settled on a total of 115 charges. Both the director's office and we as investigators knew there were far more that 115 incidents. Based solely on the statements we had collected there were over two hundred child rapes on file. But the DPP runs a cautious office and runs only with the cases where the hardest evidence exists, though all the cases were equally serious. This is something that I think is never properly explained to the general public. People hear 115 charges, and they think that's all there is to it. People hear forty-one and can too easily assume there was nothing to the remaining charges. What happens is, the abuser pleads guilty in what is known as a bargaining plea. Sample charges are taken from the file to give an overall picture of what he is pleading guilty to. Everyone in the courtroom knew that Greene was guilty of far more than the forty-one offences Dooley detailed, far more even than the 115 crimes he had originally been charged with.

The accounts written in this book of the sexual abuse Greene inflicted on his victims during his career as a serial rapist are deliberately restrained. Dooley did not have the luxury of editing what happened when he gave his evidence before Judge Matthew Deery. Acts of unbelievable depravity had to be outlined precisely so that the judge knew exactly what it was Greene was admitting he had done. At one point a young female reporter became physically sick. Judge Deery himself was forced later in the morning to adjourn for twenty minutes to compose himself as depravity piled on depravity. I can only imagine how difficult it was for the victims who showed up to see Greene sentenced, and for their mothers. No one could be anything but shaken to the very core listening to the gruesome stories John had to describe, spanning more than three decades. I felt as if I was frozen. I felt the tears inside but I couldn't cry. Having to revisit the horrors his victims had endured, while some of them sat near by, made me feel contaminated, as if the poison was spreading out across the small courtroom while John read account after sordid account. It was difficult to believe this could happen. This was a horror story beyond invention, a total degradation of human dignity and innocence.

Dooley went through the victims one by one, detailing their pain and the attempts that were made to stop Greene, as when the *Kennedy* family complained about him to Fr Hugh Bonnar. Yet despite canon law regulations that demanded the reporting of allegations of sexual abuse, Dooley had to tell the court that the diocese had no records on file. That evening RTÉ News reported that Bishop Philip Boyce, who took up the position of Bishop of Raphoe in the mid-nineties, apologised to the victims and said he shared with them the sense of betrayal of a sacred trust. He said 'his door was open to help them in any way he could'.

Some time later his predecessor Bishop Seamus Hegarty, when asked by a BBC reporter if the Catholic Church handled Eugene Greene 'appropriately' over the years, replied: 'Oh yes. Absolutely, absolutely. He had a problem all right and that was handled very professionally, very responsibly, and ah there is evidence to that effect there.' Yet the evidence was that complaints had been ignored and apparently never even brought to the attention of the bishop's office, despite what Church law demanded. The evidence was that Greene was moved from parish to parish throughout his career, where he was able to assault and rape children at will. If that was success, I dread to think what failure looks like.

Listening to Hegarty and Boyce, I wondered if these prelates of the Church, with their silks and mitres and croziers and the ornaments of spiritual and temporal power, had any real idea of the terror that went on during their watch. Their words sounded hollow; they seemed to have no real empathy for their victims, just cold calculated remarks softly spoken and easy on the ear but meaningless. Hegarty's insistence that Greene was 'handled very professionally, very responsibly' was the most arrogant and ill-informed comment I could think of in circumstances where children were stripped of their dignity, a basic tool of psychological survival. Some, I knew, had not survived. They had taken their lives because they could no longer deal with the pain. The rest were horrifically damaged, carrying mental scars that would never fully heal. Boyce issued his apology to the media the day Greene was sentenced, but he did not show up in the court to apologise in person or speak to the priest's victims or think to send a representative to do so on his behalf. In April 2002 his office confirmed that the Church had reached out of court settlements with three of Greene's twenty-six known victims. In a statement afterwards a spokesman for the bishop could not confirm if there were any plans to extend the package to all the victims affected. But while Dooley read through the evidence, the caring Church was nowhere to be seen in that courtroom, although they had had four months' notice and knew he had pleaded guilty.

When Dooley finished his evidence, two of his victims addressed the court, expressing on behalf of all those that Greene had abused their pain and betrayal. One broke down as he spoke, saying he 'hoped the priest would be put away for life, because his actions had already put him through a life sentence'. The mother of one of the victims also spoke. Listening to her was harrowing as she described how as a mother she wakened her son in the mornings so that he would be on time for morning Mass where he served as an altar boy. She spoke of the betrayal she felt years later when she found out that, unknown to her, her son was horrifically abused by the priest, someone she trusted without question. She also spoke of dealing with her own guilt, how she felt somehow responsible for having put her child in danger. It was difficult to listen to, though nowhere near as difficult as it was for her to describe her own grief, the raw pain and emotions of a mother who felt she had lost a son.

Greene sat quietly, saying nothing. His barrister read a letter from the disgraced priest expressing remorse and pleading with the judge that 'his judgment be tempered by mercy' on the grounds of his advanced age.

Sentencing Greene to twelve years, one of the longest ever handed out to a paedophile in Ireland, Judge Matthew Deery noted that some of the priest's victims had turned to drink to try and erase the pain of their childhood abuse, which he described as 'horrific'. Greene later went to the Court of Criminal Appeal to try to have his sentence reduced on the grounds of his advanced age and a drink problem, but his appeal was dismissed. He is still in prison.

Chapter 34
Shane

John Dooley's evidence in court successfully put Eugene Greene away for a long time. I could see the relief on the faces of his victims and their families afterwards, but I still could not help but think of the young men we had not been able to help.

Shane was one of those young men. I first met him shortly after I moved back to Donegal, a pleasant young man, well groomed and neatly turned out. His quiet manner and his friendliness caught my attention when I got talking to him. He impressed me as a man who could go places and I wondered that his talents were not being put to better use, somewhere where his skill in dealing with people and his natural kindness would benefit him. Nothing unusual stuck in my mind about the meeting, no signal that he might be carrying any pain inside.

A few years later when I was assigned to look into the allegations being made against Greene, I came across *Shane* again. Drink had taken over his life; he was in its grip. I had dealt with the same demons myself; I recognised the signs. During my work on night patrol, I often found him wandering around the streets late at night. When things got quiet I would drive him home, though Guards weren't supposed to do that. Some nights he came looking for me at the station, hoping for a lift. While I was afraid he might make a habit of it and land me in trouble with a sergeant or an inspector who might call on a late night check, I left him home for his own safety.

On one of those late night runs, he told me that he knew what I was investigating. He didn't have to say anything else. There was only one investigation that people didn't speak of by name. He was drunk, very drunk, but he told me he was abused as a young boy. I sat talking with him in the car outside his home. I told him I could take a statement from him, that I could set up counselling to help him deal with what happened and with his drinking, but that I could only talk to him about it when he was sober. If I took a statement from him while he was drunk, a barrister would tear him to shreds. He agreed to talk to me when he sobered up.

The next time I met him there was no way I could take a statement. He was drunk again, and we were in a public place, not somewhere I would want to be while writing up a statement, never mind one about something as serious as sexual abuse. He talked about leaving, as many others had done, disappearing to the anonymity of a foreign city. In a haze he spoke to me, giving me half jumbled details of the abuse he suffered. I could only listen and hope he would sober up another day.

Later, after the arrest and trial made Greene a public figure, *Shane*'s mother came to me, worried about his condition. She knew her son had spent time with Greene. I could listen but there was not much more I could do. I spoke to her three or four times on the phone and called to her home. She told me that Greene often took *Shane* away with him in his car on the pretence of going to Letterkenny on a shopping trip. Dooley and I decided to call out to see *Shane* early one evening before he escaped to the pub. We talked to him again, but he was a wreck. He could barely find the words to describe what had happened to him, his wounds were still too raw. We left in the hope that someday he would find the words. *Shane* carried too much pain. It held him back and dragged him deeper into alcohol. He told me it was too hard to deal with in Donegal. 'I'll feck off to Amsterdam and get work in a pub, get away from it all,' he said. His chronic addiction continued, and eventually he took his own life. He was still a young man when he died. Official statistics count him as a suicide. I know he was one of Greene's victims.

It was harrowing to see that young man in a coffin. I felt powerless. *Shane*'s funeral was one of the hardest days of my life. Knowing what I knew about him ate at my gut, the kind of hurt that is hard to describe. The hurt nagged at me, asking me if I could have done more. I knew it wasn't true, but the feeling gnawed at me none the less. I couldn't force him to sober up; he had to reach that decision himself. Until he did, a statement would have been a weapon a barrister would use against him, if the DPP even decided to use it. What *Shane* had told me about his abuse was appalling, but it was rambling and disjointed.

His family were devastated. A young priest said the Mass, gave a good sermon and spoke about the scourge of alcoholism. I wondered did he know what really happened to *Shane*, what had driven him to drink. I decided he probably didn't. He seemed a decent young priest. I could give him the benefit of the doubt that my experience in this investigation made me hold back with others.

As I sat listening to the sermon trying to control my emotions, I wanted to stand up and shout, where is the truth in all of this? Why is it always hidden? Why can't we deal with it? But that young priest probably just did not know the truth. I would do more damage by blaming everybody in a clerical collar just because they wore a collar. Not all the compassionate sermons I had to listen to were as sincere as the one this young man gave. There were people in the Church who did know about paedophiles like Greene, but it was better to keep it hidden as far as they were concerned. They hid dark secrets that the Church would do its best to protect while we struggled to open the vaults to the bright light of day. Greene wasn't the only priest in this diocese to abuse the children in his care, and Raphoe wasn't the only diocese in Ireland where paedophile priests were able to shelter in the protective arms of Mother Church. Nor was Ireland the only country where the Church stood indicted for its handling of child sexual abuse. The old common law used to define a death as a murder if it happened within a year and a day of an injury. Greene stole his victims' lives, but they took a long time to die. *Shane* wasn't the only victim I learned about who paid the ultimate price.

A few months before *Shane* took his life, a young woman called to my home. She broke down and cried as she told me that her brother had committed suicide in England, overdosing himself on drugs. Greene had befriended him, and had often taken him for rides in his car, she told me. She said that McGinley also took him on car rides, picking him up and driving him home many a time. She was still devastated by her loss although her brother had died several years earlier before we had begun our investigation. She was certain her brother had been a victim of sexual abuse, possibly a double victim. 'He was always away with Greene and with McGinley,' she told me. 'They were two paedophiles. Is there anything you can do?'

I wasn't optimistic. 'I don't want to get your hopes up,' I told her. 'I'll check with my authorities, but we have no statement from him.' She didn't want to make a statement. There was no point. All she needed was closure, an explanation from Greene or McGinley that would explain why her brother took his life. I had to explain that there was little I thought we could do, though I passed it on to the super-intendent's office. There was nothing else I could do for her.

One of McGinley's victims told me that he also had lost a brother. It was never quite clear how he died. It might have been an accident; it might have been suicide. Although he never told me so directly, I always got the sense talking to him that he felt his brother had killed himself, and had been abused just as he was.

There were others. One young man tried to hang himself, but for-tunately he didn't succeed. He still struggles with drug addiction. Dooley was able to tell me similar stories of young men who tried and sometimes succeeded in taking their lives, young men whose names he already knew since we began investigating men like Greene, McGinley and *Reilly*.

We found ten pupils McGinley had sexually abused. His eleventh victim, *Craig Thompson*, he met while working with the local youth club. Incredibly when pleading with the judge to show mercy at his trial, McGinley's barrister was instructed to cite the good work he did for the community through charity work and youth club activities. Paedophiles follow patterns, I knew. The statements we had collected against Greene and McGinley, showing the same patterns with victim after victim in different parishes and decades, were proof of that. I doubted *Craig Thompson* was the only young boy McGinley targeted at the youth club. I doubted he began his abuse when he arrived in Gort an Choirce. He was already halfway through his teach-ing career by then. How many others were there? McGinley was on a committee for a local summer college teaching students the Irish language in the Gaeltacht for the Leaving Certificate. Had young boys been scarred for life as they studied their heritage in the Gaeltacht, I wondered. Whatever chance we had of tracking down his victims in the Donegal parishes where he taught, there was no way we could research the hundreds of teenagers who travelled to Donegal every summer to improve their language skills.

It could have been stopped. It should have been stopped. There were reports about McGinley and Greene going back to the seventies. All it took was for someone in authority to listen. But no one did. No one spoke to the victims, and no one spoke out for the victims. They had no voice.

Chapter 35

Would You Investigate Your Own?

It was a quiet Saturday morning, barely gone half ten, sometime between Eugene Greene's arrest and his first court appearance. The house was quiet. My wife Bríd was enjoying a late lie-in, taking advantage of her day off after a busy week at school. The two girls Aoife and Cliodhna were sleeping in too, dead to the world after a late night disco. Nothing much was moving. The valleys and mountains were as peaceful looking as ever. I was pottering around the kitchen; my shift didn't start until late afternoon. I saw a car coming in the driveway and recognised it. I didn't know quite what to think; it was Greene's brother. I wondered what he wanted. I half expected a barracking as I opened the door.

'Hello Martin,' he said simply, unsure of what else to say in the circumstances. 'Can I come in?'

I invited him in and sat him down. Eugene Greene was in Galway, I knew, spending some time in a spiritual retreat or getting counselling; I wasn't sure exactly what.

'It's terrible, Martin. I can't believe it. When I heard about this, I had to drive down to Galway to find out for myself, to see Eugene. I wanted to know about this,' he told me. 'He told me it was true. I want to apologise to you for putting you through all this.'

I told him he had no reason to apologise. I understood he was also hurt. We sat and talked for a while, although mostly he talked and I listened. He was honest with me, devastated with what was happening. Greene's family were victims too, I realised, dealing with their own shame. His openness was a comfort and he understood I was not attacking his family. He realised this had to be investigated.

I could not understand why the Church could not be as honest as he was. When the Morris Tribunal began, we didn't think that unmasking corrupt Guards in Donegal would bring down the entire justice system. A few paedophiles will not bring down the Church. But hiding from the problem, moving problem priests from one parish to another instead of confronting what is happening does enormous damage. But it seems truth and trust have fallen out of use in the Church vocabulary and all we are left with is spin. One priest challenged me during the preparations for Greene's trial, asking me, 'Would you investigate your own?' — as if a Guard shouldn't investigate another Guard. I wondered if that truly was his attitude. Did he believe that priests should protect other priests no matter what they did, and never mind the predators who prey on the flock under their care? I'm not happy with the things that emerged from the Carty Inquiry and the Morris Tribunal when they looked at allegations of Garda corruption, but at least Carty showed that we could investigate ourselves. And thanks to Carty and Morris and the outcry their investigations raised, we have the Garda Síochána Ombudsman Commission. Of course Guards should be investigated. No one should be above the law.

Sometime after Greene's brother came to see me, my mother grew ill and I travelled home to Galway to be with her in hospital. She had a deep and simple faith and the revelations in the nineties about clerical child abuse had hurt her deeply. I think the investigation in Donegal hurt her more because her son was one of the investigators. 'Leave the priests alone,' she often told me. I knew where she was coming from. It was difficult to see her after that, it upset her so much.

When she died I was by her side. It was early morning when she slipped away. She had done so much for me, for all of us, raising us virtually single-handed for much of the time. I couldn't stop thinking of the last time we spoke, how much it had hurt her that I wouldn't 'leave the priests alone'. She must have felt I was attacking the entire Church and every priest she had ever known. Nothing was further from the truth. I had a very happy childhood and the priests in my area were great people who visited our home frequently. They were involved in every community activity and I honed my social skills as a boy because of them, mixing with others at football matches and drama groups they organised. I was an altar boy myself and I thought very highly of them.

At my mother's funeral I met a priest and spoke to him. I told him I hadn't been close to my mother at the end. 'I happen to be investigating some of you guys,' I explained. 'The last time I spoke to that woman, she ate me.' I told him I would understand if he didn't want to talk to me, given what I was doing.

'Don't ever apologise to anyone for your work,' he said to me. 'God sent you there to do that work.' It was a great relief that he understood. He lifted a great weight off my mind. I got talking to him some more. He was a 'late joiner'. He had worked in the music industry before finding his vocation. As a priest he had worked in an addiction centre in the States but was now ministering in Ireland.

There were other priests of course who were deeply troubled by the revelations about clerical sexual abuse. At the end of the week in late 2005 when the government announced an inquiry into clerical child abuse in the Dublin diocese following the publication of the Ferns Report, Letterkenny-based priest Eamonn Kelly was moved to say that while many had described the week as a black week for the Catholic Church, the black times were when the crimes were being committed against innocent children.

Local newspapers reported how he told his congregation that 'the black time was when innocence was stolen, when the confidence was robbed and when fear was instilled into wee hearts that should have remained free'. The curate said he was devastated with all that had happened and had questioned if he had chosen the right vocation.

'Most of my life I was a barman, for some years over at home and for a good number of years I worked in the bar trade in Dublin,' he said. 'Over the past week at different times, especially at night, I found myself wondering about my decision to become a priest. If I could decide again, I wondered, would I come forward for priesthood or would I remain behind the counter. And it would be tempting to go behind that counter again when I feel the disgust in my core for what has happened, or when I cringe in shame as I hear a survivor of abuse tell his or her story or when I see the tears of someone struggling to rebuild a devastated life.'

Perhaps the fact that both these priests were late vocations is significant. Having worked for a while rather than going straight from school to a seminary may have broadened their minds and made them a little more willing to speak out.

Despite how disillusioned I often felt with the Catholic Church, my own personal faith is still very important to me. Too many of Greene's priestly colleagues in Donegal were ready to look down on me for scandalising the Church. What upset me were the priests who stayed quiet about what we uncovered. It was good to know the priesthood still attracted such decent men as that priest in Galway and his colleague in Letterkenny.

Chapter 36
The Tip-Off

The most shocking event during Denis McGinley's arrest was not his casual, almost dismissive attitude when we first questioned him about his multiple acts of sexual abuse, or his continued efforts to make little of what he had done as he began to concede the seriousness of the charges he was facing. What really shook us was that he had been tipped off about the investigation.

Fr Hugh Sweeney had gone to McGinley on 30 January 2000, two weeks before his arrest, the teacher told us in custody, and effectively told him to leave the jurisdiction. 'He called me out to his car and said something to the effect that Fr Greene did wrong and that he had his chance to get lost and that he didn't, but you can't do that because of your mother,' McGinley had told us. He told us the news filled him with anxiety so that he was unable to sleep, and how relieved he felt when we showed up sixteen days later. He said he had written to Sweeney but had received no reply.

Sweeney was no longer stationed in Gort an Choirce in 2000. He had been transferred some years before and was now parish priest of Cloghan in Lifford. A native of An Fál Carrach, he frequently stayed in a holiday home he owned in the area. The towns of An Fál Carrach and Gort an Choirce are less than fifteen minutes apart. Sweeney had served as curate in Gort an Choirce during the eighties and was the curate the *Thompson* family approached when they learned about McGinley's relationship with their son. The *Thompsons* had expected Sweeney to tell his parish priest what was happening, and were surprised when McGinley was still teaching in the local national school the following September.

To corroborate the *Thompsons'* account, we had taken a statement from Sweeney. He contradicted flatly what *Rose* and *Art Thompson* said, and he denied he ever saw any letters written by McGinley that the *Thompson* family said they showed him or was told anything about a problem with McGinley.

At the time we didn't follow up on what Sweeney said. Statements from *Craig*'s parents, a close family friend *Dermot Hogan*, and a local car dealer all corroborated key elements of the allegations made against McGinley. At one point we spoke to the school principal at the time, John Gallagher, about *Craig* and other cases. He didn't want to make a formal statement but told us that he never received any complaints about McGinley. We had warned each person we approached for supporting statements that our investigation was confidential and should not be discussed with anyone. Our fear was that a loose word would get back to McGinley. We never dreamed that any of them would actually tell him he was under investigation. With that one ill-considered visit, Sweeney had jeopardised months of police work. McGinley, forearmed, had the opportunity to destroy incriminating evidence or even to flee the jurisdiction. Worse, he claimed Sweeney had advised him to do as much. What Sweeney did was potentially a criminal act, anything from obstructing a Garda in the course of his duty to conspiracy to pervert the course of justice. We knew we had to speak to Sweeney again, this time to take a cautioned statement.

There is a difference between a witness statement and a cautioned statement. Both begin with a standard formula, where the person making the statement declares what they say is the truth and 'if it is tendered in evidence I will be liable to prosecution if I state anything in it which I know to be false or do not believe to be true'. However the same Judges' Rules put in place to protect prisoners under arrest so that they have to be warned each time they are interviewed that they have a right not to incriminate themselves — the right to silence — and don't have to say anything, also cover suspects who might be arrested later. If a witness is a potential suspect, and I feel that they might be arrested at some point in the future, then as a Garda I can't take any statement without first warning them that they have a right to silence.

When Dooley and I went to see Sweeney for the second time, at his holiday home in An Fál Carrach, we knew he was a potential suspect in a criminal investigation. He could be charged with any of several crimes including obstruction. This time it wasn't simply a witness statement we were looking for. Before we wrote anything down, I cautioned him on his right to silence, that he 'was not obliged to say anything, but that anything he did say would be taken down in writing and could be given in evidence'. To an ordinary member of the public, the difference between the caution and the standard formula in witness statements might seem trivial. To a court, it made all the difference in the world.

Sweeney had denied point blank that he had any memory of being told by *Rose* and *Art Thompson* about their son and McGinley the first time we interviewed him, and said he could not recall being shown letters that McGinley had written. I suppose I expected him to say there was nothing to McGinley's claim either, especially since he had been formally cautioned. Instead, he confirmed that he had called to McGinley's home two weeks before the teacher was arrested. He told us he went to see the teacher because he was concerned about McGinley's sister's health and about their aged mother who 'obviously needed calm and peace'.

He said he confronted McGinley and asked him if there might be any reason for him to be concerned or worried about abusing boys. McGinley denied he had ever done any such thing. 'So then I told him that I had good reason to believe that the Gardaí were investigating allegations of this nature about him,' Sweeney told us. 'I went on to suggest that he should get away or get out of the family home if there was going to be an investigation on him in order to keep the attention away from his sister and his mother. I tried to suggest that if Fr Greene was in a different jurisdiction, the impact on his immediate family would have lessened, in other words that the impact on his immediate family now would be much less severe and painful if he moved himself somewhere else, but he told me that this situation could never arise as he was totally innocent, on which note we parted. He subsequently wrote me a letter confirming his total innocence in this matter. My primary concern would be for calm in the family home and should he be guilty of assaulting young boys, distancing him from the family home at this time and allowing due process of law to proceed would give those at home at least shelter and avoid immediate exposure to whatever appropriate legal procedures would be taken against him.'

I was stunned. Sweeney had as much as admitted to us that he had advised a suspected paedophile to leave the jurisdiction. Apparently he did this because he was worried about McGinley's sister and elderly mother. I wondered how he thought telling McGinley to go somewhere that the Gardaí were powerless to follow and arrest him was consistent with 'allowing due process of law to proceed'. Even if McGinley had left Ireland, we would have tried to extradite him. The local and national newspapers — even the international media —

would blare out the headline: 'Irish Police Extradite Paedophile.' It didn't sound like a good way to 'give those at home at least shelter and avoid immediate exposure to whatever appropriate legal procedures would be taken against him'.

Sweeney's statement was added to the growing file of papers in my study at home as I worked to type everything up, preparing the report for the DPP on the computer. I felt very strongly about what Sweeney had done. I felt there was a question to be answered. Perhaps Sweeney should be charged with interfering with a criminal investigation. After summarising the sorry episode in the report, I wrote: 'Fr Sweeney's actions were inexcusable and amounted to interfering in a criminal investigation. When interviewed as a witness in this case regarding letters shown to him by Mrs *Rose Thompson* he stated that he had no recollection of seeing them, which is difficult to believe. If Fr Sweeney's action amounted to a criminal act, I recommend that he be prosecuted accordingly.'

Sweeney is a controversial character, to say the least. He made the British tabloid newspaper headlines in January 2007 when the *Daily Mirror* reported how he urged Mass-goers to pray for deposed Iraqi president Saddam Hussein, including him in the list of the dead to be remembered in the prayers of the faithful at his church days after he was sent to the gallows. In 2004 he was named publicly as a tax cheat, one of 180 defaulters who reached a settlement with the Revenue Commissioners. Sweeney agreed to pay a total of €125,792 to the tax man because he was the holder of a bogus non-resident bank account. Clearly he hadn't read Our Lord's advice to the Pharisees to render unto Caesar that which is Caesar's.

The DPP never got back to me with a decision on whether to charge Sweeney with obstruction of justice. In the various letters I received from the State solicitor's office, it was never mentioned one way or the other. I never heard anything from the super's office either. Looking back, perhaps those few paragraphs about Sweeney were buried in the larger dossier on McGinley and I might have been better off preparing a separate file on him, but at the time the seriousness of what he had done stood out like a sore thumb as far as I was concerned. I did lay out the facts of the case in the McGinley file, but I can't help wondering if I should have been more forceful.

All I know for sure is that to the best of my knowledge no recommendation was ever made by the office of the DPP either to prosecute or not to prosecute Sweeney, up until the day I retired three years after I sent in the file. I don't know what decision they finally reached, or when.

Chapter 37

When is it Going to Court?

The completed investigation file on Denis McGinley along with my recommendation to bring criminal charges went up to the super's office a few months after his arrest, and all I could do was wait. It was a long wait. Before it goes to the DPP any investigation file is reviewed by the district superintendent, who checks that everything is done properly. It's a check to reduce the workload at the director's office. Files often come back to the investigating Garda with requests for another statement to clear up an ambiguity, or a report on forensics, something the original investigator may have overlooked but a fresh pair of eyes can see.

Kevin Lennon was my super at the time. Lennon had a particular reputation as a stickler for detail. He had the kind of mind that could recall at will the section and subparagraph of any Act in the criminal code while most of us had to look it up. But Lennon's mind wasn't on the job. He was distracted by the Carty Inquiry, and the investigation file sat on his desk for several weeks. Then at the end of July 2001 the Carty Report was delivered to the Garda commissioner. His response was to transfer five senior officers out of Donegal, among them Lennon, my super in Milford. Meanwhile I was listed as the lead investigator on the McGinley case by the computers in the director's office, and as deadlines passed after the arrest, the computers began spitting out requests for more information, asking when they would receive the finished files. Computers don't think; they send out letters automatically until they get answers. I didn't pay too much heed at first. There were always delays and the computer deadlines were hopelessly optimistic anyway. I don't think I ever completed a case before the computer wrote to me. Every now and then the computers in Garda HQ did the same thing. As far as I was concerned, the file was in the super's office, he would review it, then it would go to Dublin. It wasn't my problem for the moment, and wouldn't be until I got a recommendation to prosecute from the director. There was other work to do.

It had been a long day at work and I felt exhausted mentally and physically. I was working on my own, the only Garda on duty. It began with paperwork, as the day often does, processing about 300 dole forms, and I had to deal with a sudden death in the area. When I got back to the station, the phone never seemed to stop ringing, and in the evening I had to go down to the morgue. I was tired and hungry; I hadn't even had a chance to grab a cup of tea or a slice of toast all day. And there it was when I stopped by the station, another letter from a computer asking me about the McGinley investigation file. I would have ignored it, but it was forwarded to me from the super's office. But I had already sent the file up to the super's office. What the hell is going on? I wondered. Does the left hand even know what the right hand is doing?

I had to head out to the morgue in Letterkenny General Hospital, but I decided that on the way back I would swing by the district office in Milford and sort it out with the new super. The frustration and annoyance ate at me on the round trip to Letterkenny. I arrived at the super's office late in the afternoon. I went in like a bull, throwing the letter on the desk. It was not the most professional moment of my career.

'What do you mean,' I demanded, 'sending me out stuff? I have sent this file in to you. You've had it up here for the last few months.'

'What are you talking about?' he said. 'I haven't seen it.'

'How can you not have seen it?' I asked him. 'I sent it to you. I've been waiting for your reply. You signed this out to me, didn't you?' I asked, picking up the letter again. The anger took over, the frustrations I couldn't let out anywhere else. I raged at how long everything took, how everything meant another delay while victims and their families wondered what was happening and were being told nothing, how no one seemed to care about young children being abused in west Donegal. He promised to get the file taken care of, but by then I was only half listening.

When the files eventually came back to me from the DPP, the director went along with my recommendation to prosecute McGinley. I had never really expected that they wouldn't, but you never know with these things. Looking through the paperwork, I noticed that

Kevin Lennon's signature was on the covering letter sent in to the director along with my report. No wonder my new super hadn't known what I was talking about when I stormed into his office, I realised. Lennon had probably taken the file with him when he left Donegal and it had been on his desk until he signed off on it and sent it to the director.

———

An Garda Síochána runs an in-house peer support and welfare system designed to deal with officers traumatised by the job. Pretty much every officer takes advantage of it at some point. There's just too much of the dark side that we have to deal with in the job, from fatal car collisions and suicides to dealing with victims of crime who are themselves traumatised. A few days after I went to see the super, a Garda welfare officer called out to see me. I guess the super had contacted him after I left his office in a rage. The welfare officer told me he had arranged for me to go to headquarters to see a medical officer there.

Eventually the file was reviewed and went up to Dublin to the DPP, where it was reviewed again. As usual there were requests for more clarifications, statements from Guards and witnesses that required more detail and the need to expand on something we had covered in only a couple of sentences the first time round.

I took care of it, along with everything else that was going on. There was a sudden death to deal with and a fatal road collision as well as everyday routine policing duties. The road collision investigation had two teams working on it, ourselves and one from the district HQ in Milford. I couldn't help noticing the difference in available resources compared to what we had to investigate paedophiles. Statements had to be taken from eye witnesses, staff in the accident and emergency ward in Letterkenny General Hospital and the ambulance drivers. There's a lot of informal specialisation in the Guards. Some officers get a reputation for being particularly gifted in report writing. Almost every file they send in comes back with a recommendation to prosecute. Some do better on particular kinds of cases, robbery or fraud, drugs or intelligence gathering. Somehow the word had gone around that I was good on statement gathering. I tended to get everything right the first time more than most and there were fewer call backs. I became the statement specialist, so a lot of that work was sent my way. A good reputation for some particular aspect of your work isn't always a good thing to have. More jobs come your way as a result and the work seemed to pile up. At times I felt I hadn't enough time to work on the McGinley case. At other times it was good to have the distraction.

Meanwhile the victims and their families, particularly the mothers, kept in touch with me. There was no Garda liaison officer to keep them up to date with what was happening — or often, it seemed, what wasn't happening. I was the familiar face they knew, the Garda who had spoken to them, taken their statements, helped in some instances to set up professional counselling with the health board, so by default I became the liaison officer. I had only dealt with one of *Reilly's* victims, but somehow through the grapevines and informal networks by which word always seems to spread to whoever needs to know in Donegal, several of the mothers of his victims had been in touch with me too.

While legal and Garda paperwork was passed back and forth, those mothers were busy dealing with what they had learned as a result of the investigation. Support groups had been set up. I got regular calls from them asking what was happening. When is it going to court? Or if a meeting was organised I would get a call. 'It starts at 8 p.m. Would you like to come? We would like you to be there.' Always it was the mothers who called; I never saw the fathers. It was always the mothers who needed to talk.

I went to a few of the meetings, but after a while I had to stop. I knew too much. I would sit there listening as they spoke, looking across at others who just listened. There were too many details in my head, things I was told in confidence, things that sometimes didn't make it into statements, things I wasn't sure I could talk about even if I wanted to. Eventually I had to stop going.

McGinley was in counselling. He had been referred to cosc, a community-based sexual abuse treatment and prevention service organised by the North Western Health Board for sex offenders, but it wasn't going well. The reports to the court during his trial were not encouraging. He had attended some day sessions but had made only 'limited progress', and as a prerequisite to attending the group he was required to make a statement to the Gardaí, which he hadn't done.

Chapter 38
A Good Teacher

Eventually every file was completed, reviewed, amended, clarified, approved and stamped. We got our direction from the DPP and I arrested Denis McGinley for the second time just after 9 a.m. on 22 November 2000. I explained the reason for his arrest, read him his rights and explained that anything he said would be taken down in writing. 'I understand,' he answered. Dooley and I took him to the Garda station at An Fál Carrach where, after booking him, I went through the individual charges again cautioning him each time. To each charge his answer was an emotionless 'I have nothing to say.' There were a lot of charges so it took some time. From there we went to the District Court, where I gave evidence to Judge O'Donnell of what had happened that morning, again going through each charge, each caution, each reply, or rather each non-response.

McGinley sat subdued in court, his solicitor speaking on his behalf. Through his solicitor he applied for and was granted free legal aid, though he had worked throughout his career in teaching and had a generous pension. No one objected to this. Nothing of note happened as the court went through the standard procedures while he sat in silence listening to the evidence. He was then remanded on bail with independent sureties to a further sitting. The book of evidence could now be prepared and witnesses' orders made out for the victims and others who might testify at his trial.

The arrest barely caused a ripple in the national news headlines. Taxi drivers were protesting against deregulation in Dublin that day. A young RTÉ broadcaster, Uaneen Fitzsimons, was killed in a car accident, and the world was watching in fascination as George W. Bush went to the Supreme Court to overturn a Florida court decision to include manually recounted ballots in the US presidential election count. Everyone had an opinion on hanging chads and who would be the next president of the United States. *The Irish Times* reported briefly: 'A west Donegal man has been charged with 115 counts of sexual assault. The man, who cannot be named, is alleged to have committed the offences between 1978 and 1995. He was remanded to Glenties District Court.'

McGinley was back in court several times as the book of evidence was served on him, and on 26 September 2001 he was sent forward for trial in Letterkenny Circuit Court on 2 October 2001. I was there for the hearing, as were some of his victims and their families. We didn't expect much from the hearing, which was held to fix a date on the court schedule, and were shocked when one of the barristers for the prosecution team told the judge that the State intended to withdraw several charges. No explanation was given for the decision. I was shocked too. I wondered if I had done something wrong in preparing the files. While the barrister went on speaking I checked through my files, looking up the charge numbers she had struck off. The charges against *Dylan Murphy* and *Lee Nolan* were not going ahead. Every charge after 1984 had been ruled out. I looked over at the families. It was clear they didn't know this was coming any more than I did.

Dylan Murphy and *Lee Nolan* were still minors when I interviewed them and took their statements. *Dylan*'s case was one of the best documented in the book of evidence with records from the health board and statements confirming that his mother had made a complaint at the time. Ruling out those charges gave the misleading impression that McGinley's abuse was something from his past, something confined to a period in the late seventies and early eighties. I knew the abuse had gone on for years, almost until the day we began to investigate. Those cases proved it had, yet they were being deleted by an announcement from the State solicitor's office: 'I wish to withdraw charges numbers . . .'

Afterwards I caught up with the barrister and asked her what the problem was. Was it something to do with minor technical errors, some sort of confusion or a clerical mix-up in the office of the DPP? 'Ah, sure there's enough there to convict him anyhow,' she told me. Again I felt frustrated. What was I supposed to tell the victims and their families? The State never consulted anybody, never told us this was going to happen, never even sat down to explain that there was a technical error of some sort, that perhaps if the charges went ahead it might put a chance of any conviction at risk. I can see how solicitors and barristers have to remain objective, prevent their emotions from swaying their judgment, but the other side of that professionalism is a family sitting in court suddenly learning that the man who abused their son would not answer for that crime. Unless the State went ahead with those charges for the crimes committed against the two minors, they would not show that McGinley's abuse had continued for decades. A minor technical mistake could be fixed. Withdrawing the charges didn't have to be the end of it. New charges could be drafted properly. I couldn't help but feel that someone in an office somewhere saw it as just paperwork cluttering up their desk and couldn't be bothered to reintroduce the charges.

I was also worried that because McGinley was initially arrested for sexually abusing *Dylan Murphy*, and all those charges had now been withdrawn, the whole case could be put in jeopardy. A defence barrister could later argue that because there was no case against his client for what he was arrested for, therefore he had no case to answer at all since the arrest or any questions he was asked after it were somehow faulty.

The senior counsel could have had a field day at the trial. What was my client arrested for Guard? he would ask me.

Sexually abusing *Dylan Murphy*, I'd have to answer.

But Guard, I see no case here in front of me in relation to *Dylan Murphy*.

I would have no reply. I would have to stand there in the witness box looking like the stereotypical thick Guard, and after the hard work we had put into the investigation McGinley could walk out of the court a free man.

McGinley had worked in a total of seven schools in his career. Between 1959 and 1976 he worked in six different schools. From 1976 to the day he retired twenty years later he worked at his last posting in Gort an Choirce. All eleven complaints against him came from the parish of Gort an Choirce, but I had no doubt that in the other places he served as a teacher, places like Toraigh Island, Lifford, Bundoran and An Craoslach (Creeslough), he also left a trail of victims in his wake.

Shortly before I retired I met another victim, this time from Anagaire, who asked me why we hadn't investigated his school as McGinley had abused there too. I have since learned of incidents in two other schools.

McGinley's career history is suspicious. His final posting in Gort an Choirce lasted twenty years, but before that his career was disjointed

— two years here, four months there, a few years somewhere else, two very short postings, one of seven weeks and one less than a month. He was only three months in Lifford; he was barely six months in An Craoslach.

Knowing what we do now of the compulsive and repetitive patterns of child sexual abusers, the victims I had found who came forward in Gort an Choirce were unlikely to have been isolated incidents. Whilst there is no record of any allegation about him in the Department of Education, that did not mean that nothing happened in all those other places. I had to wonder why McGinley held so many teaching jobs before he finally settled in Gort an Choirce. How many more victims were there? The DPP didn't have to simply drop the charges against McGinley for what he did to *Dylan Murphy* and *Lee Nolan*. I knew they had the option to put in fresh charges properly drawn up.

I wrote up a report on what had happened for the sergeant: 'Twelve charges were withdrawn, *Lee Nolan* and *Dylan Murphy*, as apparently incorrect charges were proffered. *Dylan Murphy* was only 14 years of age when he made a witness statement. *Lee Nolan* was only 13. They were the most recent complaints against Denis McGinley. I feel the withdrawal of these charges weakens the prosecution case in that it appears that Denis McGinley did not offend since 1984 when in fact he was abusing until a short time before his retirement. Their mothers were very upset and traumatised when they learned that their sons were abused by their then teacher.'

There were times as I wrote the report when I wondered if the case would go ahead at all. First McGinley had been tipped off that we were investigating him, possibly allowing him to destroy evidence; now charges against his two youngest victims had been withdrawn. After all our efforts, would the outcome of this case boil down to a technical error without a judge or jury ever getting to hear the evidence? Technicalities have thwarted many a case over the years, for example in the Judge Brian Curtin case, where a search warrant was executed twenty-four hours too late. Surely we wouldn't suffer the same fate? Getting the paperwork right should be all it took to convict McGinley. That should be a simple matter with law officers for the State working on the case. I couldn't accept that a simple objection on some technical error would wipe out years of work and a paedophile could walk free.

I'm not sure if anyone else protested against the decision, but eventually the charges were reinstated. There were still other unknown victims out there, but at least the victims we knew about who had come forward would all have their day in court. There were more adjournments, from October to December and from there to January 2002. Finally on 7 February 2002 McGinley pleaded guilty to twenty-one sample charges out of a total of 115 brought against him and was convicted. There was one more step in the process. On 30 April 2002 I read through the details of the charges against McGinley, as Dooley had at Greene's sentencing hearing. I had spent most of the weekend writing out what I wanted to say in evidence. It ran to twenty-four handwritten foolscap pages. It took me about ninety minutes to get through it all in the witness box. Judge Matthew Deery then heard the arguments from the prosecution and defence lawyers before considering what sentence to pass. I thought I couldn't be surprised any more. I was wrong. Despite everything that came out in the court hearing, despite McGinley's guilty plea, despite the fact that when the investigation began *Lee Nolan* and *Dylan Murphy* were still minors, his latest victims in a career of abuse going back untold years, the great and the good provided character references to the court for the disgraced teacher.

Through his barrister, McGinley said he apologised for any hurt he had caused his victims. 'Unlike so many other cases, there was no real intended malice,' the barrister told the judge. Following his client's instructions, the lawyer said that his client had done good work over the years in the community, helping with the local branch of the St Vincent de Paul and at the local youth club. That particular plea for mercy took some neck, I thought to myself. It was at the local youth club that McGinley had met *Craig Thompson* as a young teenager. It was *Craig*'s decision to come forward and tell me how McGinley had raped and sexually abused him multiple times that led to the investigation that was now concluding in Letterkenny courthouse. I was reminded of the Jewish definition of the Yiddish word *chutzpah*: a man who murders his parents and then begs the court for clemency on the grounds that he is an orphan.

Judge Matthew Deery read out two glowing character references for McGinley that he had received from two priests. John McGlynn, a parish priest who presided over two paedophiles as parish priest in Gort an Choirce, his curate Greene and his teacher McGinley, wrote one of the references. Michael Sweeney, another parish priest who in 2004 was voted Donegal Person of the Year, wrote another. Apparently without irony, one of the speakers at the gala presentation dinner in Sweeney's honour said he 'had left an indelible mark on the communities he served and particularly so on young people through his great interest in football'. I wondered how the young people abused by McGinley felt that he had written in such glowing terms about their attacker.

The *Donegal News* reported that Sweeney wrote in his character reference that he 'could not imagine as kind a person such as Denis McGinley hurting anyone'. According to the report the priest added that McGinley was 'a kind, caring person and a good teacher'. I wondered if it had even registered in the priest's consciousness that this 'kind, caring person and good teacher' had pleaded guilty to sexually abusing the pupils under his care for years. It was staggering to have to listen as words of praise for a teacher who had abused the trust of parents and children were read into the court record from two school managers. Sweeney had even worked as an educator himself as headmaster of Coláiste na Croise Naofa between 1968 and 1982. He had also worked on the Diocesan College of Consultors and was a member of the vicars forane, in effect a special adviser to the Bishop of Raphoe. As Donegal Person of the Year, he was later invited into the local secondary school in An Fál Carrach to present awards to the pupils there. Some of McGinley's victims were still in school at the time and had to watch as the man who had lavished praise on their abuser was greeted as a pillar of society. I wondered what they made of that, and of the fact that nobody from the Church ever spoke up on their behalf at McGinley's trial.

McGinley had pleaded guilty in January 2002, but the sentencing arguments were not heard until April. It wasn't like there was any doubt any more. He had pleaded guilty to sexual abuse, yet still McGlynn and Sweeney felt that their duty was to give some backing to a paedophile. I wondered what the Department of Education made of it. As parish priests, these men were school managers charged with the welfare of children. Praising a paedophile's character seemed to me a dereliction of duty.

I saw something similar happen down the country with the notorious paedophile Donal Dunne, which was reported in an RTÉ *Prime Time* special about him. The former Christian Brother, who was convicted of sexually abusing two boys in different Midlands schools in the sixties and seventies, received a two year sentence in 1979. It was a familiar story. Throughout his career Dunne was moved on from school to school. Reading the Ferns Report and listening to the revelations that have come out in other court cases, it seems to be a common pattern throughout the country. Abusers were known about, yet nothing was done. They were just moved on. Paedophiles are not the only ones to exhibit repetitive and compulsive behaviour patterns. The Catholic Church does it too.

McGinley was sentenced to thirty months' imprisonment on each of the twenty-one sample charges on which he was convicted, to run concurrently. Passing sentence, Judge Deery said it had to be borne in mind that McGinley was carrying out these assaults on children of a very tender age who were very impressionable. 'The assaults were carried out on a very routine basis in front of other children,' he said. The judge also noted that when the mother of one victim did make a complaint, 'it would seem her complaints were not taken and explored the way they should have been at the time'.

That evening, as *Sandra Nolan* sat watching the report on the evening news, her son *Lee* asked her, 'What did he get?'

'Two and a half years,' she told him.

'I'll kill him when he comes out,' *Lee* said. He couldn't believe how light the sentence was.

Sandra Nolan rang me the next morning. She was crying on the phone as she told me the story of what happened the night before. 'My son shouldn't be holding so much anger,' she told me. 'Do you know who was up in McGinley's home last night? Fr Michael Sweeney called yesterday evening and stayed all night. And after dark then the local parish priest called in to support them after McGinley was sent to prison. And', she added, 'nobody came near me. Nobody called to talk to us. That finishes me from going to Mass.'

It seemed that churchmen were more willing to sympathise with the paedophile than his victims. They visited Greene's family and McGinley's family, but none of them ever came to me to ask, how are the victims doing? Do they want to see us? Can we help them? There seemed to be no concern for the children who were abused. Priests visited Greene in prison. I don't wish to criticise them for that act of charity, but only one priest that I know of ever contacted the victim support groups. I thought again about the two Donegals, the poisoned glen and the heavenly glen. There seemed to be two Churches too, one with the public image of a concerned ministry, the other hidden.

The hidden Church had known about this problem for years, from parents who complained about McGinley and Greene, and indeed about others not only in Donegal but in dioceses from Ferns to Boston. I had to wonder how much more remained hidden if just two police-men working part time in Donegal could discover so much. The hidden Church reacted to those complaints with indifference and apathy, often not even bothering to keep a written record of a potential problem. Having investigated four decades of sexual deviancy and countless dastardly acts carried out on children, I could not help thinking there was something wrong with a system that allowed this. The response of the public Church to Greene's conviction was a letter sent out from the bishop's office to be read from every pulpit in the diocese saying the Church was hurt by the revelations. It seemed so inadequate a response to the carnage that happened in this forgotten corner of Ireland to simply read out a letter and close the chapter. The public Church prom-ised to do better, adopting slogans like 'Children are our priority' and 'Our children, our Church'. Yet in private churchmen asked me, 'Is it money that they are looking for?' when I asked them about victims of sexual abuse, or suggested to paedophiles that they might leave the area before they were arrested. Which Church was I a member of? The Church spoke about protocols and protection but never apologised for what happened in Derryconnor National School on their watch, in a Catholic school managed by the local Catholic parish priest under the patronage of the Catholic bishop. I was astounded when Bishop Boyce wrote to me in 2005 and told me that McGinley's case was 'one that did not come to my notice until I read it in the newspapers. Nor did I ever hear of the letter by Fr Sweeney or any other Priest Manager you say were read out in court.' Wasn't there any system in place for parish priests to report these things to their bishops?

What we had uncovered in a few short years in Donegal should have sent shock waves through anyone with a shred of common decency, but apparently not through some priests and bishops. How could anyone write a character reference for a paedophile? Listening to the arguments for clemency in sentencing McGinley, I could barely breathe in court on that dreadful day.

Three parish priests had been served with witness orders as potential witnesses before McGinley's trial. As it happened none of them was called since he eventually pleaded guilty to the sample charges. After the case was over John McGlynn, who had given the paedophile a glowing character reference, called to my home to confront me. He demanded to know why I used his name in court during my evidence. The simple answer was he was a material witness in a criminal prosecution.

I asked him why he didn't go to court himself. He could have addressed anything that arose there himself instead of confronting me afterwards. He had written to the judge lavishing praise on a child molester, with not a word about the victims, and now he was upset because his name was used or mentioned. His arrogance astounded me.

Surely there would be urgent phone calls from the Department of Education, I thought. Surely those people would be removed from their positions as school managers. Of course they weren't. I wondered if anyone was in charge of protecting children, if anyone was willing to take responsibility.

Shortly after the court case a young lad came to me. 'Fair play to you bucks for going after him,' he told me. 'Sure he was abusing us too on Toraigh.'

'Was he?' I said. 'Why didn't you complain or come forward to anyone,' I asked.

'Aye, but he was staying with the priest in digs,' he said to me. 'Sure where would you be going?'

And that was the problem. They had nowhere to go.

Chapter 39

Sins of Omission

Six months after Denis McGinley was sentenced, BBC Northern Ireland broadcast a *Spotlight* special dealing with how the diocese of Raphoe handled Eugene Greene. Presented by Darragh MacIntyre, an award-winning investigative reporter, the programme covered the renegade priest's depraved career in Donegal, pulling no punches.

MacIntyre was no stranger to Donegal. A native of Co. Kildare, he had worked as a reporter in New York, London and Belfast and then as the Ireland producer for BBC national news, before taking a career break in Gort an Choirce for several years where he ran a local pub. As a publican he got to know many of Greene's victims personally, and when he returned to his first love of journalism, he knew he could not leave their story untold.

Broadcast on 29 October 2002, 'Sins of Omission' began with the haunting words of one of Greene's victims: 'He did rape me, and not only once but I can't count them. I just can't. And that hurt me, and hurts me yet, big time. Big time.'

The programme interviewed one of the young men Dooley and I met when we travelled to Britain to take statements in 1999. He had left Gort an Choirce several years before, at one point ending up homeless on the streets of London.

'There was one stage in my life I had nothing only the clothes I was wearing,' he told *Spotlight*. 'I wasn't even in touch with my family because I felt so ashamed. There were times that I stood on Tower Bridge, London Bridge, and said "Go on, do it. Get it over and done with, end it now." But thank God, I think somebody up there likes me and said "No, don't do it." So I didn't and I pulled myself together, which took a long time. I am now back on my feet again and I will be for the rest of my life, because that bastard is not going to beat me.'

Another interviewee, the mother of one of Greene's victims and one of the founders of a local support group for Greene's victims and their families, concisely summed up what Greene had done: 'He was an animal that preyed on little boys and took away their lives.' She had learned of her son's abuse four years earlier after we asked her if he had ever been an altar boy for Greene. With our help she tracked him down to a Salvation Army hostel in Dublin. There in a quiet café she broached the subject over a coffee when she asked him, 'Did anything ever happen to you as a small child that I don't know about?' His head dropped as he told her what Greene had done.

MacIntyre began his investigation with a series of simple questions. Was protecting the Church more important than safeguarding children? Did the diocese which employed and promoted Greene also protect him?

In addition to interviews with two of Greene's victims, *Spotlight* looked at the crucial questions: what did the Church know, when did it know it, and what did it do about it? Greene's crimes were documented as far back as the mid-sixties. The earliest complaint we had uncovered dated from 1965. Dooley and I knew that the *Kennedy* family had complained about the priest as far back as 1976, and as a result Greene had disappeared from the parish to a 'treatment centre or hospital' for several weeks. *Spotlight*, however, established that 'serious concerns' about the priest were first raised with his authorities as early as 1971 but that nothing was done to safeguard children as a result.

The then Bishop of Raphoe Anthony McFeely had appointed Greene as a curate in Cnoc Fola in 1970. Greene's behaviour in the parish worried a fellow priest and curate, who considered the reports he received so serious he passed them on to his parish priest. As a result the parish priest, who has since died, visited a number of local families making his own enquiries. Whatever the results of his enquiries were, it appeared that no report was filed in the bishop's office as a result. The failure to report any concerns to the bishop was something Dooley and I had encountered before. MacIntyre observed that 'the Church's own canon law says such a matter should have been raised with the bishop of the day. No one can explain why this appears not to have happened.'

From Cnoc Fola Greene was moved to Killybegs, from there to Leitir Mhic an Bhaird and from there to Gort an Choirce, where a second report was made about his misbehaviour. This report I already knew about; it was made to Canon Hugh Bonnar after Greene sexually abused *Henry Kennedy*. Greene disappeared for a while after that to 'some treatment centre or hospital', but after a few months he was back again. Although *Henry*'s father *Gilbert* believed at the time that the Bishop of Raphoe was aware of the complaint, again there were no records in the diocesan files. McFeely and Bonnar had since died and could not be asked what they knew or did.

In 1982 a new bishop, Seamus Hegarty, succeeded McFeely in the Raphoe diocese. Meanwhile Greene continued to prey on young boys in Glenties, then in Gaoth Dobhair, then moving on to Cill Mhic Réanáin where he was promoted to parish priest. 'Most unusually', the *Spotlight* documentary noted, 'Greene's new job was subject to a review after three years.'

In 1994 Greene moved to live in semi-retirement in Loch an Iúir. When Hegarty was moved to Derry in 1994, the diocesan vicar general Fr Dan Carr acted for a while as temporary administrator to the diocese of Raphoe, and he brought Greene out of semi-retirement as an assistant priest. *Spotlight* discovered two more complaints from this period. 'One was in a letter sent to the diocesan headquarters outlining a specific allegation', it reported. 'The priest who sent it received no reply. The other complaint was made verbally by a curate to his parish priest. The senior priest in question denies he received any complaint. Fr Dan Carr denies he received any complaints. And this diocese says it has no complaints on file about Fr Greene.'

Spotlight went on to report that 'serious worries' were circulating the following summer when Philip Boyce was appointed as bishop of Raphoe. The new bishop was told of 'grave concerns' about the priest at a special meeting in Anagaire parochial house in November 1995 called by the principal of the local primary school and the parish priest Fr Michael Herrity. In a statement to *Spotlight* the headmaster explained that 'allegations and rumours about Fr Greene and children were sweeping the parish'.

Nearly seven years later, in April 2002, McGinley was sentenced to thirty months' imprisonment by Judge Deery. That first week of April had been a difficult one for the Catholic Church in Ireland. It began with the resignation of Brendan Comiskey as Bishop of Ferns. Comiskey was severely criticised following the broadcast of a programme about his handling of the paedophile priest Fr Sean Fortune. By Thursday the Minister for Health had announced an inquiry into the Fr Fortune affair, and by the end of the week protesters were call-ing on Dubliners to boycott weekend celebrations planned to honour Edmund Rice, the founder of the Christian Brothers.

The following Sunday the parish priest in Anagaire, still Fr Michael Herrity, delivered a sermon about child sexual abuse. 'The victims and their families have suffered as well as the families of the paedophiles', he was reported as saying by the *Donegal Democrat*. The parish priest said they should also be concerned about the abusers themselves.

The report went on to state that Fr Herrity said he was aware people in the parish had been victims of lay people, not clergy, who had abused children, a reference to *John Reilly*. He made no reference to Greene, with whom he had previously shared the altar. When he was interviewed by the local newspaper, Herrity 'said he was not aware of any abuses carried out by Fr Greene in the parish' and had been shocked to learn about Greene's abuses in other areas of the county. Herrity also seemed to be unaware that there were no files on Greene in the diocesan office. 'It is not an understatement to say that the Bishops handled the whole affair so badly. Of course they did,' he told the *Democrat* reporter. 'Why don't they hand over and open up to the people the files that are being requested? There can't be much in them that we haven't imagined at this stage and I'm sure they're not as condemning as people think.'

Three years after the 1995 meeting that *Spotlight* uncovered in Anagaire, our Garda investigation began, and Greene was finally con-victed and sent to prison. The court was never told that Boyce had received complaints from Greene's parish priest and school principal in 1995. The bishop later issued a statement denying 'the existence of any records of complaints about Fr Greene on diocesan files'.

When MacIntyre confronted Boyce about the affair for the *Spotlight* programme, Boyce told him, 'I issued the statement. Did you get the statement?'

Darragh pointed out that there were serious questions to be asked about Eugene Greene.

'I just, the, there were rumours at the time and I, I explained to them and I co-operated fully with the Gardaí about it,' Boyce replied.

Darragh then pointed out that the bishop had never told the Gardaí about the meeting in Anagaire in 1995 when he was interviewed.

'That there were rumours, that there were rumours going around and there was nothing substantial that could be, that could be found and that I, em, the man was retired at the time,' Boyce said.

Darragh countered by pointing out that Greene had not retired until the Garda investigation began in 1998.

'In my, he, um, in my documents he was, he was. But anyway I left, I left this in the, I explained that in the statement and I would prefer to leave it to the statement at the moment,' the tongue-tied bishop replied.

Bishop Seamus Hegarty was similarly reticent when he too was interviewed by MacIntyre and the *Spotlight* film crew. He told the programme that Greene's four month stay at the residential treatment centre in Stroud in 1992, which offered 'therapy in a spiritual context' for priests with a range of different problems from alcohol and drugs misuse to serious sexual misconduct, was not related to any sexual problems. In a statement to the BBC programme about Greene, the Stroud centre stated that the 'recommendations we made to his bishop in 1992 were exclusively concerned with maintaining his recovery from alcoholism. With hindsight it is a matter of the deepest regret he was not treated for psychosexual problems by us', the statement from Stroud added.

What staggered me most was Hegarty's response when asked if he thought the Church had handled Greene appropriately over the years. 'Oh yes, absolutely, absolutely. He had a problem all right and that was handled very professionally, very responsibly, and ah, there is evidence to that effect there.' I wondered how the bishop could say that when so many complaints were made over the years to such little effect. Even more, I wondered how people could accept what he said.

The Dutch psychoanalyst and writer Joost A. Meerloo, in a book called *The Rape of the Mind*, a work on thought control by totalitarian governments, described how the words we use influence how we behave every day. 'The formulation of big propagandistic lies and fraudulent catchwords has a very well defined purpose in Totalitaria, and words themselves have acquired a special function in the service of power, which we may call verbocracy. . . . The task of the totalitarian propagandist is to build special pictures in the minds of the citizenry so that finally they will no longer see and hear with their own eyes and ears but will look at the world through the fog of official catchwords and will develop the automatic responses appropriate to totalitarian mythology.'

I felt I was also lost in a fog. The Church has had 2,000 years of practice in shaping words to shape minds. During two investigations

I had listened to graphic details of countless rapes and abuse on children over four decades. It amazed me that the Church response to these barbarous acts was so sparse: a letter to be read out at Masses throughout the diocese and an assurance that the Church had 'absolutely, absolutely' handled the priest 'very professionally, very responsibly'.

Sometimes it felt as if the public memory was deleted by words creating a picture in our minds. 'We weren't aware of it.' Soothing tones, and the outrage was soothed. Everyone forgot what they knew and got on with life.

Chapter 40
Cha n-ólann Denis bocht is cha gcaitheann sé

Seeing the BBC *Spotlight* special on Eugene Greene in October 2002 prompted one Donegal priest, Columba Nee, to put pen to paper. In a letter headlined 'Response to Sexual Abuse Allegations Woefully Inadequate', published in the *Donegal News* on 8 November 2002, Nee wrote about the effect that revelations about clerical sexual abuse cases had on the Church and on him personally.

'I grew up in the 1970s before the issue of child sexual abuse emerged out into the open. I remember my parents warning me about strangers offering sweets or enticing me into cars. I never considered for a second that one day I might belong to a profession that, in the eyes of many, is a haven for paedophiles', Nee's letter began.

He wrote about the snide comments he and colleagues had to face because of the Greene and other cases, but observed that the crisis the Church faced was largely self-inflicted and 'often made worse by cover-ups, lame excuses and, worst of all, silence from Church leaders'. Most priests were good men, and only a small minority has carried out 'ferocious crimes against children', including Greene, 'a serial rapist who wrecked and destroyed the lives of scores of young boys over roughly twenty-five years'. Greene's crimes, Nee wrote, were 'sickening and revolting and cannot be excused in any way'.

What upset Nee most though was the 'woeful' response of the Church to questions posed by the *Spotlight* programme. In particular the lack of diocesan files, which could explain for example why Greene was brought out of semi-retirement, troubled him.

Nee noted that the Hussey Commission into clerical abuse, chaired by retired District Court Judge Gillian Hussey, would not have to spend much time in Donegal, since it relied on paper files to get to the truth. 'Have files been destroyed or were complaints never recorded?' he asked. He described how his faith in Church leaders had been shaken by the way paedophile priests were handled. The Church needed to learn from the disaster, bring it out in the open and deal with it honestly. Those who covered up or ignored crimes shared in the guilt, as did those who 'passed the buck and made pathetic excuses in the face of sheer evil'.

Nee's words burned with passion. He spoke on behalf of many ordinary Catholics who felt shocked and betrayed by the Church, and many ordinary priests who shared their feelings. He compared their outrage to the righteous anger Jesus felt when he entered the temple in Jerusalem and found it violated by traders and money-changers. 'People need to know that many ordinary priests share their outrage and disappointment,' he concluded. 'I wonder will anything really ever change in our Church? Time will tell.'

Not every priest I spoke to saw things with Nee's piercing clarity. One said to me of McGinley: 'Cha n-ólann Denis bocht is cha gcaitheann sé.' (Sure poor Denis doesn't drink or smoke.) I couldn't see how this was a point in his favour after what he had done, but clearly the speaker felt that it excused or lessened his guilt in some way. Several people afterwards made a big thing of Greene's drink problem, but the strange argument was made that as McGinley was a Pioneer, he must in some way have been a good person because he didn't drink or smoke. It made no sense. When I spoke to another priest about my dismay at the glowing character references that two priests, John McGlynn and Michael Sweeney, had given for McGinley, his answer was 'Sure is cara mór le Fr Michael, Denis.' (Michael is a great friend of Denis.) I was even told that in one parochial house in a parish where Greene had worked as a curate, his photograph still hung prominently. Quite what the parishioner who saw the photograph of the convicted serial rapist hanging proudly on the wall thought of it, I'm not sure. The message it must send to any of Greene's victims who might see it doesn't bear thinking about.

As far as I was concerned, that seemed to be the problem. The paedophiles had 'cara mórs' everywhere. One man close to diocesan management had asked me why I was doing all these investigations, as if the seriousness of the criminal allegations I was looking into didn't warrant investigation. And through it all, no files were apparently ever kept in the diocesan offices. We had a priest who could not remember being told what was happening, could not remember being shown letters to a boy from a paedophile years before he came to our notice. It was like peering into the night, trying to see a past that no one wanted to acknowledge.

————

I remembered the night Frank Stagg died on hunger strike in England in 1976. His death captured news headlines world-wide and evoked deep emotions at home. That night I was on patrol in Portarlington along with Garda Gerry Bohan, who was later injured in the explosion that killed Michael Clerkin.

We knew there was an IRA hotbed in the area, but we were not really expecting any trouble. We had gone around the pubs at closing time, and after the crowds streamed into the streets and headed home, the town was still. The quietness of the night filled the air. Nothing much to do, I thought, just beat down the clock and another shift completed. The townsfolk were safely in their beds.

We decided to do a single patrol, scout around the wider subdistrict. It would fill a page in the patrol book at the end of the tour, show that we hadn't been idle. Gerry and I talked about Stagg's death as we drove, what it must be like for his family, whether there would be repercussions somewhere as a result. We drove around the country roads, but they were as quiet as the town we had left behind. The quietness of the night was almost eerie. We felt there was hardly any need for us to be out at all. The conversation moved on to the agenda for the next day, the usual files and reports to process, summonses endorsed, some poor devil in trouble in the District Court. It was breaking into the small hours and the clock was monotonously slow. I almost felt like an intruder in the darkness, our drive disturbing the peace and quiet of the night. We drove back into the town; there were still a few hours to punch in. A policeman can hardly ever plan his work as the unexpected can always turn up, but this didn't look like it would be that kind of night.

We turned the corner, and our jaws gaped. We could not believe our eyes. The town had been transformed since we left. I often heard about painting a town red, but in this case it was blue. There was blue paint all over the place. We first noticed the courthouse; the red bricked building had got an unnecessary facelift. There were IRA slogans everywhere. The library next to the courthouse didn't escape. Walls, bridges, it was everywhere. Outside a Garda's home, on newly surfaced tarmacadam, there were slogans with arrows pointing into the house. It was a brand new house, almost ready to move into, its owner still living in the barracks.

How could we explain this? Two Gardaí on duty and the town painted blue right under their noses. I could see the paperwork flying from the super's office. Please explain. How could we explain? Weren't we working? Not a sinner moving, yet we had wet paint dripping all over the place.

We drove around, found more slogans but saw no one. Fresh slogans were appearing, so the culprits were still at work, no doubt laughing at us from their hiding places as we drove by. Catch me if you can. The lights of our car announcing our presence were no help to us. I thought about going on foot patrol, but if I did the Garda car might be the next target. I didn't even want to imagine the sergeant's reaction if I took the patrol car back covered in blue paint. I decided on a different approach. 'Look, Gerry,' I said to my partner, 'I am going to take a risk. I'm going to drive around quietly with no headlights on. Let's see if we can spot them that way.'

There was some public lighting on Main Street but very little at the back of the town. Gerry was worried and so was I, but we agreed to give it a try. I switched off the lights and turned into a side road, neither of us speaking as I stayed close to shadows and walls, hoping to spot something. As we approached a junction I thought I saw shadows jumping over a wall. I switched on the lights suddenly, and the high beams illuminated the fields in front of us. Out of the car I bolted and jumped over the wall. There I found two people hiding, carrying a big tin of blue paint and brushes and with paint on their hands and clothes. The gambit had worked though it's not one you might find in any Garda training manual.

Locking them up for the night would serve no useful purpose. They were local lads and they were caught red handed — or in this case, blue. We took the paint and brushes as evidence and sent them home. We could have arrested them under section 30, but what was the point. They were going nowhere. Now at least we could face the skipper. When we got back to the station we woke the sergeant and told him what happened. We completed the file, got an estimate for the damage caused and brought a prosecution for vandalism and malicious damage.

———

Police work is all about gathering evidence, whether a tin of paint and some brushes or a witness statement or the paperwork from a report to a health board official or a diocesan office of suspected wrongdoing to support a criminal complaint. Yet in investigating Greene we were hampered by the lack of evidence. There were reports raising concerns in 1971, again in 1976 and twice in 1995 that I knew about, either from our own investigation or what *Spotlight* had uncovered. In November 1995 Bishop Boyce was told about the concerns over Greene's conduct, yet there was nothing in the diocesan files. Nee hit the nail on the head when he asked, 'Have files been destroyed or were complaints never recorded?'

Why was nothing ever written down? Over the years I had been given tantalising pieces of information which suggested that there was an awareness at senior levels in the diocese of the problem, even if there were no written records. One priest told me he was present when a colleague approached a senior Church official expressing some concern about what Greene might have done, only to be rebuffed with the words, 'He couldn't have. He's cured.'

Greene told us himself he was in Stroud in the early nineties. He gave us written permission to access his files there. Yet Stroud later refused to release the files on medical grounds, after consulting with the priest and his lawyers, saying he was treated for alcohol dependency, not psychosexual problems. When Greene gave us permission to get his medical records, he was under no illusion and neither were we about which files we were talking about, and he had nodded to us accordingly. We understood, as any criminal investigator would, that we were dealing with child sexual abuse and nothing else. Alcoholism was never mentioned. There was no reason to.

We could have included in his written consent an explicit confirmation that he received psychosexual therapy. It never occurred to us that we might need to. It was self-evident what we were trying to uncover. The response from Stroud to the *Spotlight* investigators was phrased in strong words: 'Recommendations we made to his bishop in 1992 were exclusively concerned with maintaining his recovery from alcoholism.' Yet I believe to this day, and so do many priests I have spoken to, that Greene did receive psychosexual therapy somewhere, if not Stroud then perhaps the Granada Institute or a similar centre in Ireland, Britain or further afield. His medical records were not given to the court when his barrister appealed his sentence, although his alcoholism was one of the reasons given when arguing for clemency. I wondered then if the records would show he had previously received psychosexual counselling somewhere, even if not during that particular visit to Stroud.

While several priests spoke to me privately about what they knew, Nee was one of the few to speak out publicly. I have heard he is now studying to become a counsellor himself.

Chapter 41
Moral Courage

Childhood abuse is the seed of a ruined life. Looking back, I wonder how much of the small-scale police work in my career might have its seeds in sexual abuse: victims dealing with their pain by burying it in alcohol and illegal drugs; public order problems from alcohol abuse; closing time arguments and fights; petty thefts, break-ins and muggings to feed a drug habit; suicides of victims who could no longer face living; domestic disputes; and assaults. Not every crime traced its roots back to that childhood trauma, of course, but it seemed an awful lot could be explained by going back to that point and tracing the long-term effects of that childhood sexual assault.

One of *John Reilly*'s victims wrote a lengthy poem in which he described some of those effects, how at one point he got drunk and broke into his abuser's home. He was seen by the authorities as a reckless troublemaker, someone 'known to the Gardaí'. But of course we didn't know the full story. We just see their lives through one pane of glass. And from the limited view we get, we tag them without knowing the full picture. The more I thought about it, the more it seemed we were faced with an iceberg and we were only aware of the tip. One senior official in the health service told me as much at a meeting where we discussed the cases when he said to me: 'While you lads did a good job, you're only scratching the surface.'

There is a reluctance in our society to face up to the hidden cancer of sexual abuse. That was my initial reaction too when I was first assigned to the detective branch in the Midlands and came across the files on a sexual abuse case. I felt as if I was intruding, looking where I should not pry, even though, oddly, I had no qualms looking through other files. Before I came to Donegal that was as close as I ever came to a child abuse case. I had read about it in the newspapers, high profile cases like Fr Brendan Smyth, but this was the first time I had to deal with the victims myself.

As much as the effects of abuse reached down the years, our investigative work had other unforeseen and long-reaching consequences too. In 2002 the Dáil set up the Morris Tribunal to look into allegations which had already been pored over by the Carty Inquiry and caused such chaos in the Buncrana and Letterkenny Garda districts in Donegal. The tribunal had several terms of reference, but the key one was the McBrearty affair where an innocent family were wrongly identified as murder suspects after a hit and run death in Raphoe. One of the Gardaí involved in the questioning of two innocent women arrested during the misguided murder inquiry was John Dooley.

In October 2005, John came forward and admitted the women, Katrina Brolly and Roisin McConnell, were mistreated while he questioned them along with Detective Sergeant John White. I cannot defend any wrongdoing by John, though I do wonder if it was right to bring such a clearly troubled man, who was traumatised by all the sexual violence he had had to deal with, before a tribunal. But what struck me about John's evidence at the tribunal was his need, before all else, to apologise for the harm he had done. When he took the stand to give evidence for the first time in March 2006, before he answered any question from the tribunal barristers, he addressed Katrina and Roisin with an apology. Overcome with emotion, he barely got a dozen words out before losing his composure. 'I would like to sincerely apologise to Mrs Brolly and Mrs McConnell for the treatment I inflicted on them when they were in custody at Letterkenny Garda Station.' He then managed to say after a few moments to gather himself: 'I regret that I hadn't the moral courage to tell the truth at the outset.'

In evidence over several days, first in the section of the tribunal dealing with Katrina Brolly's arrest and later on the section devoted to her sister Roisin McConnell, Dooley explained how he saw the senior interrogator, John White, mistreat Roisin McConnell as he ramped up the pressure in an effort to get her to confess during her arrest in early December 1996. That evening he mimicked the same tactics during the arrest and interrogation of Roisin's sister Katrina.

John's compelling need to apologise was striking. He revealed at the tribunal that he was seeing a psychiatrist and suffering from depression. He had been admitted to the Dublin County Stress Clinic run by St John of God Hospital, both to cope with the harrowing experience of dealing with so many victims of child sexual abuse, and because of other conflicts in his life. Like me, he had also had to deal with the demons of alcohol over the years.

At the tribunal John's basic need was to apologise. It was very important to him. Tribunal barrister Paul McDermott described his decision to come forward as 'a significant breaking away from the culture of lies and deceit and the unwillingness to reveal a truth adverse to a colleague that has been an unfortunate feature of this inquiry'. Dooley's decision to come forward was 'a very positive and commendable development'.

John's decision was a great help to the tribunal, I believe. It started a momentum, allowing other officers involved in the debacle in Raphoe to come forward. Thinking about his evidence, I can't help but feel that what he experienced while investigating those abuse cases with me played a key part in his decision to speak out. I think that as he listened to those victims talk about their abuse and trauma, he realised that he too had been an abuser when those women were arrested in December 1996 and he had to make amends. He could not face the thought of getting into that witness box, taking the oath and lying while they looked on. Having seen the effects on those victims in the abuse cases, I don't think he could do that. He told the truth because it was the only choice he could make.

John worked like a Trojan on those cases with me, not just investigating Greene and McGinley but dealing with *Reilly*'s victims too. At the end of a day's work he often called to my home and we would sit and talk. Exhausted, he often fell asleep on the sofa. After twenty minutes he would wake up, we would talk some more and he would then drive home. People told me he was often so drained by the day's work that he would pull over his car and sleep in a gateway on the way home.

I worked with many Guards over the years, but the partnership John and I had was one of the most successful. Something indefinable gelled between us. We got on well together. We were able to talk things through, plan where we were going. He was a consummate policeman.

Chapter 42

Missed Chances

Most of the charges against Denis McGinley were for one form or another of indecent assault because of the way he had molested so many young boys in his classroom over the years, often while other pupils looked on. The charges brought on behalf of one victim, *Craig Thompson*, were different. McGinley had met *Craig* outside the school, at a local youth club, and the abuse *Craig* suffered was chronic and lasted for several years. John Dooley and I suspected that *Craig* was not the only victim of such severe and extended sexual abuse, and as we spoke to victims and other witnesses during the inquiry, one name kept coming up, *Hector Foley*.

Hector was still a minor like *Dylan Murphy* and *Lee Nolan* when the inquiry started. Several witnesses had told us how he was often seen at lunchtime in school, coming down from the whin bushes behind the schoolhouse at the end of school breaks, crying. Just as McGinley had met *Craig* at a youth club, so we also heard reports that he frequently met young *Hector* at youth events, even after the young boy had moved out of his class. We knew we had to speak to him and approached his parents. He was still under 18; we couldn't talk to him without his parents being present.

When we approached *Hector*'s father, the meeting was not encouraging. Basically he didn't want to know. All the same, we arranged for a meeting with him and his son together. As we walked into the living room and sat down, the boy's body language was horribly familiar — the hunched shoulders, the lowered head and eyes, the crossed arms protecting his chest, the way he seemed to withdraw into his seat making himself as small as possible. We explained quietly why we were there, what we were investigating, and how sometimes we were told that maybe we should talk to a particular person. It didn't always mean anything, but we had to go and ask, hear what they had to say. Sometimes it was nothing, just someone who had got a story wrong, but sometimes it was something very important and we could put an end to it.

Hector's father loomed over him as we spoke. We finished and waited for the boy to find the courage to speak. 'Denis McGinley used to take me up the back of the fields at school,' he said hesitatingly. His father spoke before he could go any further. 'Sure just tell them nothing happened, *Hector*,' he said. 'Tell the Guards nothing happened.'

The boy looked at his father, and then at us. 'Nothing happened,' he said. His mother stayed in the background, saying nothing. There wasn't much else we could do. We were worried. We knew that McGinley had befriended the family and often visited their home. We didn't want to consider what the consequences of that might be. We spoke to the father several times afterwards, and even arranged a second visit to their home, but we got no further. We consoled ourselves that we had at least given them the chance to come forward, which was the most we could do. Because *Hector* was still a minor, we passed on his name to the child care and social services people in the health board. I don't know what they were able to do to help, if anything. The family seemed torn by what had happened for years.

There were other cases too, young men who were no longer minors, names that came up as we spoke to others. We're concerned, we told them. We're investigating child sexual abuse. Sometimes it really was nothing; sometimes they would acknowledge that we were right to call on them, but there was no way they were going to make a statement. At least we had tried. The fall-out seemed to last for years, young men who had committed suicide or who had psychiatric problems or drug and alcohol addiction.

Some were apologetic, explaining that they were newly married and didn't want their wives to know. So they said no, they didn't want to make a statement. There were so many names, so many people we spoke to, abused down the years. It was as if McGinley had a conveyor belt of victims to choose from each year as a fresh batch of children entered his classroom. Effectively the school system provided a menu for the paedophile, and he could pick and choose victims to abuse at will. It was sickening.

Chapter 43
Cell System

I first met Colm O'Gorman sometime in 2004 when I got in touch with him to see if an investigation could be started into sexual abuse in Donegal. Colm was the founder and one of the directors of One in Four, a national charity set up to support men and women who experienced sexual abuse as children. The name comes from research which shows that in Ireland just over one in four people will experience sexual abuse or sexual violence before the age of 18. In his role as a director of One in Four, he was widely credited with the establishment of the Ferns Inquiry, the first investigation by the State into clerical sexual abuse.

I hoped an investigation might also be set up in Co. Donegal to discover what the Church knew about various abuse cases in the county, when the Church knew, and what they did about it. I spoke to Colm several times on the phone. He told me if I was ever in Dublin to get in touch with him at his office. I called in to see him a couple of times.

I learned a lot from Colm. 'I was going around for years nursing this guilt,' he told me. 'When I saw a friend of mine who was also abused take a double barrelled shotgun and blow his chest out, I said that's enough. I'm going to talk. I was lucky enough. I met a decent Guard who listened to me. I wanted to parcel this guilt and hand it over. I realised afterwards it's not that simple.'

Some time later Colm came to Donegal and addressed a meeting in Anagaire organised by a local support group set up by the families of sexual abuse victims. *John Reilly* had abused several children in Anagaire. Denis McGinley had also taught there for five years in the early 1970s, although we had only prosecuted cases uncovered during an investigation in Gort an Choirce, to which McGinley moved after his time in Anagaire.

I went to the meeting in Anagaire, attended by victims, their families and partners, and listened as familiar themes were rehearsed again, from concerns about the release of convicted abusers back into the communities where their victims lived, to frustrations with the judicial process and the lack of information as cases went through the courts. The Guards came in for some stick too, and several people spoke about the difficulties in coming forward, with the abused person often suffering the wrath of society more than the abuser.

What turned my blood cold was one young man I saw sitting quietly at the back of the room. His posture was hauntingly familiar, drawn into himself as he sat, almost crouched, his hands held together, his shoulders bowed, his head hanging low. He never spoke. I had seen that posture before. I hope he left the meeting knowing at least that he was not alone and that there were people who would help him.

The support group in Anagaire worked along with the health board, not only supporting each other but also arranging professional counselling, so the lack of resources was raised several times at the meeting. O'Gorman took several phone numbers that evening. One in Four helps lobby for additional resources for victims as part of its brief.

Sexual abuse is a private pain. Few people are willing to come forward and identify themselves, so funding for the health services goes to other areas where the public demand is louder. Politicians have little incentive to devote public funds to counselling when there is little political credit to be gained.

Calls for public inquiries into the scandal of clerical sexual abuse are likely to fall on deaf ears, particularly in rural constituencies where voters are conservative and the Church still wields considerable clout. During the summer of 2007 the Education Minster, Mary Hanafin, told an RTÉ *Prime Time* programme that the government is not responsible for teachers who sexually abuse students. The day to day running of schools is a matter for boards of management, and victims abused in schools funded by the State are not entitled to compensation from the State. Think about that. The State is not responsible. That's you and me, our taxes, schools that we funded, and our government won't take responsibility. 'Is it money they're after?' Fr John McGlynn had asked me. The question had infuriated me. But counselling to heal the mental wounds of abuse doesn't come free. Either it has to be paid for privately or the health boards have to be given the resources to provide it.

Eugene Greene isn't the only priest convicted of sexual abuse in Donegal. Fr John Doherty was jailed in 2000 for sexual assaults on four young boys while he was stationed in a south Donegal parish in the 1970s. His brother Fr Daniel Doherty twice raped a 13-year-old girl in a church sacristy in 1985. His victim came forward in 2003 after seeing a television programme about clerical sexual abuse. He was sentenced to seven years in prison in October 2006.

In the past when IRA suspects were arrested, they often provided information not only about their own activities but about other operations in planning, a planned bomb attack or a bank raid. During the seventies the IRA reorganised under a 'cell system'. Operating on a need to know basis, groups of four or five terrorists were given specific tasks such as moving a car or a weapon from one place to another but never knowing the full extent of what they were involved in, so that if they were caught there was little they could tell. The key to their protection was ignorance. What they didn't know they couldn't tell us.

I wondered if a similar cell structure existed within the Catholic Church. There was no doubt that some people knew there were problems. We had statements showing that complaints had been made during the three decades in the cases we were investigating, from the seventies to the nineties. When inquiries were carried out in Boston, Los Angeles or Ferns, time and time again it was discovered that certain people within the Church were aware of abuse allegations. Yet there was a lack of reporting, a lack of paperwork, even when the Church's own canon law demanded such reports. There was a cell structure of a sort there. It made it difficult to tell who knew what was going on, and who didn't.

The commission set up to look at the treatment of clerical abuse allegations in the Ferns diocese as a result of Colm O'Gorman's campaign has already reported. There is an ongoing commission of investigation into clerical child abuse in the Dublin archdiocese. In October 2005 the Bishop of Raphoe, Dr Philip Boyce, said in a statement that €760,000 had to date been paid out in respect of nineteen allegations of abuse. Allegations of child sexual abuse had been made against ten priests in the diocese of Raphoe over the past forty years. Clearly there is a need for a properly funded official inquiry into allegations of clerical abuse in Donegal.

Chapter 44
The Swallow

I was on night patrol when I got the word over the radio. Call a given phone number for an urgent message. I rang back and arranged a place to meet.

I was back to routine policing. Eugene Greene had been sentenced and jailed by then, and Denis McGinley had pleaded guilty, but when I met *Jacob Kane*, that was what he wanted to talk to me about. *Jacob* had told me he didn't want me to call to his home. His wife didn't know what he was going to talk to me about. We arranged to meet at a country crossroads. By the time I got to see him it was the early hours of Sunday morning. I had asked him if it could wait until Monday morning. He told me it couldn't. Things were bothering him; he couldn't sleep.

Jacob came from Gaoth Dobhair. He too was one of Greene's victims. John Dooley hadn't been able to find any victims in Gaoth Dobhair when he looked there, but we knew there were probably several. Greene was too compulsive a personality to just switch off for a few years.

As soon as I realised what *Jacob* was going to tell me, I had to interrupt him. '*Jacob*,' I said, 'I've dealt with too many cases. I'm sorry, I can't deal with cases like this any more. I can talk to you about where to go for help, but you're going to have to tell your story to them.' We chatted and I gave him the name of some detectives to contact who were nominated to deal with abuse cases by the super's office and some people I knew from the health board who could arrange for counselling.

The next day *Jacob* called to see me at my home. He told me that since our talk the night before he had spoken to his wife about Greene and felt a lot better. He told me he was going to write to the Bishop of Raphoe about what had happened and would make a statement to the Gardaí. A few weeks later he got back to me again and said he was ready to make a statement. I talked to my super and he arranged an appointment so that the Gardaí could take his statement.

I found though that I couldn't let go of those cases. I couldn't sleep at night. I would wake in the middle of nightmares shouting and swinging my fists at demons. So much so that I moved into a spare room so that Brid could get some sleep. When I went to see my GP, he forwarded me to a psychiatrist. I was diagnosed with post traumatic stress disorder. He said I was so traumatised I could see nothing else but abuse.

I thought I knew what he meant. I remembered one night in particular when I had gone to clear the pubs at closing time. People were having a good time, enjoying the night. For no reason their enjoyment of the simple pleasure of a few drinks with friends infuriated me. How can they be enjoying themselves when all this is happening, I thought to myself.

Listening to the victims who did speak brought its own burdens. We had to let them find their own words, recording what was said impartially, watching them as they spoke and assessing how they would cope if we had to put them in a witness box, something the DPP would be sure to ask as he considered whether to bring a case. I felt as if I was in two places at once, listening and talking to the young (and not so young) men I spoke to, and at the same time standing back like a film director at an audition assessing their performance for the jury.

There were referrals to the Garda welfare peer support service and to the Garda medical officer, but it is only now I know how exposed Dooley and I were. British police are rotated out of sexual abuse investigations regularly and given professional counselling to deal with the trauma they encounter. Even the psychiatrists who provide counselling to the police are themselves given counselling, I learned, so deep can the trauma of repeated exposure to the pain bring. For whatever reason, whether no one appreciated how damaging it was dealing with these cases, or because it was a new field and they were still adapting, An Garda Síochána had nothing like the supports that other forces made sure were in place. Even Greene's own solicitor was astounded when Dooley told him we had never been provided with any professional counselling as a result of the horrors we had been exposed to during the paedophile investigations.

I went on sick leave in April 2002 and I was prescribed anti-depressant tablets. By the end of the summer I decided it was time to call it a day and I retired in October 2002. I could have worked for almost another two years but I felt I was in no condition to deal with anything else. I was burned out, exhausted and traumatised by the Greene and McGinley investigations. I had put my years in; it was time to go. It's never as easy as that, of course. There are some things you can't just walk away from. People still contact me, the victim support groups stay in touch, and I found that I couldn't watch a television report or read a newspaper article on child abuse without putting pen to paper. But I could enjoy a game of golf too, take care of all those jobs around the house that I had been putting off and enjoy time with my family and my new granddaughters.

Sometime in the summer of 2004 I was outside mowing the lawn. It's not as difficult a task as it used to be. These days you sit on the lawnmower and drive it around like a mini-tractor. My mind was only half focused on what I was doing. As often occurred, I was playing the criminal cases over in my mind again, when the swallow showed up. Darting left and right, high and low, it swooped everywhere but away from me, no doubt attracted by the food I had inadvertently provided as the lawnmower disturbed insects resting in the grass. I switched off the motor and watched. Sitting there in the stillness, watching the swallow hunt on the wing, the words just came and I had to go inside and write them down.

The swallow is but a lovely dream
That fills with fascination
It weaves with ease with its spanning wings
Stillness is forgotten.
The air it breathes, you cannot see
But like God we take it for granted
Like an ease of mind that is held within
In chambers that once were rotten.
But like my dreams, the swallows disappear
And you think are gone forever
But are courted back by the summer breeze
I wish I could court these dreams forever.

It's not going to win any prizes, but I found that the words helped calm me. I've written several more poems since, ranging from satire to laments. More than simple prose, the poetry in Irish and English somehow focuses the emotions I feel and gives me a place to put them to rest.

Chapter 45
The Day I Met a Miracle

D ays, weeks and months passed by and eventually turned into years. I wondered what had happened to *Craig Thompson*. I had lost touch with him, as with so many, in the years since I retired. He was the one who had opened up the case against Denis McGinley, coming forward with his story, able to provide details that we could check up by talking to others, his parents, family, friends, a car dealer. It seemed like it was only yesterday that he had knocked on my door, where I found him half huddled in the corner outside hiding in the shadows. I knew how difficult it was for him to come forward. As he said at the time, 'I thought hard and long about it for the past year.'

Those memories still preyed on his mind years after he got out of Donegal. The abuse had messed up his life and that of his family, in particular his mother. Our investigation showed that what was happening was reported to the school management — the parish priest — back in the middle eighties, yet nothing was done and the abuser went on to abuse for another eleven years before the Gardaí eventually caught up with him.

Again in the middle nineties McGinley's activities were reported to the school management, but again the authorities charged with the protection of children under their care had failed to respond adequately. The priority seemed to be to hide those things, cover them up with a quiet word and hope it wouldn't happen again. The protection of children didn't seem to matter as much as the need to avoid a scandal.

Craig's harrowing story of abuse was gruesome. He had gone on a journey through hell; the carnage left was hard to deal with. He had revealed to me personal things in his life that had affected him greatly. He was traumatised, trapped in despair and buried under years of shame and guilt. When John Dooley and I met him together, we spent long hours trawling through the years of abuse with him. It was a draining exercise.

Craig had moved away from home to Dublin, away from his childhood torture chamber, though it followed him anyway. He didn't want us to meet him in his city centre flat since he shared rooms with others, people who might wonder what was going on, people who might find out. I knew there was no point in even mentioning a Garda station. Not one of the victims I spoke to over the years ever went near a Garda station. Anything to do with an institution of power was seen as some sort of enemy. They had been let down by institutions; they felt they had been abused by them as much as by individuals. They felt they weren't wanted, left to deal alone with their hurt. The stories they told did not fit into the image that society had created of safe schools, safe churches, idyllic rural lives. Society didn't want to deal with those issues. People learned that quickly; those issues were not to be spoken about. It was too shameful to talk about child sexual abuse; it was much easier to pretend it didn't happen. Come forward and you were an unwelcome intruder, attacking those pillars of respectable Irish society, the priest and the teacher. Small communities don't want to deal with issues like child sexual abuse when they are so immediate. Let it happen somewhere else. Let it be something to read about in the papers, not something right here, not on our doorstep. As a result victims were often left on a ledge of despair, at the edges of society, feeling they weren't wanted. It was easier to leave. But even in Dublin, *Craig* didn't want to go near a Garda station, and I didn't fancy the idea of a semi-public meeting in a hotel somewhere. Fortunately I was given the use of a private house, thanks to my brother.

It was one less worry and the privacy of a home in the suburbs meant there was no hurry and we could deal with *Craig* at his leisure. His life was in disarray, but at least in the peaceful, tranquil estate where we met he could go through his story undisturbed. At last he could talk after all those years. Afterwards we took him out for a meal. I couldn't help noticing how frail he was.

Craig's courage in making the decision to talk to us started an avalanche. We spoke to several more of McGinley's victims afterwards, and we were able to build a case showing he had abused for years. We arranged appointments with the health boards for several of those witnesses including *Craig*.

I kept in touch with *Craig* after McGinley was arrested, letting him know how the case was going as it wound its way through court hearings, pleadings and legal arguments, until the day came when McGinley pleaded guilty to twenty-one sample charges.

Craig had told me he would be in court for the sentencing of his abuser. When that day came I gazed around the courtroom before I gave evidence. I spotted several people I knew but I couldn't see *Craig*. I tried unsuccessfully over the next number of days to contact him. He had switched off his mobile phone and no one seemed to know where he was. A few weeks went by and I wondered how he was doing. Eventually I made contact and asked him what had happened.

'I was on the way down to court,' he told me. 'I switched off my mobile and I headed north instead and I went on a tear. I couldn't face him.' It was hard to blame him. I knew how much the past still hurt him. To face McGinley again was asking a lot, even if it was to see him sent to jail.

Time moved on. I lost *Craig's* number, but still he was on my mind. Five years passed, but I still remembered vividly the trembling young man I found huddled at my doorway one night. One day in May I parked my car in town, and as I got out I saw a face. I thought I should know the face, but this person was bright looking. '*Craig*?' I asked, almost a question as much as a greeting.

His face lit up. 'Martin,' he said, 'how are you?'

I was so glad to see him, even more to see how much he had changed. We sat into the car and we had a chat. 'How are you getting on?' I asked.

'I am doing great now,' he told me. Then he laughed. 'It was a good job I left Donegal, otherwise I would be in prison. I would have killed that bastard. But I don't need to think like that any more, thank God. I got two years of intense counselling. I've broken through the barriers of shame and guilt. I can see the other side now.'

It was wonderful to hear those words. I felt as if I was in the presence of a miracle. This was an individual whose life had been destroyed, but through the right intervention he had become an enriched young man.

'I am down for a while,' he said, 'looking after my mother.'

That too was good to hear. *Craig's* mother had gone through her own hell when she learned about the abuse her son suffered. She had also become a victim, living with her son's pain. I thought of the other mothers I had spoken to, brave women who had supported their sons, talked to me when they could not get through any longer, and set up support groups to help each other. There were times when it seemed as if the mothers were the only people in society who cared. They were hurting, their children were hurting, and they felt responsible. It was good to know *Craig* had the strength now to take over the caring role for a while and ease his mother's burden.

I exchanged phone numbers with *Craig* and watched as he got out of the car. Walking down the street into the bright early summer sunshine, his shoulders straight and his head held high, I knew he would never have to hide in the shadows again.

Self-help Contacts

- **One in Four Ireland** is a registered charity that provides support to women and men who have experienced sexual abuse and/or sexual violence either as adults or children.

  Address: 2 Holles Street, Dublin 2
  Telephone: 01 662 4070
  Fax: 01 611 4650
  E-mail: info@oneinfour.org
  Web: www.oneinfour.org

- **Samaritans** offer completely confidential, non-judgmental emotional support 24-hours a day, every day.

  24-hour telephone helpline: 1850 60 90 90
  24-hour e-mail helpline: jo@samaritans.org
  Web: www.samaritans.ie

- The **Dublin Rape Crisis Centre** offers a confidential, national 24-hour telephone helpline, 7 days a week, staffed by trained counsellors who are available to listen to you and any concerns you may have in regard to issues of rape, sexual assault, harassment, sexual harassment, bullying or childhood sexual abuse.

  Telephone: 1 800 778 888
  E-mail: rcc@indigo.ie
  Web: www.drcc.ie/